A LITTLE BIT SIDEWAYS

VICTORIA LANDIS

Fiction Titles by Author:
Alias: Mitzi & Mack
Blinke it Away

Amazon Author Central Page:
http://www.amazon.com/author/VictoriaLandis

Facebook Page:
http://www.facebook.com/pages/Victoria-
Landis/356968881052071?ref=hl

Writing Website:
www.victorialandis.com

Artist Website:
www.landisdesignresource.com/

Cover and Illustrations by Victoria Landis
Book Interior Design by Gregg E. Brickman

CONTENTS

There are many ways to conquer human emotion. I've managed to overcome searing grief, stabbing heartbreaks, severe loneliness, primal fear, and overwhelming rage. And lots of rejection. All without hitting or killing anyone, though I have to admit wanting to at times.

But, because of its constant-everyday-in-your-face nature, I find frustration to be the most challenging to endure—and the funniest.

"If we couldn't laugh, we would all go insane." – Jimmy Buffet

***

This book is a collection of humor columns I wrote over the last decade.

They are not meant to be taken seriously.

It's hard to fathom that I have to explain this, but it has been pointed out to me there are people who don't understand that one of the best ways to tell a story is to exaggerate. And invent. And twist. I make up stories around real life. Any resemblance to actual, living persons in this collection is coincidental. Except for my parents. Mom gave her permission to have all the fun I want with them. – Victoria Landis

FOOD

WE SAY POTATO

Among the delicious array of foods we eat at Thanksgiving is the humble potato. Idahos, russets, reds, whites, yams, and sweet potatoes. Whipped into soufflés. Layered with marshmallows. Baked into pies. Kneaded into bread dough. The image of creamy, fluffy, mashed potatoes swimming in butter and gravy says *home* to Americans in a way those upstart pretenders to the throne, like jicama and quinoa, could never hope to duplicate or understand. Of course, it also says heart by-pass surgery, but that's not the innocent potato's fault. And jicama and quinoa technically were domesticated food stuffs long before spuds, but we Americans tend to not know that. It's a rare occasion when we allow facts to get in the way of a good story.

The history of this bland starchy staple is probably not something you've thought much about. Until recently, neither had I. But that was before my brother decided to go on a quest. My brother's doctorate is in nutrition. How seriously does he take his job? Last year, he gave a Distinguished Lecture on the Tomato. When my teenaged son saw the invite/announcement, he quite literally didn't know if it was a joke. I told him his uncle was an intense vegetable scholar, indeed. I'm glad my brother didn't see the glazed look of disbelief. My brother's kids call him Dr. Vegetables. A quick note to fact-check nerds—to save you the helpful and informative email you no doubt were already composing in your head—yes, I know, the tomato is actually a fruit.

Back to Veggie Dad. It may be more accurate to call him—The Potato Whisperer. In search of the potato's roots—the genetic and the physical—my brother ventured to South America. Accompanied by gangly, bespectacled, and geeky college students, armed with video cameras and more brains than money, he traipsed all over the continent, starting in the high Andes mountains, seeking the elusive wild varieties. They camped near Machu Picchu, in the frigid overnight temperatures, among the spiders and beetles, enduring any number of deprivations. For the record, he did invite interested family members along. As much as I want to someday see Machu Picchu (definitely on my bucket list), there was no way I was sleeping outdoors on the cold lumpy ground—no matter how exciting the long days of digging up wild purple potato roots might be. Call me wimpy, but room service is my idea of camping. The South American trip produced enough material for a documentary. Haven't seen it yet, but I'm told it's riveting. Not to hurt my brother's feelings, but somehow I don't think Martin Scorsese has anything to worry about.

My brother's quest did make me wonder about the potato. Who knew such a lowly and commonplace vegetable could claim such a storied past? It's the Wonder Spud. The Spaniards brought it back to Spain in 1570, where it was mocked and viewed with great disdain. Many snickered and called it *Earth's testicles*. It slowly made its way to England, then the rest of Europe, but not without a few mishaps. The first French chefs tasked with preparing potatoes for the French court cooked the stems and leaves and tossed the tubers. Oops. The stems and leaves are poisonous, as are the

4

ones that are cooked and eaten while still green—which is where the fatal green potato chip legend came from. Anyway, the stems and leaves made all the courtiers quite ill, and the potato was unceremoniously jettisoned from the kitchens. In 1598, a Swiss botanist claimed that the consumption of potatoes caused leprosy and induced a fierce amount of wind (gas, not hurricanes). If that weren't bad enough, he also declared that potatoes *incited Venus*. That must have struck panic in the hearts of the French. For if any people on Earth didn't need sexual incitement, it was the French. Lord knows, their history is choked with scandalous goings-on. A vegetable that made people hornier than usual had to be seen as the path to destruction, the downfall of their society. Doom and gloom predictions about incorporating a tuberous Viagra into the diet spread like wildfire. Now that I think about it, maybe there is something to that claim. It is credited with enabling nothing less than the Industrial Revolution. Why, you ask? As a supremely reliable food source, it doubled Europe's population. Hmmm . . . My parents had six children. My dad insisted on potatoes at every meal. Wow. Could it be after all this time, the potato actually is an aphrodisiac?

In taking the potato for granted, we forget how many aspects of our lives pay tribute to it. I think I'll start a petition calling for the potato to be our National Vegetable. Ireland calls it their National Vegetable, but since we did them a huge favor by taking in millions of Irish citizens because of the potato blight during the 1800s, they shouldn't argue too much if we steal it. It's kind of weird for them to choose it anyway, isn't it? You'd think they'd never want to see another one after what they went through. The potato famine caused them to lose half their population in four years—either by emigration or starvation. If they had any sense, they'd be courting those lonely step-sisters, jicama and quinoa.

Lots of people are couch potatoes. Mr. and Mrs. Potato Head owe their existence to it. Potato-white starch perks up wilted restaurant lettuce—an arcane fact that they really *don't* want you to know. There's a potato museum in Brussels, Belgium. Once a year, a sweet teenage girl gets crowned the Potato Queen in a small USA town and gets to ride high atop a hay wagon in the local parade, doing the Queen's wave while the other girls secretly pray for a sudden downpour.

Potatoes might be involved in ninety percent of all middle-school science projects. They can be turned into clocks. They're used in the faux-painting trade. And there's a company now claiming that a chemical in the potato skin makes you feel fuller than you are—can you say *amazing new diet pill?* Ah, the majestic potato. Bet this Thanksgiving, you'll eat yours with a little more respect.

DONATE YOUR UNEATEN MINCEMEAT PIE TO A NEEDY CROCODILE

My grandmother loved mincemeat pie. She brought one to every Thanksgiving dinner. As a kid, I didn't understand why *anyone* would want to eat a dessert made from meat. And mystery meat at that. She practically cooed over the danged thing. "Nothing better than mincemeat pie." She'd repeat that phrase ad nauseam the whole day. Yet she never convinced any of us kids. We went out of our way to avoid trying it.

I don't think she understood what ran through our heads when we heard it mentioned. All I could think of was the cartoon where Klondike Kat would threaten—"I'm going to make mincemeat out of that mouse." No way anybody was getting me to eat ground up mice for dessert, no matter how much sugar or alcohol was added to it. As a teenager, it was finally divulged to me that, in fact, there wasn't (and never had been) meat of any kind in Grandmom's pie. Just the fruits, spices, and liquor. But by then, I was an adamant and unrepentant mincemeat hater.

Now, as an adult and self-proclaimed repository of useless but fascinating trivia, I realize I have exhibited a woeful lack of interest in mincemeat. Given Grandmom's unabashed enthusiasm for the stuff, it should have been on my radar screen for closer scrutiny long ago. I apologize, for I know my loyal readers count on me to keep them informed.

My crack investigative team (Google and Bing) uncovered all sorts of fun facts about mincemeat. Recipes from the 1500s to the 1700s did indeed require meat chopped very fine. Any kind. They weren't picky. Road kill would suffice quite nicely, if you happened to be fortunate enough to stumble upon it. And yes, there *was* such a thing as road kill back then. You'd be surprised how many references there are for wildlife meeting unfortunate ends by colliding with careening carriages.

Due to meat's tendency to go bad or rancid, they added wine or brandy—to preserve it—and the fruits and spices masked the nasty gamey smell and taste. The alcohol also broke down the proteins (not that they had a clue what that was) and tenderized the tough and stringy meat. What's amazing is—properly stored—the stuff could last ten years. Might be a safe bet the originators of Spam knew a thing or two about mincemeat history.

As though all this weren't already turning your stomach (sorry, but we hard-hitting reporters must soldier on and be thorough), I discovered a recipe—posted recently no less—for mincemeat fruitcake. Holy figs and dates. There is a person out there who thought, *Hmmm . . . my fruitcake isn't quite revolting enough. I know. I'll add decaying meat!* Morticia Adams is apparently alive and well in an Internet kitchen.

You may be intrigued to find out who could be the biggest fans of mincemeat today. Crocodile hatchlings. They devour it. Well, by definition, their coarse table manners dictate the devouring part. Hmmm . . . I wonder if they prefer it with wine or brandy? But the little carnivorous darlings are at the mercy of the person preparing the delicacy. If the mix doesn't have enough bone in it, they'll get calcium deficiencies. And that could lead to kinky tails. I found all kinds of helpful information like this on a !Crocodile Fun Facts! page. Although—*fun*—is not how I'd categorize them. A more apt title—!Crocodiles WILL Eat You!—might garner the site a few more visits.

Crocodiles have earned a villainous reputation for good reason. They can outrun the average human on land. They can see in the dark. They can eat underwater. And—they will happily eat *you* if presented with the opportunity. So, that explains the panic aboard a small aircraft in 2010 that was approaching Bandundu airport in the Democratic Republic of Congo. Some nimrod smuggled a crocodile aboard in his sports bag. Just before landing, the croc tore through the bag, causing a stampede of passengers toward one end of the plane. It tipped and crashed into a house, killing nineteen people. One person survived—as did the crocodile. Now, *that's* a fun fact.

Back to our poor flesh-eating babies who don't eat enough bones. Their teeth could turn diaphanous—like glass. Imagine that. You're traipsing along the Tárcoles River in Costa Rica, just minding your own business, when a sixteen-foot crocodile with a ninety-degree kink in its tail springs from the surrounding brush and bares his crystalline teeth at you. Why, anyone in their right mind would come to the logical conclusion that those ancient aliens with the crystal skulls had mated with the crocs. Betcha never saw *that* on the History Channel. I smell a cover up.

The lesson today? If there's a chance of a croc crossing your path, carry a leftover mincemeat pie with you. It has a crazy-long shelf life. Now that we know crocs love the stuff, just fling it at them. The life you save could be your own.

MAGIC BEANS

It's amazing what humans will eat when they believe a food (and I'm using the term *food* in a rather broad way here) enables certain *health* benefits. For thousands of years, cultures have propagated myths about some plants and animals.

Now, many of them actually had/have curative properties. Such as the willow bark tea from 2000 BCE that the Egyptians used to reduce fevers. The compounds in willow bark led to aspirin. There are lots of great discoveries just like that. Go us! Er, them. (Pretty sure not a single ancestor of mine did a thing to advance the cause, although they probably made significant contributions to cirrhosis studies.)

But not all the medicinal lore passed through the ages was good. Or even safe. Some was outright batpoop crazy. Quite frankly, it's a miracle anyone survived to tell about the weirdest ones. All societies had hits and misses. Mostly, the misses went by the wayside, dumped into the compost heap of humanity's historical failures, as science made larger and larger leaps.

What happened to the bad ones that kept going, despite being disproven by modern technology? Funny you should ask. Because most of them are still alive and thriving in one place. One huge, populous, ancient, and stubborn-as-heck country. China.

Yes, the country that is whupping us with daily twenty-first century cyber attacks on our businesses and government (and spanking our students in math and science) is also the biggest throwback and user of *stuff-that-never-worked-but-we-refuse-to-believe-it* from the first century. Even other Chinese have proverbs about their countrymen. In Northern China, they say the Cantonese 'eat anything with four legs and is not a chair, and anything that flies and is not a plane.' I'll hit some of the highlights, because the list of whacked-out edibles is a long one. I'd be here until martini time tallying them.

Let me be absolutely clear—the following claims are not true. Do not try these at home. Or even in a Chinese restaurant. Which you couldn't do anyway, because apparently, there is a secret code for ordering exotic and endangered species as a meal. Nope. Not kidding. Supposedly, you order a certain type of duck dish with a *wink-wink,* and they charge you triple and bring you exotics instead. I only hope that the restaurants' owners are perpetuating a huge fraud, and instead of serving what that customer what he *thinks* he's getting, they bring him chicken. Everything tastes like chicken anyway, right? I hope they're laughing themselves silly back in the kitchen.

Eating owl is supposed to sharpen one's eyesight. Seahorse will help asthma, heart disease, and improve one's manhood, if you get my drift . . . Fresh snake blood—is an aphrodisiac and improves one's manhood. Every part of the poor little pangolin—imagine an anteater with scales—is used. For arthritis. For asthma. (Honestly? Asthma a big problem there? Take a look around Beijing lately, guys? Could all the breathing issues be solved by less air pollution?) Eating pangolin is even thought to reduce infant drooling. And, of course, male impotence.

Tortoise flippers for longer life. Golden turtles for cancer. Bears, especially their paws, for one-hundred-twenty-three different medicines. And burns. And liver ailments. And impotence. Rhino horn? Stops convulsions, helps asthma, and—improves one's manhood.

I'm certain Chinese women have worn themselves to a frazzle from constantly rolling their eyes when their men fret over such things. Clearly, the Chinese men have a collective fear of underperforming. Which makes absolutely no sense. I mean, look at the population problems they've created. If anything, they've over performed. China has no worries there. So, it's got to be about them *feeling* inadequate, right? Instead of slaughtering innocent animals to try and help their fragile male egos, why not import self-help gurus?

No, no, no. Not to be eaten, although many here in this country would applaud that. There's an absolute goldmine awaiting the self-help expert who can crack the code with Chinese men about their precious manhood. I'd like the book concession. Actually, that gives me a great idea. I think I'll write (under a male pseudonym of course) THE be-all, end-all self-help book for them.

Suddenly, I have a most urgent task at hand. The book will practically write itself. *Don't Eat That—Read This! Real Men Don't Eat Seahorse. Eat Prey—No Love.* But what to call me? What do you think? Hardy McRocky?

B.A. Mann? Excuse me, please. I have some Mandarin to brush up on.

GLORK DISCOVERS BEER!

Here's a headline for you: Beer was discovered, not invented. Yes. As seems absolutely appropriate, man stumbled into beer.

Around 10,000 BCE, humans finally figured out that life might be easier if they grew their food in one place instead of endlessly wandering to gather it. Hoping to scrounge up enough grain and berries every day had to be rough. Nothing like we go through now, of course, endlessly wandering through superstores the size of the Pentagon, trying to decide on which eight-thousand-ounce box of cereal grain to drag home. Our ancestors had been living in small nomadic bands of up to fifty for over thirty-thousand years—hauling their animal skin tents, bows and arrows, fishhooks, and needles over hills, through storms, and in the blistering sun. No wonder they died around thirty—toothless and looking like the crypt keeper.

What probably happened was the women got fed up, put their walking-weary feet down, and insisted Glork and Erg stop and ask for directions already. At any rate, once they settled into the first villages, some fool—most likely the aforementioned, directionally challenged Glork—declared himself in charge of things, becoming the first mayor and stumbling into inventing politics. Aren't we grateful for that? Especially this year, when some of the candidates do seem to be channeling the empty-headed and ego-filled Glork, blundering and gaffing their way through.

Planting barley and wheat produced a problem. Where to store the surplus grain after harvest? Underground pits were the first storage units, keeping the food protected from animals and nature. Except the rain, of course. Thank the alcohol fairies, too, because it led to the discovery that, when soaked in water, grain starts to sprout and tastes sweet. Enzymes converted starch into maltose sugar, or malt. They made a gruel from it. And, no doubt because of an argument over whose turn it was to scrape the leftovers out of those nasty rotting wood bowls, the gruel sat around for a few more days and became slightly fizzy. Glork's mate, Gerk, mad at him because she had a long day of hauling water, tending to animals, weaving baskets, and tanning hides—all with a screaming, leaking (imagine a diaper made of animal skin) baby tied to her back—made him eat the fizzy gruel.

And Glork got drunk. The wild yeasts in the air had fermented the maltose into alcohol. Beer. Glork then felt happy. Merry. Playfully slapped Gerk on the butt and made jokes about their desperate existence. Damn. Thanks to beer, Glork invented stand-up, too.

Now, people had experienced accidental intoxication before, by trying to store fruit or honey. But without pottery, which wouldn't be invented for 4,000 years, they couldn't store the accidental wine or mead without it spoiling. Malted barley changed everything.

Beer making caught on fast. Through trial and error (lots of errors) humans found ways to brew it. Thorough cooking of the gruel made beer stronger. They cooked it in pitch-lined baskets, leather bags or animal stomachs— think of the piquant flavor notes *that* would add. There is an argument to be made that in several of today's commercial beers, they've preserved that primal essence of pitch or stomach. They used anything—large shells, stone vessels, and even hollowed-out trees—to cook the mash. No wonder the Keebler elves always seem so merry.

Malted barley mixed with water and brought to a boil was the key to the beverage that would launch humankind forward. They soon discovered people got sick less and stopped that annoying drop-dead-at-thirty thing. They didn't know why, but they knew plain water could kill. (Might have had something to do with rinsing the animal skin diapers.)

As patriarchy reigned supreme, somehow beer-making became women's work—along with everything else they did. At least they got some benefit from this duty—a woman was a more valued mate, so brought a higher dowry (a pig *and* a goat, versus just the goat), if she made a good beer.

Thank God for Glork. Because as we stumble into politics this year, beer can make us merry while we watch the stand-up comedians lampoon the stumbling, ego-filled politicians.

HOMEMADE GOODIES

My mom made it her mission in life to provide the six of us kids with good, warm memories. She and my father both grew up in less than ideal circumstances—absent parents, neglected preventative care, poor housing, and ketchup sandwiches as a treat. Never having had the heart-warming Norman Rockwell-type holidays, Mom went out of her way to insure we did.

She morphed herself into a cross between Julia Child and Martha Stewart. And it was wonderful. Really a great way to grow up. Everything was made from scratch. Of course, back in the late fifties and early sixties, there weren't many prepared foods available. TV dinners had hit the market, but my mother declared them inedible. There were canned goods and frozen vegetables, but that was about it. No slice and bake cookie dough yet. The Pillsbury Dough Boy was but a mischievous twinkle in the eye of an ad man at the Leo Burnett Ad Agency. Mad men, indeed.

Near Christmas one year, several neighbor couples were invited for dinner. Mom made a delicious-smelling chocolate layer cake. She hadn't quite mastered the art of icing the outsides and top without getting crumbs in the final coat of icing. Crumbs visible in the icing were a *major* cooking faux pas at the time. Shameful. Enough to cause whispers among the female guests. Anyway, Mom read a tip in one of her magazines—put the cake in the freezer before icing and crumbs will stay put.

The home freezer in the mud room pantry (1850s house, there was a warren of little rooms off the kitchen), packed to bursting with the latest meat order (remember the freezer orders they'd deliver?), had just enough space for the cake. Unfortunately, the popsicles were kept in that freezer. And yes, even in the cold winters, we played outside more than in, and popsicles were *always* fine with us. About an hour later, the back door slammed, children's footsteps pounded into the mud room, and then came a crash. My brother and sister had pulled out the box of popsicles, which caused a package of frozen steaks to slide forward, which pushed the cake.

Mom ran, but it was too late. The cake lay smushed, upside-down on the floor. It was three o'clock. Her guests were due at six. There was still most of the work to do on the main meal, and my father had the car. Even if there were time to drive to a bakery, she couldn't.

She knelt by the cake and assessed the damage. Most of it hadn't touched the linoleum. She told me to bring a knife. Taking it, she carefully sliced across the layer that had hit, leaving about an inch of what was the top layer on the floor. The plate it had sat on was unbreakable, so she righted what was left and carried it to the kitchen counter. She thought for a moment, got out a round clear glass bowl, and cut the cake into pieces. She layered softened vanilla ice cream and chocolate chips with the cake pieces, then put it back into the freezer, locking the mud room door. Just before serving, she mixed up some fresh whipped cream, and the dessert was declared a masterpiece.

I don't know what real sugarplums are, but Mom made a confection she called sugarplums. Not a speck of fruit or anything remotely nutritious in them. A meringue of egg whites and sugar, baked in little mounds that melted in your mouth. We loved them. One year, Mom agreed to send in sugarplums for my third grade and my sister's fourth grade Christmas parties. Being a busy person, Mom was distracted the night before and set the oven on broil instead of bake. Burnt a whole batch. She stayed up very late making another batch. Then my evil older sister sabotaged the tins. She wanted more, so she put all the good ones in her tin, and loaded up mine with the burnt ones. (Yep, the same sister who hid her mashed potatoes and peas in my glass of milk.)

Once, a fairly large spider lowered itself by its silk thread right into Mom's mixing bowl. We noticed just as the beaters hit and dragged him under. Mom didn't blink an eye, just kept the beaters whirring and said, "Protein." The severe and constant lack of time to redo anything was a big factor. Since time immemorial, frenetically busy moms have always turned a blind eye to such trivial inconveniences—it's just nobody ever talks about it. This particular cake happened to be for my evil older sister's birthday. I didn't have any of it and decided I would always be present when Mom made *my* birthday cakes.

Every Christmas, we had homemade chocolate chip cookies, peanut-butter cookies, sugar cookies, and shortbread cookies made by squeezing the dough through a special Christmas-tree shaped nozzle. Pies made with crust from scratch and fresh fruit. No cans, ever. Mom had perfected desserts and all the kids in the neighborhood loved them. I'd eaten at their houses, too, and their moms were not as good in the kitchen. So it shouldn't have surprised me when dozens of Mom's cookies disappeared. Turns out evil older sister wanted to make some money, so she sold the cookies in wax-papered bundles of four to other kids for ten cents. Such a young entrepreneur. She also sold rides in our elevator (It was quite a house.) for a nickel.

I've spoiled my children in the food category also. I didn't mean to, but I wanted them to know from-scratch cooking like I did. Now, they won't eat jarred spaghetti sauce or birthday cake from a grocery. When I do buy cookies from the store, they sit in the pantry until they're stale and thrown away. But I draw the line at blending insects into my batters. And I don't care about sealing the crumbs when I ice my triple-chocolate cake. I figure if someone actually has the time or inclination to notice such a thing these days, God bless 'em.

VICTORIA LANDIS

LIVING IN FLORIDA

FLORIDA RETAINS ITS TITLE

Well, it's another January and before we go about the business of 2015, a round-up of 2014 seems to be in order. As usual, Florida reigns supreme over everyone else in the stupid/crazy category, a source of great pride for all writers in the state.

First up—people getting naked and doing bizarre things. We top the charts worldwide for misadventures without clothes on. I can only surmise that our weather is to blame. My totally speculative reasoning relies on the research. My whip-sharp team (Bing & Google—take your annual bow) proves it with the locations involved. I saw no incidents in northern Florida, and the reports of such antics became more prevalent the further south I looked—ending up with the highest numbers in—Ta-Da! South Florida—where it's the warmest. Yay, us.

I doubt anything will ever top the naked man on the side of the freeway trying to eat the face of another man, but—in Orange County, the police rescued a man whose car wound up in a lake. When they pulled him out, he was not wearing clothing. They're *guessing* alcohol might have been involved. A man pretending to be a cop entered an IHOP, mooned everyone and demanded a free meal. A man (sorry, men out there, but your gender seems compelled to do this stuff) entered a store in Orlando wearing only socks. Another man entered a store naked and attempted to steal socks. Only socks. Huh? Another man who shed his skivvies caused a neighborhood disturbance (ya think?) and slapped the face of the officer who arrived to take him away.

Normally in our animal division, alligators and pythons hog the headlines. But this year, five black bears dragged trash cans out of a Lake Mary garage to forage in them. When the lady of the house went outside (Let's assume she didn't *see* the bears feasting in her driveway, because why would anyone in their right mind take a single step near *five* hungry bears? Then again, we are talking Florida.), one of the bears attacked her. She needed thirty staples and ten stitches in her head. The Florida Fish & Wildlife guys came, and for some reason, tried to convince the aggressive bear to desist. No, I'm not kidding. The man was quoted as saying they shouted at the bear, clapped their hands in its direction, and yelled, "Bad bear" at it. It's incredible to think that, despite them giving the creature the royal Tinkerbell treatment, the bear didn't *care* about being labeled as *bad*. Why, it's like he had no shame at all. Then again, thinking back, that particular method had little to no effect on my sons when they misbehaved. Why would it work on a bear?

We have crocodiles. Not a ton of them, but they're here. They live in the brackish water of canals and waterways. A three-hundred pounder named Poncho was known to hang out near Coral Gables. A young man and his girlfriend, while visiting friends, decided to go swimming in the backyard canal at 2:30 in the morning. In the first ever reported-in-the-USA crocodile attack, Poncho gave the man lacerations on his shoulders and torso and shredded one hand to bits. No guessing here as to whether this wise choice involved alcohol—and maybe a few other substances.

A tiger bit off the thumb of a construction worker in Jupiter. The man was working at the animal center and stuck his hand into the tiger's enclosure on purpose. Okay, this one belongs with the stupid human tricks, too. Everyone I asked said the tiger gets a pass.

Imagine one woman's surprise when she saw a baby kangaroo hopping around her Orlando neighborhood. Animal control captured the little roo. Another woman came to claim him. It wasn't hers, though. She was hired to babysit him. She didn't live in the neighborhood, but the kangaroo did. I'd love to see the Craigslist ad for that service. As a bonus, that happened in a suburb called Christmas.

Back to people behaving poorly without the added dimension of the animal kingdom, at a baptism party in North Miami Beach, someone posted about the party on social media. A group of uninvited men showed up and were very upset when there were no utensils left and the food was almost gone. A nasty fight broke out. Two lessons for modern times, I guess? If you must tell your friends via social websites that you're at a party they are not invited to, better have extra food? And, if you insist on crashing said party, bring your own fork and knife? I dunno. I'm kind of at a loss here, having grown up in the Miss Manners and Emily Post era.

There was so much more to report for 2014, but I don't want your head to explode. Just go to bed tonight safe in the knowledge that our title as Crazy Capital of the Country is assured for another year.

WHEN ABUNDANT SHOWERS MAKE ME COWER

I remember a cartoon when I was a child about April showers bringing May flowers. It might have been Little Lulu. She sang a happy song regarding the rain, then the sun appeared, and beautiful masses of flowers sprung up in full bloom. The birds and their nestlings chirped along. Maybe a singing cow or horse was in it, too.

After decades of adult years (weather seemed inconsequential until I had to go to work in it), I've yet to see anyone singing with delight about a deluge in any season. Once in a great while, a soft, gentle rain falls—pattering a hypnotic tune on the roof. But I live in South Florida, a place not known for subtlety, even when it comes to weather. The majority of our rainfall feels like a giant is standing over your house pouring bucket after bucket on top of you. And he's laughing with stereotypical fiendish glee—bwa-ha-ha.

Rather than produce vibrant displays of colored blooms, when our rain stops, it leaves delicate ornamental plants smashed to smithereens. The weeds, however, explode in an exuberant spectacle. Mosquito larvae spring to life, then soar in a celebratory ritual of sucking blood from anything with sweat glands. I used to keep close to my ex-husband when we stepped outside during these times. The mosquitoes loved him, and if he was near, they'd leave me alone. He was also the best at finding stray sewing pins on the floor. No matter what, he'd be the only one to step on one and have it pierce his foot. It's strange—the things you discover you miss about someone. But I digress.

The bumper crop that pops up in my yard after a hard rain is mushrooms. Within hours, the fungi grow at breakneck speeds. I've seen broad orange ones spotted with brown. Skinny stemmed white ones. Pink, yes—pink, ones. Brown ones. Some of them stink so bad the neighbors' dogs won't go near.

The animals seem to know what will hurt them. I can't say the same for humans. More than once, I've heard giggling and rustling noises near the shrooms—young adults searching for 'magic' mushrooms after the rain. Tempting as it is to have some fun as the 'get off my lawn' shrew, I resist. Instead, I turn on the lights, open the front door, and call for an imaginary cat. It's usually enough to scare the scavengers into the next yard. The next day I knock down and smash all the mushrooms I can find. I'm pretty certain that real hallucinogenic fungi need manure to grow. My yard is mostly sand, but why take a chance some whiz-bang lawyer could make a case against me because I didn't protect his clients, now drooling on themselves in front of a jury, from my pop-up mushrooms.

Back to our crazy heavy rains. This past summer, to prepare for a new type of sod, I tore out the few remaining clusters of St. Augustine grass and the thick, deep, entrenched weeds in my front lawn leaving a bare expanse of exposed sand. There was a smattering of black dirt specks visible in the mix. Not enough to say I actually had topsoil. One day, it rained five inches in under four hours. It was a tumult. When the sky cleared, every precious black soil particle had floated to the top of the sand, sailed downhill on the newly formed river of run off, and deposited itself on the front sidewalk. There were two inches of thick, sticky, dark silt covering the concrete for at least thirty feet.

I panicked. The only dirt I had to nourish the new sod now looked like a dislocated mud bog, the kind where they find mummified remains in Europe. Of course, I'd just paid to have the sidewalk pressure cleaned a week earlier. That giant with the buckets had to be doubled over with laughter at what he'd done to me. There was no way I'd pay to haul in more topsoil for the new grass. The sod stretched my budget as it was. Plus, my for-the-most-part patient neighbors would complain for sure.

So, I had to move the mud. Using a square-front shovel, I scraped up the muck inch by inch and flung it as far as I could back onto the sand. Took me a few hours. Then no more than an hour after I'd finished, it rained again. Scrape, rinse, repeat.

All in all, I love living in South Florida. I've lived in New Jersey, Georgia, Texas, California, the Florida Panhandle, and Hawaii. This may be the most entertaining place there is. Between the crazy weather and the silly human shenanigans in the daily news, I may have found nirvana for humor writers.

'LEAF'ING IT ALL BEHIND

Having fun in the fall means something different in South Florida than it does up north. For instance, the annual ritual of jumping in a hilly mass of leaves. Try and explain that to a ten-year-old here. They look at you like you're sprouting cabbage from your ear. No doubt they're imagining a pile of trimmed palm fronds laying by the curb waiting for pick-up. Is it any wonder they think we're strange?

When we lived up north, at least once in the season, we'd go into the mountains to enjoy the changing colors. Kids in South Florida don't know a maple leaf from a bottle of maple syrup. They do see changing colors, but of a very different nature. Local television stations provide a non-stop broadcast of updates when a storm's brewing. The salmon color of the tropical storm watch gives way to the screaming pink of the hurricane watch that can morph into the hot red of a hurricane warning which complements the green of the coastal flood warning so well. The piquant red and green combo takes us on a smooth glide through the close of hurricane season at the end of November straight into the Christmas season. Breathing enormous sighs of relief, we then go forth and spend like crazy, doing our part for Florida's economy. Or in more challenging economic times, try to find clever ways to turn unused hurricane supplies into holiday gifts.

There were farms in those autumn mountains up north

that allowed people to search the fields and pick their own pumpkins. We'd pack the trunk full, cart them home, and try to outdo each other when carving faces in them. Brightly lit from within, they occupied the porch for a week or two before Halloween in a display with a collection of bizarrely figured gourds, miniature hay bales, and the ubiquitous cute homemade scarecrow. Everyone's porch looked like a cover photo shoot from *Southern Living* magazine.

Ah, but the price we pay for our warm weather. In South Florida, it's best to wait until a couple of days before Halloween when selecting one's seasonal gourds. That way you'll pick the ones most likely to last. If they haven't rotted by then, the odds are good they'll stay intact for another twenty-four to forty-eight hours. And don't even *think* of carving them until the day of, or, at most, the day before. I found out the hard way about that fact—children crying buckets because the precious pumpkin they spent an hour choosing (in front of Publix) has acquired a nasty case of rotting flesh and, not only can't be lit, must be trashed immediately—or else the orange gooey slime leaks and soaks into anything within a five-foot radius. We also discovered that ants, cockroaches, lizards, and frogs can sense pumpkin ooze from a mile away. It's ambrosia to them. Want to make a horror film? Smash a few pumpkins in your driveway and film what happens in the next few days.

Back on the idyllic farm, hayrides on horse-led wagons meandered on dirt roads. Hot or cold fresh cider awaited your return. The air was clear, crisp, and smells of earth and crushed leaves joined with the fresh breeze. Our October South Florida air tends to be thick and humid. It has the signature odor of the sulfurous water pumped from wells to water our lawns.

On the other hand. Waxing nostalgic about leaf piles is one thing. To actually do all that raking is a literal pain in the patookie. And the back. You buy hotpads and coolpacks and ibuprofen by the gross. Sometimes it poured rain before you could get to the raking, causing the leaves to pancake down and compress into thick, wet blankets of muck. That required twice as much work. With the rake tines, you dug in until you saw the grass, then grabbed at the matted section with a gloved hand and lifted as much as you could, revealing a world of writhing worms and beetles. Then you screamed, shivered, and recoiled in disgust as you dropped the section and headed into the house for a drink. All those wet leaves would've made the leaf bags too heavy anyway. They'd rip apart on the way to the curb. Someone—usually one of the neighbors who raked all theirs before the rain, the ones whose yard and children always looked ridiculously perfect and their porch was really the only one that looked like the magazine cover— helpfully pointed out that if the leaves were left in place until they dried out, the lawn would die. No wonder I moved to Florida.

You know what? You can visit autumn colors and leaves. There are fantastic pictures of them on the Internet, too. Nothing competes with sitting on the warm beach in October enjoying the aqua water, refreshing breezes, and white puffy clouds sailing by. Especially when you realize your northern counterparts are clad in corduroy and wool, installing new weather stripping, and buying long johns, calcium chloride deicer, and snow tires. Oh, yeah, and peeling up thick layers of decomposing plant matter.

In truth, those guys who ran that pumpkin farm did bear a disturbing likeness to some characters from *Deliverance*. If banjo music had suddenly started playing, we'd have dropped the pumpkins in the field, and been in the car in a minute, tops. And while the kids here don't know the fun of leaf diving, they do have year-round biking, camping, fishing, swimming, and a gazillion sports. That doesn't sound too bad to me. Not too bad at all.

NUCLEAR CRABGRASS

The return of summer to South Florida heralds the perennial problems of living in the sub-tropics and having a yard to maintain. During the short winter—or what passes for winter here—the local flora grows at a somewhat manageable pace. More like what happens up north in their summertime. Trees and shrubs elegantly sprout new tendrils that become branches and pretty leaves. Day by day, the beautiful process can be admired and appreciated while sipping fancy-flavored morning coffee on the porch, like in the TV commercials. Over a few weeks' time, the flowering shrubs have produced the showy colors that will endure until fall. It's a lovely thing, to watch nature unfold like that.

Unfortunately, that Norman Rockwell picture I just painted for you is only possible down here for a matter of weeks. Blink, and you'll miss it. The rest of our year is technically summer, and it's like the plant life gobbled steroids. Lots of 'em. In fact, judging from the overgrowth in my yard, they're suffering from all-out 'roid rage'. My bougainvillea grows—I swear—three to four feet a week. The areca palms, recently chopped down to a modest eight-foot height, are now sporting five-foot extensions. And the weeds are once again completely out of control. I can't fathom what they'd all be like if I had actual real soil instead of a ninety-percent sand mix.

I am in serious denial about my green-thumb abilities. In

my mind, I don't see the black soot and spider infestations covering the gardenias. I see lush bushes with fragrant flowers. I see the potential of my yard. My HOA, however, refuses to wear my rose-colored glasses.

If you've read my column over the years, you're familiar with the fact that, along with the famous brown thumb, I also have insanely bad luck with the flora of my yard. I plant little trees the guy at the nursery place assures me *I cannot kill*, and within months they're on life support. Insects attack. Animals burrow into roots. Lightning strikes. The latest weird thing to happen in my yard—in the front, of course, on proud display right where the HOA guy drives by in his important little golf cart wearing a jaunty little hat—is an incredible outbreak of monster crabgrass. It's taking over.

I called a pro, and he sprayed the entire yard. Said it would take some time to work. I waited. And watched an amazing array of weeds spread further—especially the crabgrass. And waited. Finally, after two months of the crabgrass pretty much flipping me the bird, I bought some Weed & Feed and spread it myself. And waited. Still, nothing. Zip. Didn't kill a single weed. You're not supposed to treat lawns very often, so I waited another two months and tried a different brand. You guessed it. Nothing. Killed a few of the minor weeds, but not a dent in the crabgrass. It's as though all these treatments were super-vitamin pills for it. It's growing at a ridiculous rate.

So, I've gone old-school. I'm spending an hour each morning on my kneeling pad, hacking out the nasty things with a three-prong tool. And I'm beginning to understand why nothing else has worked. The root balls of the monstrous weeds are twelve to fourteen inches in diameter! They are the cockroaches of the botanical world. They are the nuclear survivors. They refuse to die.

My neighbors are being quite polite when they pass by walking their dogs. They make comments like, "My, that sure looks like a lot of work", when I know for a fact most of them think of me as that *eccentric writer/artist lady*. They're probably wondering—why on earth don't I just have somebody come in and treat the lawn? If they asked, I'd relay the reason, but they don't linger long enough to hear my tale of woe.

Oh, well. Every neighborhood needs an eccentric creative type.

WE ARE NOT ALONE

Oh, Florida. How do we love you? Let us count the ways. Nah, can't do it. There are too many. But one of the favorites is celebrating our weirdness. We love to make fun of ourselves and our fellow citizens. But we are not alone. Thanks to global connectivity, people all over the world appreciate the special artisanal blend of goofy-crazy that is so unique to this state. We're bringing needed comic relief to many. And that is a noble calling.

Take the 'Florida Man' meme that's so popular on the Internet. Every day, some intellectually challenged Sunshine-Stater proves that fact is way stranger than fiction.

Is it the balmy (humid) air that affects us? Or the lilt of foreign languages surrounding us everywhere we go? Perhaps it's the constant threat of having our innocent little doggies attacked by alligators while traipsing along the canals?

Florida Man Kills Roommate for Forgetting to Buy Toilet Paper. Florida Man Leaves Phone At the Scene of the Crime: Asks For it Back. Florida Man Run Over by Own Truck During Road Rage Incident. Florida Man Gets Attacked by 300+ LB Fish. Florida Man Sets Neighbor's House on Fire Because it Was Ugly. Florida Man and His Trusty Sidekicks Steal Food in Their Underwear. Oy.

And just so you know I'm not discriminating against the male gender, there's also a 'Florida Woman' meme. Women don't seem to do as many ridiculous things as the guys, but they are out there trying their best to keep up. Florida Woman Brands Her Children for Identification: Says She Forgot How Much She Loves Fire. Florida Woman Sues Family Health Centers for Not Being Hired to Do a Job She Said She Wouldn't Do. Florida Woman, Enraged When Duck Won't Eat Her Candy, Runs it Over With Car.

It *is* wonderfully fun, isn't it? Except—wait a gosh darn minute. It so happens that we're not the only state with very silly people residing in it. Turns out some of the other states have some real gems. So, why don't they get the national headlines? Somehow, maybe it's just not as much fun when it doesn't happen here?

For example, I saw this recently—Seattle Man Sets House on Fire While Trying to Kill a Spider. How about—Michigan Woman Blames Zoo for Losing a Finger When She Tried to Pet a Caged Lion. Or—Man Sentenced for Drunken Driving in SUV Full of Chickens. That one happened in Grand Island, Nebraska. (Wanna bet the spider guy is actually from here?)

I think the nation likes to gang up on Florida because so many other states have to deal with the cold, ice, sleet, black ice, tornadoes, earthquakes, and dead leaden skies for five months of the year. It's natural for them to be jealous of a place that's known for sunshine, beach days in the middle of winter, eighty-plus degree water temps, golf courses, and impossibly good-looking people everywhere. For them, it must seem so unfair that we have all that pretty much year-round.

So just like in families when one sibling is gorgeous, smart, and makes a ton of money, everyone dumps on that person—under the guise of kidding around. It's a little passive–aggressive thing that helps them manage their feelings of inadequacy. The armchair psychiatrist in me believes it.

And that's okay. We can take it. Go ahead and poke all the fun you want at us. Because we will sit poolside with a smug look on our faces as we check the news and see that another storm has just dumped two more feet of snow onto the driveway you worked so hard to shovel out the day before. Because we will build sandcastles with our kids on the beach on the same day that you spent four hours chopping firewood to heat your home when the wires froze and snapped. And because we will have a terrific time playing golf, riding bicycles, stand up paddling, gardening, or just enjoy dining al fresco with friends while you are shivering.

Yup. Face it. We are the smart ones in the family. No hard feelings, right?

HURRICANE SHUDDERS

Every year in June in South Florida, wild weather season starts. The television and radio stations flood the air waves with information on hurricane preparedness. Unless you've lived here for less than a year, there is no excuse for not knowing the basics. Keep a stock of dried foods, water, flashlights, and a battery-operated TV or radio. Experienced hurricane survivors also keep a few extra gallons of gas, chlorine, work gloves—we could *yada yada* the rest. We know the drill.

First, I'd like to praise and thank my fellow responsible Floridians who take precautions. Most of us do. Yay, for us! We're the boring ones, but Florida would be one catastrophic mess without us.

The rest of the populace provide us and the national news audience with great entertainment. Preparation procrastinators pay double and triple for plywood sheets—which, by the way, I do not recommend. Our feisty Wilma in 2005 tore a friend's plywood—secured with Tapcon screws no less—right off every window. And that was during the supposedly kinder first half of the storm. (Wilma blew so hard, I had white-caps in my pool.) In the supermarkets, women wearing spandex and four-inch heels tussle over the last loaf of bread and bottle of water. People stare nervously at the sky in hours-long gas lines as the wind begins to howl.

Meanwhile, eager surfers run for the bigger swells,

disregarding the lifeguards' warnings, cheered on by the drunken revelers in the bars across the street. Denizens of trailer parks shrug away the reporters' concerns. "I've ridden through these storms the last thirty years," they say. "Ain't nothing but a little wind."

Then the very first day, hours even, after a hurricane blows through, the news shows groups of citizens who complain about not having anything to eat, not having any water, not having gas. I'm not talking about the poor folks who lost their homes or really need ice—everybody wants to help them ASAP. But their needs get obscured by the *oops, I forgot* crowd. When asked, some complainers say they *meant* to buy supplies—just couldn't get to it. Others didn't expect it to be so bad. We have citizens who fire up their SUVs and idle for hours with the air conditioning running, using up what gas they do have waiting in a line for a bag of ice. Not because their child is diabetic and medication must be kept cold, either. One woman was asked by a reporter why she waited so long in line for ice. She giggled and said her husband didn't like warm beer. My neighbor threw a worn out drill bit at the battery TV when he saw that.

Back to the first day. Somebody's missing off their boat. A tree crashed into a car out driving in the middle of it (my friend's husband wanted to see what it was like *out there*.) The roof of the mobile home peeled back like the top of a sardine can. The bar patrons, wet and hungover, had the scare of their lives.

And the unprepared ask, "Why isn't the government doing anything?" demanding attention with tears welling in their eyes. On the first day? Yikes. The roads are covered with trees, debris, dead animals, and downed electrical wires. Traffic lights not only don't work, but lots of them are smashed on the ground. What do they expect? Where were these people for the week leading up to the storm? Don't tell me they don't watch TV. The government—state and local, all the news stations, plus the hunky guys at the Weather Channel nagged us ad nauseam to prepare to be on our own for at least a few days, if not a week.

So while the rest of us sit by lantern light munching our peanut butter and jelly sandwiches or granola bars and sipping warm Gatorade watching our battery television, these foolish people are screeching their outrage, demanding personal attention. What I want to know is why the TV stations don't send crews to neighborhoods like mine, where everybody's chipping in to help each other. Okay, I know the reason. Tragedy and controversy lead, and *we* are boring. But, I'd love for the nation to see it. We take a lot a grief from our friends and family about Florida. Can't tell you how many laughing-hysterically phone calls I got about the 2000 vote. Nothing like being the butt of a national joke.

After the storm, there are puddles. Big ones. Mini lakes. We've been told not to let the kids play in them. There might be a hidden live power line. Or snakes. Baby gators. Or floating animal feces. Enough nasty stuff to boost the *yuck* meter off the chart.

But playing with puddles is irresistible. So when his parental units weren't looking, a ten-year-old boy grabbed his fishing pole and headed for the four foot deep swollen swale. He imagined there were fish, just like in the canal. When his line hooked on something near the bottom, he yanked so hard, he lost his balance and fell in. He screamed, and Dad came running. The boy, after his dunking in filth, sputtered his way up the bank and threw up.

Then he cried because his pole was still stuck at the bottom. His father felt bad for the kid. Instead of waiting a few days for the water to drain, Dad waded in to fetch it for him. As he reached down into the dark fetid depths, his hand feeling for the pole, a sharp jolt of pain hit him. He cursed and jumped from the water, holding his bleeding finger. He swears it wasn't the fish hook—something bit him, he insists.

The boy's doctor's office had no electricity yet, so the Mom called a friend's pediatrician whose office did have power. She took her son to check for any rare tropical fungus or disease that thrives in muck. Apparently, she didn't care what her husband had been exposed to. He got a raging infection in his finger. And a divorce. Mom left Dad and now lives with the new pediatrician. See? The experts were right. Puddles *are* dangerous.

Every man in Florida wants to own a chainsaw, if he doesn't already. But not every guy is cut out to wear the lumberjack plaid. Accidents with chainsaws skyrocket in the days after a hurricane. One unfortunate fellow electrocuted himself when he hit a power line. Another didn't die, but had to be hospitalized when the connection between the power cord and the extension cord was dragged through wet grass. And still another fell thirty feet from a tree while cutting a limb, breaking several of his own limbs. He says he's just lucky the saw didn't land on him.

MAKE LIKE A TREE AND LEAF

I have a love/hate relationship. With a tree. A really big tree. In my front yard. It is magnificent. It thinks it's a New England tree, but it's a little ferblunjit with the timing. It just finished dropping all its leaves. While everywhere else on my block looks like summer in South Florida, my yard is Vermont in October. My neighbors snicker at me raking when they stroll by. They think I don't hear them as I'm stuffing bag after bag after bag, but I do. The yard guys are zero help. As many times as I've asked them not to, they *helpfully* use their blowers to force tons of leaves under the other plants, which prevents enough water from reaching their roots that they can die. The modern day yard guy has probably never seen the exotic tool called a rake.

Someone once told me the name of my tree (botanical, not his real name—which is Fred), but I neglected to write it down and have since forgotten it. Fred has many massive, easy-to-climb branches. My youngest used to take his homework up there and study while nestled in a comfortable seat formed by two branches, enjoying the breeze and the view. In all, everyone loves Fred. Fred really is beautiful.

I am nearly finished getting the gazillions of leaves off the lawn, from under the begonias and shrubs (where they are hard-packed by the blowers), and out of the gutters. Yes, my weekends are so very glamorous. You'd think I'd be celebrating. Nope. Because the next phase is worse. About fifteen minutes after the last leaf drops, Fred sprouts the new, shiny, pretty, little yellow-green baby leaves. Fifteen minutes after that, tiny blossoms erupt forth. They are so teensy, when you look up into Fred's canopy, you can't even see them.

So it comes as a huge surprise (to those experiencing their first encounter with Fred's relatives) when, a week later, billions of these blossoms start dropping. I do mean billions. And they keep dropping for weeks. They stick to the sidewalk and the bottoms of your shoes. Try scraping them off on the sisal doormat—the suckers wedge themselves in and clog it. You can't rake them, they happily glide right though the tines. So, they must be swept. Which works well until it rains or the sprinklers come on. Then they stick like glue to the driveway and sidewalks and become *slippery* as heck. Which means lawsuit if anybody slips and falls because of them.

Those of us who haven't hired a tree service to hack the freaking tree down hustle out nearly every day to at least sweep or scrape the dingblamed blossoms from the walking areas. And yes, the neighbors are snickering again. It's all to no avail, though. Literally an hour later, so many more have fallen it seems like you imagined all that scraping. Time for the orange traffic cones. Set 'em up at the drop zone ends, because by the time you get home from work, the blossoms will be an inch deep again.

You're probably beginning to understand the love/hate thing. Now add to the messy mix that if the wet blossoms sit for longer than a day or two, they begin to rot. And stink. And draw flies.

I think I'd better stop now. Plotting Fred's demise is becoming a lurid temptation.

ISN'T IT ROMANTIC

MY FUNNY VALENTINE

Perfume. Chocolate. Jewelry. Flowers. The four can't-go-wrong items to give women for Valentine's Day. Granted, there are women who don't care for any of the above, but in general, they get the ball over the goal line, gift-wise.

Some tokens of affection given in Cupid's name are Hall of Fame worthy. Others, the Hall of Shame. A man gave his wife a luxury car. Topped with an enormous red bow like it escaped from a game show, it had five dozen long stemmed red roses inside. However, what if you're not loaded? News flash—it's not about the amount you spend. Not if she loves you. If she doesn't love you, then monetary values are big, really, really big. Do not skimp.

Another man gathered wild flowers, wrapped them in a pink satin ribbon, and wrote a heartfelt love note he tucked inside. His girlfriend cried, she was so touched, and of course she immediately texted her best friend. Okay, granted—best friend's boyfriend now hates Mr. Flower-Picker for making him look extra-cheesy with his quickie box of dimestore chocolates. And—that was in Florida where we *have* flowers blooming in February, but men everywhere can go to a green market or florist and pick individual stems.

The point was he took the time to do it. And that, my dear gentleman friends who might read this, is the key.

To everything. The key to her heart *and* the key to getting lucky on a consistent basis. Go out of your way to do something that shows you care. Washing her car without being asked could melt the most frozen of icicles. Want to be her hero? Do all the laundry (and do it well) for an entire week. Don't know how? Look it up. You Google everything else.

Knowing full well the above pearl of wisdom will no doubt fall on mostly deaf ears, let's move on to the Hall of Shame, shall we? Here are some just awful *gifts*.

Anything that can be picked up at a drugstore fifteen minutes before you give it to her. Think she won't know? Wrong. That travel manicure set? She's seen it a thousand times in the personal care aisle. And she soooo does not want the bath salts and poof set. Ditto for the teddy bear wearing an I-heart-you T-shirt, which is meant for teenage boys to give teenage girls.

Appliances. Women are not like men. (Might help if you recite that phrase as you shop.) We don't want tools as gifts. This isn't 1935, when a gift of a washing machine was manna from heaven because it saved her from untold hours of scrubbing laundry, an aching back, and sore, red, chapped hands. These days, appliances are part and parcel of the household, meaning you'd buy them anyway. So, not a real gift.

Supermarket flower bouquets in white-lace printed plastic sleeves. For the same reason as the drugstore gift above. It reeks of last minute panic. The *oh-my-God-I-forgot-to-get-her-a-gift* gift.

The only exception to the aforementioned examples is if the gift is from a child to his or her mother. Anything the children pick themselves (except for a kitten or puppy—more on that later) is A-Okay. Now here are a few unique presents that fell flat.

Fencing lessons. Yes, epées and en garde and parry and all that sort of Frenchiness. Mary's fiancé had always wanted to learn to fence. So he paid for ten private lessons for her (a surprise gift!), although she'd never uttered any interest in or desire to try fencing. With a positive smile, she endured the first one. Turned out fencing was all about being in a semi-crouch the entire time. Her thighs ached. Mary hated it. But, to not hurt her honey's feelings, she gamely went back for the second lesson. This time, in addition to her male instructor, another instructor—a woman—was teaching a class. Mary found she couldn't take her eyes off the woman's bulging thighs. The instructor was a thin woman with gams the size of Christmas hams. When Mary discovered that huge thighs were as much a part of fencing as the white beekeeper helmet-thingie (which she didn't like either), respect for honey's feelings bailed out the window. Mary told him she wasn't going back—so sorry—and Mr. Fiancé gallantly suggested that he should take the remaining lessons. The more cynical of her friends intimated perhaps that was his goal all along.

A mop head. A wood attachment for a mop handle, its white cotton tendrils flowing from the base like Rapunzel's tresses, greeted Sarah as her husband walked in the door. Seriously. The man presented her with the (unwrapped, not that anyone would wrap such a thing) gift. Whereupon she looked at him in confusion.

"Happy Valentine's Day," he said, smiling. Sarah had no clue what he'd been smoking. The following Halloween, under great revenge pressure from Sarah, hubby wore the untouched mop head as a wig. Lesson—don't buy a gift for your wife while under the influence of any alcohol or drugs.

A bottle of the perfume your last girlfriend wore. Oh, no, no, no. Never do this. Especially if the new girlfriend knows the former girlfriend. Nothing tells a woman she's not your first choice better than a thinly veiled attempt to make her smell like the prior one. This led to a break up, broken glass, and a few stitches.

And last but not least—a pet. Do not give a live animal (although dead or stuffed ones are probably not a smart option, either) to your sweetie. Even if your honey says she wants a puppy, drive her there and let her choose. Tiffany loved those cute little tea-cup pups. Her husband wanted a dog, too. Convinced she didn't know what she truly wanted (how could she possibly know her own mind?), he surprised her with a German shepherd. She liked the puppy just fine until he grew into what she never wanted—a large, strong, slobbery dog with big poop. Her husband traveled a lot, so guess who had the walking, cleaning, poop-scooping duty? It led to fights, and, *yada yada*, four years later they divorced. The ruined couch, stained rug, and the dog went with the husband.

OH, ROMEO

Whenever the subject of love stories emerges, Romeo and Juliet is the first that comes to mind. We all longed for a much different ending to the tale. So, for this Valentine's Day, I'm granting your wish. With apologies to William Shakespeare, I present to you alternative endings to literature's most tragic love story.

Ending number I. (It happens in Italy, hence the Roman numerals)

Juliet's nurse complains constantly about being tired and achy—a perfect role for Mel Brooks in drag, if you ask me. Impulsive and spoiled Juliet never listens to her anyway, so when she and Romeo meet and fall into instant lust when he crashes her family's party, she easily misleads and dodges her weary nurse. She and Romeo have a teenage tryst behind the stables. Meanwhile, Verona's most eligible bachelor, Paris, has set his sights on the fair Juliet. Mr. Capulet, Juliet's father, agrees to the marriage. Juliet re-enters the party picking hay and grass from her mussed hair—her face flushed, lips swollen, her dress rumpled. Her father tells her she's betrothed to Paris, and she stomps up to her chambers in protest.

Paris is good-looking and rich, but she's smitten with Romeo, which she can't tell her family because he is a Montague—the long-time rival family to the Capulets. Conflicting emotions whirl in her head making her dizzy.

55

She's only thirteen, how the heck does she know what she wants? Unable to make a good argument against marrying Paris, she agrees. She knows her father will reject any idea of consorting with a Montague. As the wedding date nears, it becomes apparent that she'll soon be a parent. Too frightened to tell anyone, she simply hopes no one will notice at the wedding. A predicament like this does make me speculate—perhaps that is how the Empire-waisted dress trend began. Juliet will have lots of sex with Paris, then convince him the baby arrived early. The nurse has cataracts and merely thought she'd finally been successful at getting the skinny girl to eat something.

At a dinner the night before the wedding, Paris asks for a word with Juliet in private. Alone in her father's study, he kisses her, presents her with a beautiful necklace, and cops a quick feel up her dress. He freaks out, storms from the room, and screams about damaged goods, accusing the Capulets of trickery. Juliet's father demands to know who de-flowered his daughter and ruined his extremely profitable alliance with Paris' family. Romeo Montague is found and frog-marched to face the Capulets. Tybalt wants to kill him, but Mr. Capulet sends for Friar Laurence. Juliet will marry Romeo, then he'll send them both packing off to the Montagues. He figures the whole mess is their problem now. Romeo doesn't want to marry a girl he barely knows, and he sure as heck doesn't want a baby at this stage in his young life. With the help of his best friend Mercutio, he makes a break for it and escapes to the countryside, where rumor had it he made his way to Spain to see who he could de-flower there. Okay, it's not a happy ending, but at least everybody's still alive, right?

Ending number II

Romeo and Juliet do get married because of the pregnancy. They live with his parents. Juliet's mother-in-law can't stand her. Juliet's not too fond of his mother, either. Her time comes, and she delivers triplet boys. Romeo runs for the hills.

Ending number III

Romeo and Juliet stay married and live with his parents. Romeo has an over-sized libido, and the couple have four more children. All girls. The triplet boys, Mario, Luigi, and Yoshi, grow into unruly, spoiled teenagers. Juliet's exhausted. It seems she can't go a day without Romeo trying to get into her pants. She's twenty-eight, the mother of seven, and her mother-in-law never sprang for any household help for her, much less nurses for the children. Her teeth are rotting, her breasts are sagging to her navel, and the dark bags under her eyes make her look like she's sixty. On one particularly bad day, young Mario—who inherited the Montague libido—insults the Prince of Verona by making a pass at his niece and winds up in jail, Yoshi declares he wants to become an actor, and Luigi is found lying with the stable boy—by his grandfather Montague, who grabs a pitchfork and chases the buck-naked kid into the woods. That night, when Romeo approaches Juliet with *that* look in his eye—the one that means she won't be getting any of her very much needed sleep, she freaks, bolts from the room, and—runs for the hills.

On second thought, maybe the *happy dagger* was the best ending after all.

CHOCOLATE WORKS

Gentlemen, if you wish to enhance the likelihood of a lusty Valentine's canoodling, pay attention.

While long-stemmed red roses are the cliché classic, you can do better. Add chocolate. You know we love it. "But wait," you say. "I do give her chocolates, and the canoodling, if I can get any, is iffy at best."

Well, if you've done the check list of pre-date tasks (helpfully listed below), and you haven't recently compared her unfavorably to your mother or an ex-girlfriend, then your problem is you bought cheapo drugstore bargain chocolate. You might as well have given her a bottle of sewer water instead of perfume. Listen now and take notes.

There is a valid and scientific reason to give chocolate to your sweetie on Valentine's Day. Women react to and crave chocolate more than men do. I dare say we crave it in lieu of men at times. Science has discovered why. It has theobromine and phenylethylamine in it, and apparently females are more sensitive to them. But what the heck are those things, you ask? Trust me, while I did do the arduous research, the explanations and reasons are complicated and pretty much boring enough to be an effective anesthetic. I fell asleep while reading what I printed out. Twice. Simply accept the miracle I'm sharing.

They call phenylethylamine the 'Love Drug'. I've seen three different spellings for it—even the experts can't stay awake long enough to get it right or agree with each other. (Obviously, neither they, nor I, had the sense to eat chocolate while tackling this.) And no matter which way I type it, my dear friend Bill Gates (Word) tells me I've got it wrong. I also don't know how to pronounce it. So, I'm nicknaming it Penny-Ethel. No wonder nobody reports on this. It's way too tedious, and all anyone really cares about is eating the end results. Because of Penny-Ethel, a man's chances of getting some serious nookie on Valentine's Day are much better. Penny-Ethel is a dopamine booster. Makes her feel euphoric and excited. Couple that with the caffeine-like effects of the theobromine and before you can say melt in your mouth, your honey will melt into your arms.

Here's the catch. (There's always a catch.) You have to open the wallet and spring for the good stuff. Cheapo chocolate just won't work. The higher quality of the cacao, the more magical Penny-Ethel in it. It is worth searching out the best—chocolate made from the Criollo variety in Venezuela is the ultimate.

Another catch is you must attend to your personal grooming. Get a close shave. And for God's sake, trim those nasty, wiry, out-of-control nose, ear, and eyebrow hairs. Take a shower. Use deodorant. Brush and floss your teeth. Don't eat garlic that day. Wear unwrinkled, clean clothing with no rips or stains. I know, I know— what a pain in the patookie. But a crinkled two-inch hair protruding from your ear is enough to make us run scared—after snagging the chocolate, of course.

Unfortunately, there is yet one more catch. One I didn't know existed until a friend pointed it out. To get lucky, you have to do *everything else* right, too, if you believe what you see on television. Or rather, what *she's* seen on television. **Everything.** Like choosing the right flowers, making a dinner reservation at the right restaurant, wearing the right clothes, smelling of the right aftershave, and so on. None of that ever seemed to matter to anyone in real life that I knew, but I've come to learn after many years that we—where I grew up—were not, in fact, hip. So, tiptoe over those eggshells, boys, and increase your odds with my chocolate advice.

Or—dump the high-maintenance chick with the attitude and addiction to crappy television, and find one who'll be thrilled you thought of her. It is a made-up holiday, after all. But you still have to pluck. Sorry.

JUST A GIGOLO

Trying desperately to become the next mover/shaker/local mucky-muck, the brother of a friend (we called him Jim-the-weasel) some years back thought he had found the way. If the crumbles of his dream weren't so pathetically bogus, the whole affair might have been tragic.

Jim wanted into the 'in' crowd so bad he could feel it vibrating in the silk threads of his Eton dress shirts. He tried running for city council and failed. He frequented the trendiest bars and restaurants in hopes of rubbing elbows with the city's *beautiful* people. He contributed to campaigns and volunteered his off hours to their causes.

None of it worked. The harder he tried to schmooze, the less he was included in the A-lists of parties. He took dancing lessons. He memorized details about posh resorts, the latest trends, the expensive cars and cigars. He told funny but clean jokes. Perfected his table manners. He opened doors and pulled out chairs for women.

All we could figure—from our decidedly middle-class and content-to-be-on-the-C-list observation posts—was desperation and need emanated from Jim. And the A-listers could feel it, smell it, see it radiating off him like heat waves from an overheating dilapidated truck stuck on the side of the road. Poor Jim may as well have doused himself in skunk juice. Seems the *beautiful* people could spot a wanna-be from a polo field away. The mayor's widowed sister turned out to be his Waterloo. Jim saw her as, finally, *the way* that he'd wedge himself into the upper crust.

Jim didn't come from money, but he was quite handsome. In that particular city at that particular time, the who's who la-dee-das valued two things—money and power. Looks came in a distant third and were by no means enough to compensate for lack of the first two.

Jim's pursuit of 'Lila', the mayor's sister, came about when her family dined at the restaurant Jim haunted. He perched at the bar, talking up a self-aggrandizing storm to a couple who waited for a table. The bartender mentioned to them that none other than the mayor himself sat nearby, and with him was his pretty, widowed sister. Lila's husband, a French tycoon, had expired in a skiing accident near Gstaad one year earlier. She'd moved back home from France shortly after. The social elite of the city fawned over her.

Lila was ten years older than Jim, in her forties, but that didn't give him pause. Opportunity was knocking, screaming at him in a deafening roar, and Jim-the-weasel was powerless to resist it. He sent a drink to her table and smiled with charm when she nodded her acknowledgement. Under the pretense of being on his way out the door, he stopped by to pay his regards to such a lovely woman. He feigned surprise upon discovering her brother was the mayor when she introduced them. She gave him her number.

Jim borrowed a BMW (he'd tried for a Mercedes, but

that friend said no) and took Lila out for dinner. He knew the chef at a private supper club and finagled a table at prime-dining time on a Saturday night. It cost him not only mega-bucks for the dinner and the grease-the-palm requirement to the owner, but said owner milked it for more.

Jim believed Lila enjoyed their evening. She laughed, smiled, and in her intense gaze into his gorgeous dark eyes he saw longing and the promise of romance. When he walked her to her door, he kissed her on the cheek and asked to see her again. She agreed. He left feeling jubilant, knowing his charm and his weasel-y plan were working as he predicted.

The next morning, while a huge bouquet of long-stem red roses were being delivered to Lila's door, Jim paid the piper. The supper club owner's fee was for Jim to play chauffeur for the owner and his wife on Sunday morning. So Jim wore a suit, and when he arrived at their home in his Honda Accord, the supper club owner smirked and handed him a chauffeur's cap.

Their destination was a fund-raising brunch at the city's premier art museum. Jim dropped the couple at the entrance, then moved the Mercedes to wait for them. He watched the well-heeled attendees arrive in their fancy cars, salivating over the possibility he might soon belong in their ranks. A Rolls-Royce stopped under the entry portico, its driver exited, then opened the rear passenger door. Out stepped a pair of long, beautiful legs wearing stilettos. His gaze traveled up and, to his dismay, it was Lila. Shocked, Jim pulled the cap over his eyes and slumped in his seat, afraid she'd spot him. A distinguished older man came out the other side of the Rolls, took her arm, and escorted her into the building.

More determined than ever and not about to let some old man disrupt his delusional plan for wealth and easy living, Jim parked his Honda several blocks away from Lila's that afternoon and walked to her door. After all, what woman would choose a crusty dodger over a young, energetic lover? Especially when he possessed Jim's good looks? He spun her a yarn about how he realized her home just happened to be on his jogging route. She invited him in. Sparks flew, and before you could say phony-baloney, they did the horizontal tango.

Their hot and heavy affair went on for several months. Jim fostered his illusion by taking her places in rented and borrowed cars, spending oodles of cash. Jim's sister earned a verbal smack-down by pointing out that Lila continued to attend all the society events, but hadn't invited Jim to be her date at a single one.

The day arrived when Jim felt he'd hooked Lila and reeled her in but good. He maxed out his credit cards and bought an engagement ring. On his knees, his eyes filled with hope for a lifetime of travel, servants, gourmet food, pictures in the society pages, and all-around ostentatious consumption, Jim recited his eloquent speech asking Lila to marry him.

Poor Jim. She laughed. Actually laughed at him, and said, "Oh, Jim. Don't be ridiculous. You don't love me anymore than I love you. And I already have a puppy."

Ouch. Turns out Lila was a champion weasel from the big-leagues.

LETTERS OF LOVE

Many moons ago, we humans used a form of communication called writing. Our parents lectured us on the crazy expense of long distance phone calls. According to them, one call to the friend who'd moved to California would send them into debtor's prison. So we wrote—with a pen or pencil on actual paper—letters. It's a quaint notion now, but one I wish we could bring back. And believe me, so does the Post Office. The US Post Office was awesome then. They used to allow almost anything as an envelope. We mailed coconuts with the addresses written in black marker right on the husk. When McDonalds came out with the hot apple pie, it was sold in a red cardboard sleeve, and we sent letters in those, too. Our keen eyes began to see every object as having envelope potential. Guess we thought it was cool. And the more we liked someone, the more inventive we became.

There were a lot of letters exchanged. And—this should put a permanent cringed expression on the face of every friend and ex-beau of mine—I saved all of them. Yes. All. If any of you become amazingly famous, I could cash in big-time. Don't know if I would. I'd have to consider it on a case by case basis and the amount of moolah it might bring. There's no need for panic, though. Figuring out where the darned things wound up after the last move could take a while. Heaven knows what box they could be hibernating in.

Returning to the non-larcenous take on my spiel, about a decade ago, my mom was in one of her cleaning modes. It can be a very dangerous mode, and it's another one of the genes I did not inherit from her—football fanatic being the biggest other. If you know anyone who values strict organization above all else, then you understand. Mom can't stand having *stuff* around. So much so that she's constantly trying to give the six of us kids back the tchotchkies we gave her as presents over many, many years. *Here, honey, I know you're going to want this.* No, Mom, I don't. *I gave it to you.* In some cases, she'll swear I gave her some weird object that I have no recollection of ever seeing. Much less buying. Much, much less *ever* considering as a gift to my beloved mother. I think she just wants to get rid of it so much, she'll convince me it was my fault it now sits in her cabinet and hopes I simply don't remember. Oy.

Recently, I received a sizable box in the mail. Unexpected and from my mom. It wasn't Christmas or my birthday. I opened it and unloaded it item by item. Stuff. Stuff you couldn't pay me to take. The further I got, the whackier it was. Old and tattered organza shaped to look like roses and meant to hold candles. *There*'s a tragic fire just waiting to happen, huh? Strange plates with dancing cows and daisies. A white satin Jackie O-style dress with a little matching jacket. If I can get a couple of aged stains out, it might be worth something. A yard of monkey-print fabric. Pez dispensers. But not in the original packages and obviously used. The entire box was jammed with junk that should have spent its declining years adorning a landfill. Although I do have a friend who *loves* monkeys, and I suppose I could make her a pillow. Now I'll have to distract her from reading this or I'll be committed.

Anyway, during a tornado-like sweep of the upper shelves of the front hall closet, Mom found a bag filled with old letters. Apparently, she'd deposited every letter each of us kids wrote to our parents after we went to college or moved away. Pleas for money. Notes from my grandmothers and aunts and uncles. Descriptions of family events and disasters. She saved serious missives from my brother (fondly known as Dr. Vegetables) during his doctorate studies.

I happened to be visiting that day and luckily glimpsed inside the bag by the garage door, meant for the garbage can. I asked what it was, and when she told me, I grabbed it and squirreled it away. It made the move to Florida with me and years later, I finally tackled it. Boy, did I hit the motherlode. I have enough good fodder to last for quite some time, and, as a bonus, plenty of embarrassing evidence to blow my siblings away if they ever get too big for their britches. Not that I'd ever do that, but it's always a good idea to have leverage with your brothers and sisters. You never know when it'll come in handy.

There were some poignant cards and letters in the bag. Tender sentiments from good and bad times. And it got me to thinking how—oops—I wrote earnest letters to those I loved. I sure hope they had the good sense to throw mine away.

THE KENSPECKLE SYNDROME

Ah, l'amour. Pepe Le Pew (the cartoon skunk) spots his perfect female from across the park and charges into full-on courting mode. He's instantly in love and makes a total shnook of himself only to find she's really a cat with a paint stripe on her tail. In her own non-verbal cartoonish way, she *did* try to tell him the truth. Blinded by his ardor, Pepe wouldn't see or listen.

It's a child's cartoon. Or a dead-on warning to all humans who fall into the love-is-blind trap. And what a wascally, deceptive trap it is, too. Years later, otherwise smart and savvy people slap themselves silly and say, "What was I thinking?"

Most of us have made complete idiots of ourselves. How many friends have we all watched plunge into the deep-end of the emotional swamp of (supposed) true love without so much as a backward glance? At the very least they could have handed their valuables to a friend to hold for safekeeping before climbing onto the high dive. But no. Their stories are legend. Here is one from the annals of disastrous pairings. Grab a glass of wine and a box of tissues.

There's no fool like an old fool. Boy, ain't that the truth? I knew a wealthy (I mean—the loaded, could-book-a-flight-into-space-orbit-with-Sir-Richard-Branson kind of rich) man who had been married four times already. Except for the first wife, who'd been his same age when they wed at age twenty-five, the wives got progressively younger. I really liked him. He was a very nice man, but not by anyone's measure was he good-looking. As he aged, he didn't stay in shape either. So then he was sixty, pale and paunchy, with a waddle of a double chin, and he wanted to meet another woman. Unfortunately, the only women who caught his attention were twenty or thirty-somethings with model-perfect faces and enormous augmented chests. He harbored the common delusion among wealthy men that he was so fascinating, a woman like that could fall into true love with him. Now, I'm not just picking on men. I'm aware that women can delude themselves with considerable aplomb as well.

Back to our modern-day Pepe Le Pew. If he hadn't driven the top-end Mercedes (and owned a Lamborghini, Ferrari, and a Porsche), lived in a mansion on the ocean with hot-and-cold running servants, owned a yacht, and done things like jet over to Cannes for the weekend, I doubt any of these young ladies would have wasted a single glue-on batted eyelash on him. Seriously, look at some of the rich men in the news who have major-babe wives. You think the ladies would have married those guys if it meant living in average-land? The man who drives a Chevy or a Ford, fixes his own lawnmower, and worries about how he'll pay for his kids' college educations? You don't see them with super-babes.

Anyway, about my delusional rich friend? After the first four wives took him to the cleaners (but don't worry, he made more money—lots of it), he decided to require wife number five to sign a pre-nup. But wife number five's lawyer insisted on a clause that specified a six-year limit on the pre-nup. If the marriage lasted over six years, then the pre-nup no longer existed. If he didn't agree to it, she said she wouldn't marry him. My friend—blinded by mad lust, he was crazed over this woman—agreed, thinking six years was a great test of true devotion. I sure do wish he'd checked with a few of his friends first. I know I would have told him to forget that clause.

For those six years, she played the part of adoring wife to perfection. He totally believed she loved him in return. They went to dinner at the most expensive restaurant in three counties to celebrate their sixth anniversary. She cooed and cried when he presented her with the diamond and sapphire necklace from Harry Winston. He'd personally picked out the flowers he gave her. They had a wonderful time in the bedroom that night— or he thought they both did.

I'm afraid you can guess what happened next. Uh-huh. The day after—not a year, not a month, not even a week—the six-year pre-nup expired, she filed for divorce. The poor guy was devastated. Unlike everyone else in his life (heck, the household staff had bets going—and by the way, the gardener won), he never saw it coming.

He was the kind of man you had to get to know before you'd appreciate him. The kind of man who grew on you, so that as you fell in love, he'd become better and better looking. Problem was, he wanted to jump into the sack almost immediately with whomever he dated. And the only women who'll do that right away—with a man they don't know, who's overweight and on the cusp of ugly—are the women who are after his money.

I made up a technical term for this phenomenon. The Kenspeckle Syndrome. Whereas everyone but you sees the blatantly obvious truth. I understand young people making the mistake of slipping into the dreaded KS, but you'd think that by the time a person is over fifty, they'd have wised up just a tad. Well, you'd think wrong. Apparently, there are no limits to the human ego. We believe what we want to believe, no matter the evidence to the contrary. So, is it any wonder there are others who would prey upon the trusting?

Is there a moral to this precautionary tale? Nah. What would be the point? The ones who are aware of their own egos don't need it, and the ones who do need it won't recognize themselves. My wealthy friend has since married a sixth time—I kid you not. But if only for basic humanity's sake—beware of felines with a faux stripe on their tails.

FOR MEN—A ROMANTIC PRIMER

My new editor asked me to write my February column about romance. Borrowing from the great Bugs Bunny – "She don't know me very well, do she?" Poor thing probably hasn't had time to read many back issues and doesn't realize what my track record is.

But I take pride in doing what I'm told (sometimes). And I relish relaying romantic tales. So here goes.

Valentine's Day means a lot. To women. Not so much to men. Most men do what they're told to do by their woman in order to maintain the household peace. This I know with certainty, because I have three adult sons and have had three semi-adult husbands. I believe this makes me an expert in the romantic gifts and gestures department, or—perhaps more accurately—what *not* to give the woman in your life if you ever expect to have intimate relations again.

After all, every man hopes that giving the right gift will lead to what we women call *romance*. The men call it something else that I can't say here. The smart ones realize that a thoughtful, mushy gift will open a woman's heart and make her feel all warm and tingly inside. Which leads to a long walk in the woods, then some playful swapping of baseball caps, then a relaxing soak in twin bathtubs outside in the yard while watching the sunset. Oh. Wait. No. That's a special pill commercial.

Most men these days do know that most women are wired differently and require a little schmoozing. They don't understand it—because, honestly, all they need is a simple nod toward the bedroom, and they'll be out of their boxers and under the sheets before you take three steps down the hall—but if some affectionate gestures and canoodling make his woman want to jump his bones, a man will comply. But this is where some of the worst stories come into the picture. Seems that even what comprises those gestures is a mystery to men. Just when they think they've got it nailed and are doing something romantic, it can all blow up in their faces, poor things. A few things *not to do*:

Shoulder rubs are wonderful and most women will welcome one—but not when standing at the kitchen sink scrubbing pots—you're likely to get hit over the head with a frying pan. Better idea? Gently nudge her away from the sink, dry her hands, pour her a glass of wine, and *you* finish the job. By the way, this only works if you do a *good* job of it, not the old—*I'll do a crummy job, and she'll never ask me to do it again* ploy. Because that just pisses her off worse and gets you further from your goal. Much further. You have no idea how much further. One of the best pieces of advice for a male cohabitating with a female is to learn early on *how* she likes certain household tasks done, then actually *do* them that way. If more nookie is what you're after, listen and follow my directions. Doing chores badly only makes her think of you as she would an irresponsible teenager. Someone she needs to supervise—so she's still on duty, not relaxed. And if your woman is the weird exception that finds a grown man who acts like a petulant teenager a turn-on, well, it's up to you of course, but I say there's a whole lotta trouble coming your way. If you stay, then you deserve what you get. Don't say I didn't warn you.

Don't tell her you've planned a romantic evening, have the wine poured, get her all comfy on the sofa, then have a porn movie start playing when you hit the remote. (Unless you know, for a very, very, solid fact, that she's into it. Come to think of it, get that in writing and have it notarized.) Women will compare themselves with the gorgeous, but anorexic, girl with huge boobs on the screen and wonder why you need to look at her to get turned on. Which leads to massive feelings of inadequacy and lower confidence and not so much fun in the bedroom—if the door hasn't been slammed in your face already.

Do not write her a *poem* that has *any* words rhyming with bucket. Just don't.

In addition, do not give her the following 'gifts'—all courtesy of my exes: Rubber grippie-things to help open jars. A box of real coal chunks in a pretty box from the most expensive jeweler in town. No jewelry hidden inside, just the chunks. A used coffee mug. A scrub brush for the car. And a framed picture of her mother-in-law.

You are welcome.

WEIRD HISTORY

OOPS – DIDN'T KNOW THAT WOULD HAPPEN

At some point, early man said, "Enough of the nomad stuff, I'm tired." Inspired no doubt by his spousal unit, Girg—"*You're* tired? Listen to me, Grog. *I'm* the one schlepping these bags with three kids on my back from one end of the plains to the other. For what? A couple of scrawny antelope and a branch of berries? It's up with the tent, then scrounging for kindling. Take down the tent, pack it all up again. I'm done. There's a nice view of the valley here. A lovely stream. I'm staying put." Grog wisely decided to stay and garden to augment his hunting and gathering, though he most likely delegated the grunt work to Girg. At their first Paleolithic garden club meeting, I envision Girg sitting in silence and rolling her eyes as Grog takes the credit for their prize-winning beets. Year after year, the competition grew—because that's how we humans operate—and the race for biggest and the best was on.

In response to man's efforts, the natural world seemed to laugh and say, "Oh, yeah? Watch this." It's time to explore the unintended consequences of improving on nature.

There are ample examples of good intentions gone screwy. Florida, as you probably know, had some major goof-ups. Hawaii, however, has some unique instances. Being islands and isolated, nature ran amok (like the dinosaurs in Jurassic Park).

Hawaii really was a paradise—before humans got there. No snakes, rats, or mosquitoes. Lots of pretty yellow and red feathered birds flitting from treetop to treetop, happily minding their own business. Then, century by century, men tried to improve circumstances on the islands. When the Tahitians arrived, they brought small Asian pigs. Rats, too—on purpose. They were a tiny species (weighing about three ounces), the Pacific rat, and they used them for sport. Target practice, actually. The Tahitians made mini bows and arrows to shoot the teeny vermin. Legend has it they made quite a tasty pupu (Hawaiian for appetizer).

When Captain Cook found the islands—I won't say discovered—he brought goats and let some loose. Rats skittered ashore, probably lured by the tantalizing aroma of fresh papayas, mangoes, and bananas. Imagine what the dregs of such a ship's hold, after an ocean crossing, smelled like. Can you blame the creatures? Soon the whaling ships made regular stops in Hawaii. Their stowaways were the big Norway rats and the roof rats. With no natural predators on the islands, they multiplied faster than that Duggar family from Arkansas with the nineteen kids. They were terrific climbers (the rats—I don't know about the Duggars), and conducted shock-and-awe nighttime raids on the poor little pretty birds' eggs in their nests.

Now the birds were already having a hard go, because the Hawaiian royals developed a fanatical love for their yellow and red feathers. The royal capes and headdresses were enormous and beautiful. And made exclusively of the tiny feathers. You can see some of them at the

Bishop Museum in Honolulu. As you can imagine, it took a lot of Tweety-Birds to make just one goofy hat. Alas, we're back to that human *keep up with the Jones' and I'm better than you* garbage. Anyway, the birds are long extinct.

In 1827, the Wellington, a whaler, came to Hawaii. It hadn't done well. The barrels in its hold were still filled with water as ballast, instead of the expected whale blubber. The water in the barrels teemed with mosquito larvae. They emptied the barrels into a river. If I could borrow Dr. Peabody's Way-Back machine (Rocky and Bullwinkle show—look it up), and could go back in time to anywhere I wanted, I'd go try and stop those fools from introducing mosquitoes to the islands. Just like everything else introduced in paradise, the darn pests have flourished. They morphed into huge dive-bombing blood suckers.

The subsequent trading vessels brought large feral pigs that mated with the little Asian ones, and now there are two-hundred pound boars roaming—well, anywhere they want, quite frankly—but mostly in the middle elevations. The pakalolo (marijuana) growers plant on the mountain slopes in hopes of evading the police—the down side being their crop is subject to trampling or uprooting by boars. Maybe the boars ingest some of the plant while they're uprooting and searching for tasty grubs and roots. That would sure explain a run-in I had with one. In Hawaiian, lolo means crazy. A giant boar with nasty-looking tusks wandered into my (sea-level) yard on the North Shore of Oahu. He seemed dazed and confused (hence the he-ate-pot theory) like he had no clue how he wound up there. I'd just stepped out of the house and onto the lanai when he emerged from the tall California grass and sauntered into the driveway. I froze. He froze. I backed toward the door and reached for the handle behind me. Guess he didn't like the way I did that, because he snorted, then charged. I screamed, fled into the house, slammed the door, and ran to the window. Halfway to the lanai steps, he changed course and raced for three palm trees in the center of the lawn. He circled them a few times, then headed for the road, Kamehameha Highway. Dodging the passing cars, he crossed and disappeared into the woods on the other side.

Back to the rats. Sugar cane became the money crop, and the rats loved the sugar cane. So the sugar companies imported seventy-two mongoose from Jamaica (who'd gotten them from India) and set them free. Just an eensy problem came to light. Rats are nocturnal. The mongoose hunts during the day. So now, there are gazillions of rats and mongooses enjoying the lush life of sunny days and mild nights. Both animals carry leptospirosis. It's in their droppings, and poisons the streams and water supplies. Oh, and the mongooses eat bird eggs, too. Oops.

YOU AND ME AND TEA

I once went to a Fourth of July celebration concert with an English friend. When I invited her, she said, "Oh, sure. Gloating's far more fun when the losers are present."

Huh. I hadn't thought about the Fourth from a British person's perspective. It made me consider how little we modern day Americans know about the personalities of the people who were responsible for that little tiff we call the American Revolution.

We were ticked off by King George's government treating the American colonies as though they were property. As if! How dare they! Oh, wait. Technically, the colonies were. But still. The British had the nerve to levy taxes on needed supplies like paper, paint, glass, and tea. Never mind that the taxes were supposed to help pay off the debt from the French and Indian War. In North America and the Caribbean, it was a battle against the French for control of those colonies. The American colonists hated the notion of the French taking over, so England really was fighting for their cause as well. And it was pretty darn pricey. In fact, so staggering a debt that it nearly destroyed the English government.

The colonists didn't care. Already, the fledgling soon-to-be rebellious ones conveniently forgot they almost had to learn French and seriously step up their game in the kitchen. And who wouldn't want to forget? That's a lot of pressure—going from preparing basic grub (Sorry, English) to excelling in wine reductions, crème fraiche, and escargot. King George III was a little unstable—not completely mad yet. But King Louis XV? Despite being known as *the beloved*, Louis wasn't. (It's kind of like how every North Korean *adores* Kim Jong Un.) Louis was—as were all the Louies—weird. And surprisingly progressive by today's standards. He was the first one to send a transvestite to spy on the Russians. Luckily for us, Louis never met a war he couldn't lose. Might it have had something to do with too much wine and men wearing silk stockings?

Back to our British overlords. By 1770, only the tea tax remained. Big deal, right? Depends on how much you know about human beverage history. And lucky for you, I've done extensive research. Tea was the first non-alcoholic drink in the Western world that wouldn't make you sick. See, back in those days, everybody knew if you drank water, you could die. They didn't understand the why. Until tea, everybody drank beer or wine. Seriously. Even the kids. It's a miracle the human race didn't stagger its way into cave walls and off cliffs, stab themselves with poisoned arrows, and get dizzy and tumble down the pyramids to extinction. So tea was a big deal. It enabled the Industrial Revolution, because sober people can be trusted around machinery. Drunk people, not so much.

But perhaps England's biggest mistake in all of this was allowing volunteers to go populate the New World in the first place. They should have assigned people to go instead. Because the people who would volunteer to leave everyone and everything they know to sail for months to an uncertain fate carry a certain daring adventure *gene*. Yes—I know it's not *really* a gene. Don't make me roll my eyes at you. All of us Americans, back then and now, carry this *thing* I'm calling a gene. Americans come from ancestors who dared to leave home and try something new. People seeking freedom from other people telling them what to do or believe.

As a result, by default—we Americans are independent. Curious. Brave. Brash. Restless. Self-motivated. Inventive. It's why our spirit is admired around the world. The most adventurous people from all the other countries *chose* to come here, effectively diminishing their home country's gene pools of such traits. We can't help being rebellious. It's in our blood. So, of course that pesky tea tax was going to piss them off royally. There was a bit more to it than that, but I don't want to overstay my welcome in the history aisle.

My fellow Americans, this is an awesome responsibility. Our demanding that *they*—whoever *they* are (Oops, it's the government, don't tell anyone)—*do something* (This is outrageous!) is constantly at war with our inner rebel that doesn't want anybody messing with our lives. Until we break an axle in a deep pothole. *Why the heck can't these fools manage to fill a hole?!* Or dozens of people fall ill from salmonella in a restaurant. *Why can't THEY make sure these places serve safe food?!* Or your baby gets lead poisoning from chewing on an imported toy. *Why can't THEY test these things before they allow them into our country?!*

Nothing's changed. We want it both ways. And that's impossible. Happy Fourth of July, you rebel, you.

MAYBE YOU'RE A BLUEBLOOD, OR MAYBE NOT

Why get married? These days, it's because two people are in love—or at least in deep-like. It wasn't always this way. Being in love with—heck, actually having *met*— your intended is a relatively new phenomenon. Tales of defiance and even death spring from accounts of marriages that maybe pushed the fickle finger of fate a tad too far.

The stories range from mere pranks—*gee, it seemed funny at the time, Dad*—to real in-your-face defiance and murder. They start way back—when people were often made to marry for political or financial reasons. Marriage was a business contract, and many such contracts garnered zero interest from the betrothed ones. It wasn't uncommon for children as young as twelve to be married off by their elders for the family's gain. So now, imagine a teenager, we'll call him Reynard. He's rich with hot-and-cold running servants, and he has to marry someone he's never laid eyes on. At fourteen, he's a spoiled little shit. And if his spies return from a surreptitious mission to the guest house and report that the intended bride is not particularly fetching? Easy. Have a band of disguised (yeah, like nobody in town knew who they were) hooligans break into her bath and cart her off naked, eventually dumping her into a vat of blue dye. This being France, naturally it was a *fabulous* dye. Nine months after the escapade, two of the bride's deflowered attendants gave birth. Seems the kids turned that night into quite a party. Those darned horny teenagers. The actual marriage produced twelve children. Not a one of them blue. Jeepers, how many offspring they would have had if Reynard had actually been attracted to her? It does make you wonder if that's where the expression *blueblood* comes from.

In some cases, the entourage escorting the bride-to-be would need to be housed for a month or more. When there weren't enough guest quarters, things were improvised. Barns were mucked out, or if the weather was mild, tents sufficed. If the incoming bride was uber-rich or important, then the groom's family surrendered relatives' rooms and shuttled poor old Aunt Gertrude into a horse stall. Now the bride has to marry some guy she never met *and* Aunt Gertie's pissed off at her. How true were the rumors that the old warted hag was a witch? What if the groom was the male version, physically, of Gert? They were related, after all.

If the bride or groom were good-looking, they might be enticingly paraded in front of the reluctant party. All complaints ceased, and sometimes the date moved up. More than once, in a fit of middle-age-crazy lust, a widowed (or hastily divorced) father stole his son's arranged bride for himself, then assigned the homely sister to his kid. For a bride to remain hidden until the wedding day could signify humility, modesty, or shyness—it wasn't always a *beware of the dog* clue. It's possible her father didn't want the groom's father spoiling the arrangement, and keeping her beauty under wraps was a protection. But internal alarm bells sounded when the groom stayed sequestered or out on peasant-supervising duties (can't collect that dung or haul the harvest properly without some big shot shouting orders from under a shady tree, now can you?) until the big day. Seriously, what young man skips out on a full month of sanctioned constant partying and despoiling chamber maids? That meant the groom likely was horrifyingly ugly or had a skin disease. Or weak. Or blatantly gay. Edward II had to be carried away from his partying boyfriends and forced by his father's guards—into his marriage bed with Isabella of France. What if the groom was decrepit with rheumy eyes and no teeth—and in those days, that could be age fifty. (Fifty was the new eighty?) They didn't want the girl committing suicide or fleeing to take her chances in the forest—which was probably the real story of Snow White—before the deed was done.

One rumored tale had a nobleman participating in his own marriage by proxy. He didn't appear until he came to a darkened marriage chamber that night and every night until his wife announced her first pregnancy. She'd never seen him, but told her ladies he was an attentive lover, and she was amply pleased (like, wow!) with her mystery man. Once the baby boy was born, her husband allowed her to see him. He was unathletic and really ugly. After that, they went to bed with the candles lit. She was pretty. He liked seeing her. She reported that her husband's touch had changed, things weren't as . . . er, bountiful, and he was now a selfish lout in bed. Hamlets are notoriously terrible places for secrets. Eventually, the wife heard through the rampant village potato vine about a studly young man—all the young maidens doted on him—who'd been given a large sum by her husband the nobleman to explore the world and make his fortune. Had the nobleman simply wanted to improve his gene pool and take the credit for a better-looking heir? Their subsequent children unfortunately resembled daddy.

Many times, an older woman—widowed, perhaps with sons already, arrived to marry a boy. A proven male-heir bearer was a valuable commodity. This was before anyone knew it was the man's contribution that determined a child's gender. In those days, if there was no son, it was the woman's fault. Failing to produce the expected boy meant likely divorce, possible banishment, an occasional beheading, or worse—belittling constant abuse from her mother-in-law. Once the wise, older women produced an heir or two, deadly poison often made its way into the meatloaf, or the husband and his mother fell ill from the most mysterious causes, and the wife ruled the kingdom or the family as mother of the heir. Until someone conspired against her, and so it went.

History's a hoot because people don't change. Even back then, potential mates lied about their age and posted deceiving pictures. Take Henry VIII's fourth marriage, to Anne of Cleves, the daughter of the Duke of Cleves in Germany and arguably the most famous mail-order bride in history and maybe the instigator of online dating deception. Not trusting other people's taste, Henry sent the painter Hans Holbein to do portraits of Anne and her sister. When the portraits came to England, he chose Anne. Anne in the flesh apparently didn't measure up to the picture. Henry found her so unattractive, he couldn't consummate the marriage. Not wouldn't. Couldn't. And she had a personal odor problem. Or so went the royal court gossip.

Wives who took advantage of the private services of good-looking servants, who then disappeared. Husbands who arranged quickie divorces and marriages to legitimize babies. Impregnated daughters married off to a nobleman (not the baby's father) with a wink and a nod and a huge sum of money? People sneaking in and out of bedchambers. Yikes. Is anyone's family tree accurate?

Anyway, if your great-great-grandfather swore you were descended from William the Conqueror, and if that actually matters to you—you might want to do a little digging into your DNA pool.

MAY DAY FESTIVITIES

When I was a kid—yeesch, I sound like my dad now—our tiny town's grammar school (elementary—K through 8—the town was too miniscule to have a middle school) made us dress up in our best clothes and prance around a maypole on May 1st. I kid you not. The girls wore frilly dresses, lacy anklets, and patent leather Mary Janes. The boys wore suits (some with snappy plaid bowties) and polished shoes. Moms, grandmoms, and aunties—hair permanent-waved or in tight buns, wearing matronly house frocks, sensible orthopedics, and cat-eye glasses—gathered to ooh and ah at how cute we were. It was as if somebody had poked a hole into the television screen and all of Mayberry spilled out.

We had no idea why skipping around a pole inspired such enthusiasm. They never bothered to explain if there was any meaning to it. We were the little children of the early sixties and simply did what we were told. Walk single file in the hallways. Bang erasers together and inhale the chalk dust. Scraped and bloody knees from the rough asphalt playground surface? Stop fussing, put a bandage on, and go back outside. Climb this rope. Jump that rope. Tug this rope with five other people and knock down the opposing team—on asphalt.

At any rate, to celebrate spring, some of the doddering spinster teachers thought it would be lovely to have the children put on a pageant. We clutched long satin ribbons attached to the top of the pole and performed the steps they taught us. The first part of the ritual was over when the ribbons were completely entwined. The second part was to 'unwind' them by reversing the steps. And it never worked. It was always a tangled mess. Everyone politely hee-hawed while Miss Bessie Mingleton spent ten minutes with a frozen smile undoing the tangle as Miss Evie Tripp banged away on the piano to fill the time, all so the next group of kids could come out and dazzle the crowd.

I should mention that, although they seemed like obedient robots, the boys especially hated the maypole dancing. Faces scrubbed, hair slicked back, and having to touch girly ribbons made them squirm more than usual. A secret game of cootie tag was always in play under the teachers' noses. A certain boy, who we'll call Ralph, made it his solemn duty to ensure the worst ribbon tangle poor Miss Mingleton had ever encountered. And invariably, some boy would manage to get a hold of a girl's hemline and whoosh her skirt upwards to expose her underwear—and make it look like an accident.

I wonder now how many of the adults who put us up to re-enacting Pagan rituals realized just how sexually suggestive the whole maypole thing was designed to be. Yes—designed. An old Germanic custom, also observed by the Druids, Beltane (the night of April 30 to May 1) was all about worshiping phallic symbols and fertility. In ancient days, hundreds of men and women went into the forests on that night to gather plants and flowers to make wreaths and decorations. Yes, at night. I did mention it was a Pagan thing, right? There are historical texts that estimate that two-thirds of the women who went into the woods as virgins, emerged in a very different condition. The babies conceived on that night were traditionally not recognized by their fathers. Those infants were known as Merry-begats and were said to have been fathered by a god.

Blatant debauchery prevailed for many years. Every town erected permanent maypoles and constantly upgraded them if a neighboring burg put up a bigger one. Of course, each time a new pole was brought in, there *had* to be great festivals—and *flower gathering.* One account reported an eighty-foot high pole. Can't imagine what that was about. The townspeople were having way too much fun, because, shockingly enough, when the Puritans took over in England, they outlawed Beltane and maypole festivities in 1644. Makes you want to see population charts, doesn't it? They probably had a big drop in the birth rate. I can see the Puritan leaders scratching their lice-infested heads over that one. They also thought bathing led to promiscuity and immorality, and it invited diseases.

Going back to the mid-twentieth century, it all seemed very innocent to me. Of course, at eight, my sheltered Mayberry-like life hadn't exposed me to anything remotely sexual. Heck, on television, Lucy and Ricky Ricardo and Rob and Laura Petry all slept in twin beds. What did I know? It seems a sure bet that Miss Mingleton, Miss Tripp, and our parents didn't have much interest in history. I like to think that there was at least one person at the school or in our town who understood the symbolism of maypole festivities. I hope that person stood in the back of the auditorium shaking his head and silently laughing as I am now.

RAISING KIDS

THAT SMARTS

How humbling is it to admit your child is no genius? Depends on who your friends and family are, I suppose. And how comfortable you are with denial.

We all know people whose kids play like Mozart on the piano, draw like Michelangelo, dance like Baryshnikov, and reason like Einstein. In their parents' minds, of course. They play the home videos for us to watch their genius in action, usually after dinner and drinks when we're good and toasted, can't fight back, and haven't got the energy to leave the sofa.

Statistically, a certain percentage of the population will be born with high IQs. Another percentage with average IQs, and another with below average. Now, I know the IQ test doesn't measure many things—like character and determination—but there are just some people not destined to cure cancer or build our colony on Mars. What I don't understand is why some parents cannot accept that their prodigy doesn't possess a brilliant mind.

It's as though they've failed some genetic test by passing on an average gene. It's personal to them. And therefore, embarrassing. So they put blinders on and only see what they want to. Which then provides the rest of us with entertainment. Especially people with average genes, like me.

I want to point out that I love kids. All kids. Smart.

Dumb. Athletic. Spastic. Doesn't matter. I look into their little faces, their eyes, and I see love and potential. They all have potential, just different kinds. None is more valuable than any other, since we need all sorts of people and abilities to make our society work. Denial by hyper-fanatic parents, however, makes for some serious humor.

'Janie' had her daughter, 'Flaxen', tested for gifted abilities when the child was four. The private psychologist doing the testing arrived at the expected and paid-for result. Flaxen was *indeed* very gifted, and placed in the local school's gifted kindergarten the following August. While volunteering for the gifted class, a friend—'Darla'— observed Flaxen's behavior. The class used their safety scissors to cut colored shapes from construction paper, then pasted them to the word that spelled the shape. No line-drawing shape outlines to help them. If they didn't know the word, they wouldn't be able to complete the assignment.

Except every other kid looked at the other's papers and figured it out, if they didn't know the word. Flaxen didn't bother. She didn't seem interested. As much as Darla and the teacher told her not to, Flaxen kept eating the paste off the spatula-like applicator, smiling adorably the whole time.

Then there was 'Delroy', the son of a friend's friend. Delroy, according to his Fortune 500 company executive mother, had abilities light-years beyond his peers. The boy went to the birthday party of a third grade classmate. The hit of the party was a scavenger hunt. Each child had a list of items to find within certain rooms of the house and a bag to put them in.

Delroy misread the list. In the chaos, he went into the birthday boy's sister's room. Her name was Kaitlyn. Delroy grabbed what he needed, put it in the bag, then searched for the rest. When time was called, the kids dumped their bags in front of them on the family room carpet. The others had a paper clip. Delroy had a crumbled potato chip. The others found several Captain Underpants books. Delroy, with a very puzzled expression, held up Kaitlyn's underpants. Poor kid. Until that moment, no one had the courage to stand up to his intimidating parents and insist he needed remedial help.

A little girl named 'Jilly', at the insistence of her mother, entered an expressive modern dance class. Before long, every time someone visited the house, Jilly's mom dragged the child out of her room to perform her latest routine, because her daughter showed *all signs of being the next Janet Jackson!* Jilly's mom's face filled with excitement, pride, and joy. The rest of us faked it. Jilly was a cutie-pie, no doubt about it, but her dancing was worse than awful. Picture someone who's sunburned the bottoms of her feet and attempting to wrestle free from a straight-jacket—and you can imagine the bizarre hopping, wriggling style. Midway through her performance her mother exclaimed, "She made up the whole routine herself. Can you believe it?" Why, yes. We could. And did.

If you have *average* children, take heart. They can do incomprehensible things that make you wonder about their future. My brother once attempted to chase a wasp away from my sister by picking up a length of rope—and then lashing the end of it at the wasp. All the neighbor saw was my sister—who lived in the excitable state of an endless sugar high anyway—shrieking at the top of her lungs and running around the yard, being chased and whipped by my brother. That brother now holds a doctorate and is a university professor.

I've witnessed so many goofy stunts, it's hard to narrow them down. Stuffing small Legos up their noses. Eating leaves off the shrubbery because they're pretending to be cows. Filling a baseball cap with Cheetos and wearing it. Jumping on the bed and hitting their head on the rotating ceiling fan. Running around in the yard wearing a football helmet, cowboy boots, and his sister's ballet tutu. Pogo-sticking on ice. Hanging ten on the ironing board top as it shoots down the stairs.

It's hard to keep up with them and absolutely baffling to decipher why they do what they do. The best kicker I've heard in answer to the question, "Why would you do such a thing?" was, "You didn't tell me not to." I have to say, it never occurred to me to tell my children not to cram a Lego up their nose or surf on my ironing board, but I did tell them not to eat the plants. They did anyway. And though they will probably never admit it, all those parents of the *brilliant* kids most likely have stranger stories than we do. You know their kids must do ridiculous things, too. I just wish they'd break down and tell 'em to me. Then we could all laugh together.

MAYDAY! MAYDAY!

May, May, go away. Oh wait, that's rain. Nevertheless, if you have school-age children, you might secretly want May to disappear. You are not alone.

On the surface, and before you know any better, May seems to be such a happy month. It even sounds happy. Say it now. Feels like prancing barefoot in a soft field of daisies, doesn't it? Not like February, which not only sounds sharp-edged and icy cold, many people can't pronounce it or spell it correctly. Nobody *ever* misspells May.

Alas, the more children you have, and the older they get, the more you dread even the mere mention of that deceptively named evil month. It starts innocently enough, mind you. You've got a kindergarten kid, and the room mother asks you to call the other moms to contribute to an end-of-the-year gift card for the teacher and her classroom aide. Ten dollars per child sounds easy enough, so you say *sure, why not?*

Leave pleasant request messages for twenty to thirty parents. Four call back and tell you they're in. You make second calls. Get three more commitments. After a week, you collect a total of ninety dollars. You chip in an extra ten so the teacher and aide will each have a fifty-dollar gift card. But the teacher and aide both know that ten bucks per kid is the norm. They can do math. That means they know that half, or less than half, of the parents didn't contribute. That makes them feel unappreciated. Really unappreciated, considering they've been spending money from their own underpaid pockets all year long for supplies the school board says they can't afford. So, you go back to the few parents you know who are sympathetic and well-heeled enough to boost the amount up to one-hundred dollars each, therefore avoiding the embarrassment for both sides.

Problem solved, right? Oh, no, no, no. Silly you. Problem just starting. Because now you purchase the gifts. You thought Visa gift cards would be great—they could spend them anywhere. Then, at the end of year class party, which is attended by nearly all the parents, several of them back you into a corner. I would like to interject at this point that there are *way* too many adults dependent on happy pills, and they tend to be the *least* happy people. Doesn't take long to figure out which ones they are. They are the biggest and loudest complainers, nearly bursting with indignance. Another segue here—why are the people who don't volunteer the hardest on those who do?

One mom demands to know why she wasn't asked or consulted about a gift. You discover their number on the class roster actually belongs to her miserable, disgusting, and sneaky ex. After hearing all about his slimy affair, during which you frantically dig for tissues in your purse because now she's sobbing, you find out he never answers such calls, and why didn't you double check it? Another tells you she thinks giving teacher gifts are wrong and how dare you sign her name to it? Still another, who wears a ten-thousand-dollar watch and drives a spanking new Mercedes SUV, is upset because *everyone* knows you should only give gift cards to office or craft supply stores. Yeah, let's give teachers a gift they can use to buy more stuff for your child.

In the little children's classes, they need decorations and snacks for their party. I'm a well-known artsy-fartsy type, so I was pressured to do the decorations. No problem, thought I. Easy-peasy. Cut out some construction paper flowers and string some pastel crepe paper rolls around.

Nope. The room mother, we'll call her Gwen, decided my elementary ideas were not up to snuff. Unbeknownst to me, there was a contest for best spring decorations in the school. Gwen *needed* me to step it up. To win what, exactly?

May becomes a nightmare of class trips, proms, and graduations, all requiring ample parent participation. And every year sucks you in deeper. All that work, all those hours, and when your child gets to high school, they are embarrassed to admit they *have* a mother, much less one who *actually shows up* in their school to do something.

May gives me a headache.

GIVE A CHEER FOR NEBRASKA

I read an article in the paper recently. The headline said something about Nebraska law allowing parents to drop off any underage child they want. Or rather, don't want. Like, abandon them. And the state will take care of them. Underage meaning under the age of nineteen.

Hold the phone.

Other states have a 'safe-haven' law. You can drop off an unwanted newborn at any hospital within seventy-two hours of birth, and the state will assume custody of that child. No penalties or prosecutions. The intention being to keep desperate mothers from dropping their newborns into dumpsters, I think it's a wonderful law.

But Nebraska says you can drop off any child under nineteen?

I have three sons, two of whom are now in their twenties. Where the heck were these lawmakers when I needed them? During the *I know everything, you know nothing, and Oh My God – you are so lame, Mom* teenage years?

The social service people in Nebraska better brace themselves. They're about to be overrun by unruly, defiant, and hormonal teenagers. The hospitals that accept the waifs will soon need a drive-through-and-drop-off lane for the hoards of crazed parents who'd love a year or two off from the burden of enduring adolescents.

I have to admit, I have great kids. They've never been in trouble, at school or anywhere else. They remember their manners—when they're not home—and I often get compliments from other parents about how polite they are.

Despite the glowing reports, my boys were testy during the hormone years. I'd read more than once that young men almost *have* to rebel against and challenge their parents. The primitive instinct of readying themselves to leave the nest sort of thing. Primal urges. My guys had that stuff in spades. Plus, my ex told me that it's common for a teenage boy to not even want to admit he *has* a mother. It's way not cool. When my oldest was in high-school, my fondest fantasy involved the words *military boarding school.*

Not having had any, I can't speak to the female teenager scenario, but I've had friends who've compared their high-school daughters to the green slime spewing, rotating head girl in *The Exorcist.* Once, my friend took her very pretty sixteen-year-old out to dinner. There was a cute busboy who, after the girl went to the ladies' room, asked my friend if the girl had a boyfriend. My friend laughed and said, "Oh, you don't want her. She's a witch." Only she used the 'b' word.

I met someone from Nebraska once. It was while I lived in Hawaii. He seemed very nice, well-mannered, unassuming, and well, kind of Radar O'Reilly-ish. Innocent. Sweet. Totally not the sort of person who would know how to handle the obnoxious verbal assault a teenager can dish out. Maybe teens in Nebraska are sweeter, like the young man I met. Maybe these naïve lawmakers are under the impression that all teens are like the ones they know. Somebody should warn them that Nebraska could become a national dumping ground for harried baby boomers' kids.

Which makes me wonder, does that state then help these kids through college? Do they have a program like we do in Florida where the lottery funds college tuition and fees if the kids get good grades? Wow. You could abandon your child and save quite a bundle when you add it all up. Teenagers are expensive long before they fill out their first college application. Just the savings on the water and energy bill would motivate me. My middle son took three twenty-five minute showers a day. Their computers never have a moment's rest, and their lights and fans don't seem to have an off switch. Don't get me started on clothes and shoes.

Even if they don't supply the college funds, I still have a thirteen-year-old at home, and moving to Nebraska sounds very do-able to me. I hear the summers can be quite pleasant in Omaha. Anybody there need a great artist and writer?

A PROPOSAL

Sometimes, I'm a little late to the party. Okay, maybe a lot late. Now that the latest prom season has folded up like the last tent at the traveling circus, I get wind of a new trend.

I just heard about prom proposals. As if marriage proposal videos on YouTube weren't bad enough already—making normal guys who don't come up with contrived and corny gimmicks feel inadequate. Complicated dance sequences are now practically a requirement. Now I see, on a fluffy morning show (which I *have* to watch, lest I no longer qualify as your intrepid reporter on the ridiculous), that high school boys are spending an average of $350.00 on their prom proposals. What in tarnation?

Before this trend takes hold, let's stop it. Stop it right now. Parents of teenagers, put your feet down and say no. Oh, wait. I forgot. The kids who are pushing this trend probably have parents who can't say no to them, because they want to be their kids' *friend* and they think every blasted move junior makes is YouTube and Facebook worthy. And Mom's already out buying her outfit to appear on a morning show because the proposal is sure to go viral.

But what if the girl says no? Won't that crush junior's little heart? Does that mean he has to spend another $350.00 to ask the next girl? Does he have to come up with another original idea, or does he repeat the same one? In which case, girl number two will no doubt hear (it *is* high school after all) that she was number two *and* didn't even deserve her own unique proposal? She got the rerun? That'll go over as well as asking her to hold the pom-poms while he kisses the cheerleader. So, this makes me think that girl number one has to be in on it from the beginning. He's got to confirm in advance that she'll say yes. Her job is to polish up her acting skills and pretend it's all a big surprise for the camera. The whole thing is a mini reality show for them. It's icky on so many levels. But it's just high school kids, right?

There is a bigger, far more ominous picture, though.

What if this leads to everything else in life becoming video proposal-worthy? This is a dangerous column I'm writing here. If the floral and balloon (to say nothing of the personalized promotional products) industries catch wind of this, before you can say *Proposal Packages for All Occasions*, we've got a whole 'nuther layer of social pressure breaking our backs. Not to mention what the treacherous minds at Hallmark might do.

Anyone in the position of being able to choose who they'll work or partner with—on anything—can be wooed with this outright display of showmanship. Will you be my mentor? My website designer? May I have this job? Will you be my piano teacher? My contractor? Will you be my plumber? (This could be the hardest sell of all. Good, reasonably priced, and dependable plumbers are next to impossible to find. I hear they like daisies.)

Is all of life going to come down to who presented the best—most social media sticking—proposal? This could doom our species. Or at least America. The US already has the largest percentage of the world's complacent people. Folks who are obsessed with celebrity instead of actual issues that affect our future. Our politics are a mess because the engaged citizenry can't get the unengaged to pay attention. They're too busy celebrating—and emulating—the last-name-begins-with-K people. (Sorry, I have a tough time mentioning a particular family who is best known for big booties, inane patter, and wasting scads of dollars on TV.)

Yikes. The best jobs and choices will go to the most creative and gregarious, whose proposals will absolutely blow the less imaginative straight into the dumpster. I am not saying this out of envy, mind you. I *am* a creative. An artist and a writer. For the entirety of my life, I've knocked the stuffings out of the creative competition. But we really, really don't want people like me running things. Creatives have a place, but—trust me—you do not want me as your lawyer or your tax accountant or an infrastructure engineer. Some jobs are best suited for the pragmatic people who look at a tree and think, *nice tree*, instead of, *wow, I could build a really cool fort in that tree, and what if it really has elves inside—would it disturb them, but maybe they'd like hanging out with me, and . . .* Yeah. You get the picture.

Popularity on YouTube may be fun, but it's no way to run a country. Or a business. Or get through high school, for that matter.

THE CUB SCOUT BUS

Philanthropy is wonderful. Thank goodness for the wealthy who contribute to the common cause. I've never been in the position to actually *give* money away. A lot of it, I mean. I always throw a dollar or two into the fireman's boot—more if it's a he and he's cute. Some goes to the Salvation Army bell ringer's kettle and the Veteran's jar in front of Wal-Mart. I proudly display my tiny red paper poppy on my rear-view mirror. But sending oodles of cash to a children's hospital or medical research? No. I do think I'd be very good at it, should the chance arrive. I'll keep buying my lottery tickets.

Those of us who care but can't do the money thing—volunteer. I've logged thousands of volunteer hours over the last thirty-odd years. When my two oldest sons were happy, eager Cub Scouts, our Pack Committee Chairman quit. Pleas went out at the Pack meeting for someone to step up and help. Crickets chirped in the resulting silence. No one dared step out of the room, lest they be appointed in absentia. Ours was one of the largest Packs in Atlanta with lots of sub-committees and parents. Not one wanted to become the new chairman.

I was already a den mother, but decided not to let the Pack collapse. Oh, dopey me. A week later, I said I'd do it and soon found out why the last chairman quit.

To be a Pack Committee Chairman, you had to go to an all-day training session. People from all over Georgia attended. At eight on a Saturday morning, about a hundred of us trudged into a room in the convention center. The organizers meant well, but the presentations couldn't have been more boring. Everyone on the Cub Scout bus, they said, needed this information. So— necessary, but boring. During the breaks, they tried to revive the group with rousing Cub Scout cheers and little ditties which we were supposed to cheer and sing along with.

There were eight people who were so gung-ho and happy, just stamping and cheering and loving the heck out of it. The rest of us looked at each other and shrugged. Yes, the little Cubs loved these things, and yes, we did them with enthusiasm during our Pack meetings. But, golly. The fervor, the passion, of these eight was just plain weird. They put drunken football fans to shame.

During the lunch break, another woman and I sat on a concrete planter edge in a lobby area, balancing old boiled hot dogs in stale buns on paper plates in our laps and squeezing mustard and relish from little plastic packets, when some Atlanta police-persons entered. They were followed by several convention center security people. The group of eight had settled some distance away, thankfully, because their behavior had become raucous, louder, and lewd.

As the police approached them, a quick shuffle occurred, then two of the eight ran-walked into the bathroom. My companion raised her eyebrows. Two officers followed them. The rest couldn't control themselves and argued with the police. A small melee ensued, knocking over potted palms, and scattering other attendees trying to avoid getting swept up in it. Hot dogs, fries, and plates flew. When a hot dog hit the tree in the planter behind us, we scurried out of the way. The gang of eight were forcibly removed from the premises.

After lunch we re-assembled, and the leader gave us a brief explanation. The contingent had carpooled together from a rural county, apparently drank on the drive to Atlanta, drank during the morning sessions from hip flasks, and smoked an illegal substance which was found on their persons. Then he said, "The Cub Scout bus has no room for alcoholics and drug abusers."

Back in Atlanta, I hurried to implement the recommended guidelines for our various sub-committees. I discovered our previous chairman either slept through the training or purposely didn't bother to do any of it. The phone calls started. "What do you think you're doing?" Uh, what the head Cub Scout dude told me to. "Why are you changing things?" Um, because our Pack isn't organized. "You're not doing it the right way. If I were doing it . . ." Tee-hee. Loved that phrase.

One of the best things I learned from the head Cub Scout dude was to delegate. Never try to run it all by yourself for two reasons. You'll get burned out fast—a lá our ex-chairman, and, if you happen to get *run over* by the Cub Scout bus (his actual words—he used the Cub Scout bus reference a lot), others can easily pick up where you left off. After experiencing for myself some of the irate and irrational calls, I'm guessing our former chairman only wished he could be so lucky as to get run over by said bus. So when I heard, "If I were doing it . . .", lickety-split that caller was my new fund-raising committee chair. Then all the crazy calls regarding fund-raising car washes, candy bars, and popcorn were her problem. Delegating was fun.

As for those I couldn't pawn off on someone else, there were some doozies. A parent called regarding the skit her son's den presented at the previous Pack meeting. The complaint was her son didn't have a big enough part. The den mother wouldn't return her calls. I sympathized, told her I thought her son was brilliant in the part he did have. Still she yelled. Finally I tried another tack. "Jeez-O-Pete, lady," I said. "I'm a volunteer. Don't scream at me. On behalf of your child, I gave up a whole Saturday, risked salmonella and listeria poisoning, and had to sit near a fair number of overweight men in tight green shorts, who'd eaten bad fast food for lunch."

During the lull while the caller no doubt envisioned that, I suggested perhaps she could become the den mother. I knew the den mother in question wanted out, anyway. Then my caller would control all such things within her fiefdom.

She did it. And she turned out to be pretty good at it, too.

THE TRUTH ABOUT SPRING BREAK

Spring in South Florida is a whole different animal compared to the rest of the country. Even if our winter (like this one) didn't have many beach days, March is sure to bring them. And with that certainty, it also brings young people from the north anxious to get a jump on their competition for the earliest tan, escape from their parents' *let's-all-drive-to-Dollywood-during-your-school-hiatus* trip, and meet-up with their peers in a dazzling display of courtship rituals.

In other words, Spring Break.

Few occurrences in modern times rival Spring Break for entertainment value. The combination of raging hormones and cheap beer foster a spectacle of grand proportions. Hoteliers and merchants alternately cheer and complain about the half-naked dancing bodies swirling about in a hazy horde on the beach road. If the kids are buying T-shirts and trinkets, it's all good. If they're sandwiched in, twelve-to-a-room, getting sick in the hallways, and spilling out onto the sidewalks—then, um, no.

It's easy to determine which people are profiting from Spring Break. They're the ones, when interviewed by the local news, who say the kids are just letting off a little steam. That's all. No harm done. The person ranting about immoral behaviors probably just had to pay a Hazmat crew overtime fees to expunge bodily fluids from multiple motel rooms.

I get a kick out of parents who are in denial about their college-age kids. They know someone is causing all kinds of ruckus down there in Florida, but it isn't *their* child. Their child is abstaining from drinking, smoking pot, and entering wet T-shirt contests. Their child has standards. They *trust* their child implicitly. Okay.

For those of us who've survived the kids-in-college stage, the big fun comes years later when said angel-children fess up to their crimes and misdemeanors. Once they arrive in their mid-twenties, socializing with both their parents and old classmates at the same time becomes acceptable. At those gatherings they tend to reminisce about the college years. Priceless doesn't begin to describe the facial expressions on Mom and Dad Perfect when they find out what little precious did in during those supposedly innocuous vacations.

Young men diving from second or third story balconies—hopefully into the pool, but sometimes not. That's the most common scenario that comes to my mind when conjuring stories for the Spring Break Follies. I'm actually not sure if the stupid drunken diving is fact or mostly myth. There have been disastrous falls from balconies, heaven only knows if the poor soul thought he was diving.

It's not just the male gender, either. The reason boys love Spring Break is because girls, when they drink, become as uninhibited as the boys. It's been reported that while participating in Spring Break, young men consume an average of eighteen drinks per day. Young women—ten. Forty percent of them, both genders, drink until they pass out.

When they're conscious, the kids are amazingly inventive. Lost your Frisbee? No problem. Heck, just borrow some trash can lids. The larger size makes them easier to catch. Tell that to the kid who went home with a hematoma the size of an ostrich egg on his forehead. Bored with the rides on the pier? Those same trash can lids can double as bobsleds for racing down the stairwells. They also make great shields when engaged in a light saber battle. In a pinch, the metal ones serve as a fire pit, beer cooler, or when strung by drapery cords from a palm tree, whimsical oversized wind chimes.

Underwear gets abandoned on the sand, in the rooms, and at the top of flagpoles. Hair gets bleached, braided and beaded. Belly buttons get pierced. Tattoos magically appear above derrieres. And everywhere, every morning, the beach clean-up crews tsk-tsk while shaking their heads at the remnants from midnight madness. Cigarette butts. Beer cans. Plastic hurricane glasses. Breath mint wrappers. More undies. Condoms.

Inline skating while toasted is a daily occurrence at the beach. Group inline skating while toasted, scantily-clad, and texting leads to obscenity charges. The young ladies in question accepted a dare via text. If they stripped off their bikini tops, skated four abreast (forgive the pun) down the wide sidewalk towards him—just long enough for him to get a picture, no big deal—then he'd buy them all a steak dinner that night. No doubt the video captured on his cell camera would have been on YouTube within hours. As luck would have it, there was a cop who rounded the corner at that moment. Why the instigator sent his request via text versus just asking them, I don't understand. Kids text each other in the next room now. It's a generational thing, I guess.

But it got me thinking—what if there had been YouTube and the Internet in these kids' parent's time? Twenty-five years later, the ghosts of their Spring Break embarrassments would still be floating in cyberspace for their kids to find. How would you explain your own exploits and maintain any kind of moral authority? *Yes, darling, that is Mummy leaning backward while Aunt Kiki pours tequila down her throat. And no, that was not a tramp stamp. It was only a henna dye. Times were different then. I forbid you to do that. As a matter of fact, I've changed my mind. You are going to Dollywood with us. Period.* Fast forward another two decades. Holy smokes, will these kids have to confiscate all their children's e-gadgets.

Looking back, I'm ecstatic no one filmed my most knuckled-headed moments. I wouldn't revisit those days if you paid me. But, to be honest, I think if men over fifty could still get away with staying for a week—on a beach —surrounded by inebriated nearly naked nubile women who smile a lot—knowing there would be little or no consequences—they'd be there in a heartbeat. We women over fifty? Not a chance. The beer goggles never did fit us very well.

I'M TIRED

Mothers in August are either exhilarated or exhausted. Depending on whether their children go for weeks of sleep-away camp or stay home, moms in August look fresh, rested, and feel terrific—or—the dark rings under their eyes make the raccoons in the neighborhood jealous.

I was always in the latter category, looking on with envy at the first group, the Free Moms—those whose children slept away. To be polite, you had to ask the obligatory, *And what are Sarah and Jason doing this summer?* But we knew. The physical, dead giveaways told us which of us moms were footloose and partying. Hair that gleamed and stayed coifed. Makeup perfectly applied. Tennis whites and sneakers without crusty macaroni and cheese smears. Their teeth looked whiter, their eyes brighter. Free Moms had energy, that zest for life I remembered with an aching, growing fondness.

It dawned on me hours later that the sparkle in their eyes meant something else entirely. The rediscovery of romance with their spouses. Amy, my best friend in the neighborhood, and I let go a collective sigh as we realized the truth of our lives. If we were lucky, we'd recapture the romantic aspect of our relationships when the youngest went to college. For Amy, that was twelve years away. For me, eleven.

But like the loyal and weary soldier-friends we were, we'd

guzzle spiked iced tea while listening to the Free Moms by the mailbox—the neighborhood water cooler—in the late afternoons. One Free Mom in particular, Mrs. Paderndern we'll call her, delighted in reciting the hectic schedule of her child-free summer days. Tennis at nine—before it got too hot. Lunch at the club, followed by a manicure and pedicure—hoping to get the *good* Vietnamese girl, not the one who never smiled and couldn't file symmetrically. A nap in the afternoon before meeting up with hubby for drinks and dinner downtown. Amy and I bet each other a quarter that Mrs. Paderndern didn't take all those afternoon naps alone, judging from the unbelievably fortuitous timing of the pool guy's arrivals.

Then she'd toss her perfect hair, release a perfect sigh, and proceed to tell us how much she missed her little scamps and couldn't wait to get them back home again. Yeah, right. Amy and I exchanged knowing looks. Said Paderndern scamps were notorious for their manipulative skills. During many after-dinner walks we heard the tantrum screams of tweens emanating from their home. Maybe it was a good thing Sarah and Jason's parents could afford to send them to camp. Heaven knows I'd have needed a break from the high-tension in that house. Without summer camp for Paderndern's kids, I might be writing a far different, and not the least bit amusing, story involving weapons, crime scene tape, medical examiners, and police detectives.

I remember being exhausted by the time school started again. Pooped. Worn out. Tired. Tired like Madeline Kahn's character in *Blazing Saddles*—Lilly Von Schtupp—singing *I'm Tired*. Amy agreed that Lilly represented our overall enthusiasm level. We were her. Except we didn't own, much less wear, the spicy bustier get-up, and we didn't have Harvey Korman, or anyone else for that matter, hanging on our every utterance.

While Mrs. Paderndern spent her summer in child-free bliss, we trudged through our days. Laundry, cooking, cleaning. Driving the kids to the pool, the beach, the movies. Our little scamps required all-hours trips to the ER. They got mud in their eyes. Shoved pebbles or Legos up their noses. Fell from trees. They accidentally hit each other with sticks, plastic golf clubs, croquet balls, and rubber snakes—I had no idea how far one of those things could stretch via centrifugal force when swung overhead. They attempted to leap—Evel Knievel style—while on their bicycles over the bodies of two of their friends. Mine were the daredevils, Amy's were the hapless potential roadkill lying on the sidewalk, waiting to be jumped over. The darlings stayed up late watching scary movies, then roused their parents because of nightmares at three in the morning.

Off in the horizon, the glimmer of school being back in session taunted us. The ads in the paper started featuring specials on lunchboxes, notebooks, and protractors. I did ask my oldest once if he'd ever used the ubiquitous protractor that was perennially on the supplies list. He answered, "What's a protractor?" I took that as a 'no'. Quite often, my children came home from the first day of school and dumped half of their listed required items onto the table. "My teacher said we didn't need these." So, who made up the list? Made me wonder if somewhere, in North Dakota maybe, there was a Bureau of Lists We'd Rather Not Bother to Update that had been re-issuing the same supplies list since 1979.

But I digress. Soon it would be our turn to catch a break. Mrs. Paderndern's kids would come home and, while they also went to school, they came home every afternoon to drive their mother crazy. For her, the school year was one long slog of accommodating her kids. For us, it was a huge relief to have some time to ourselves. Maybe even take a nap. Too bad neither Amy or I owned a pool.

VICTORIA LANDIS

WHEN I WAS A KID

CABIN FEVER

As a child, I lived up north. In New Jersey. Not Snooki's Jersey. (By the way, I heard she's from Staten Island. For you who aren't familiar with the area, Staten Island is in New York.) The good New Jersey—where postage-stamp sized towns had great schools, everyone had hydrangeas in the yard, barbeques meant horseshoes and volleyball in the backyard, and the tomatoes and sweet corn were (and still are) the best in the world. The winter holidays meant skating on the ponds and rivers, building snowmen, and stuffing our faces with more homemade cookies than June Cleaver ever gave Wally and the Beav. And rum balls, too. I think the rum balls were given on purpose to knock us out when we finally came in at dark. Sort of like Dimetapp these days.

After the holiday whirl settled down and school reopened, I remember the malaise that descended. The whole of January, February, and most of March lay ahead, like a vast, cold, empty wasteland. The fun and busyness of the holidays had kept us from dwelling on the unrelenting bleak skies and the bitter cold. We went back to rising at six, shivering through the early hours as the radiators clanged and banged bringing a pathetic amount of heat to the old house. Walking to school (or trudging depending on the snow situation) meant cold wet hands and feet. Our boots always let snow in, and since waterproof fabrics hadn't been invented yet, mittens and gloves were wool. The rich kids had boots that cinched in tight at the top and leather or suede gloves. We made fun of those kids and called them wussies.

Occasionally, there'd be a heavy snowstorm that closed the schools and made snow forts possible. We could get away with a near murder then, as long as it was outdoors. Having just gotten us back into school, our moms did everything they could to keep us out of the house. If cooped up inside fighting over the TV or the Monopoly game, we'd drive them crazy. Acts of cruelty toward younger siblings that might normally earn the perpetrator a two-week grounding were let go with a stern wag of the finger. Unless we were a certifiably blue color, under no circumstances did mom want us back in the house before dinner. In defense of these women, you need to understand the neighborhood. We had six kids. Next door had four. Other side had five. Behind us had eight. And across the street? Twelve. That's thirty-five kids within a five house range. Only two of the families were Catholic, so there might be a little something to Snooki's version of Jersey—a whole lot of people with a serious interest in nookie.

So we-the-banished invented all sorts of games, some of which—looking back—were downright dangerous. There was the unicycle ice challenge. A boy from down the street borrowed his brother's unicycle, and we all tried to ride it across a huge frozen puddle in the front driveway. Only one girl wound up with a split lip. (She got to stay inside after that.) There was the icicle swallow. Find the largest icicles and pretend to be a sword swallower with them. That game wasn't very popular because it tended to trigger the gag reflex, causing a disturbing amount of up-chucking. Snowpile was the most popular game, because anybody could do it, but it was the most exhausting. Just like with a leaf pile, we'd gather snow under a tree branch into a huge mound, then take turns climbing the tree (not easy with boots and snowpants on), and jumping into it. It had to be rebuilt nearly every time. We tended to get tired before everybody got a turn, which meant the younger kids never got a chance to jump because—in the kid kingdom—they were the lowest ranks. One of them would turn tail, cry, and run into their house. That particular mom would venture out, arms wrapped around her, clamping her cardigan close, take a few tentative steps into the snow, and yell at us for not including the little ones. Why didn't we just have a nice old-fashioned snowball fight?

It was like permission from God. We divided into two teams. Made piles of snowballs. Just as we'd negotiated the rules of engagement, the dinner bells started. Every house had its own. A cattle ranch triangle. A real bell. Ours was an old taxi horn.

The next day, war games resumed. Overnight, the snowballs developed splendid icy crusts. And although our teams had equal numbers of the junior warriors, our team's neophytes were hopelessly outmaneuvered. Unfortunately, the first blood was spilled by my little sister—Janie-the-screamer. She got hit in the cheek (needed two stitches). Within a minute, every mom on the block tore out of their kitchen door and high-tailed it for our yard. Mom led Janie, still howling, into the house. The other moms scolded us. Having had enough of the guilt, I went inside under the pretense of concern for my sister.

Janie's screams had subsided into sobs. My mother asked why I'd let it happen. A question I didn't understand, since I hadn't launched the weapon in question. Before I could stammer a statement of innocence, though, my father sauntered in and asked what the delicious smell was. On reflex, all heads turned toward the stove. There was nothing on it or in the oven. A look of alarm filled mom's face. She handed me the washcloth she'd been holding to Janie's cheek and flew up the stairs.

A few minutes later, she came back down holding something in her palm. She showed it to my father, who totally didn't get the signal he should not let on, and made a loud joke about turtle soup for dinner. My brother had thought Janie's tiny pet turtle looked cold, so he put it on the radiator to warm up. Two seconds later, Janie understood what must have happened, and the hysterical screaming started again. I went back outside.

I really can't imagine why my mother hated snow days.

CLOTHES MAKE THE GIRL

Going back to school each fall was a big deal when we were kids. Parts of it we loved—seeing friends after a long summer, wondering who'd be in our class (the cute boy who liked us last year?), what teacher we'd have. Parts of it we really, really dreaded—making our own book covers from paper grocery bags (yes, this *was* back in the stone age, and Wilma Flintstone sends her regards), and walking to school in the bitter cold while carrying all our books. You need to understand that, back then, the only people who owned backpacks were serious hiking enthusiasts. We literally carried a stack of textbooks in our arms. And the horrible box of hand-me-down clothes waited in the attic for us.

Looming above our heads on the third floor and reeking of moth balls, the big cardboard hand-me-down box made its entrance into my parents' bedroom about a week before school started. Always quicker on the uptake than I, my evil older sister, Susan, had a sixth sense of when my mother would carry that box down one flight and summon us to her room. Susan would disappear. I, like a fool, obediently went to Mom's room when called and managed to be genuinely surprised that it was clothing try-on day. That's what happens to kids like me, wandering around for the summer months in our own little universe—marveling at the clouds, spellbound by creeks, working in earnest to build a tiny town for the ants out of pebbles, twigs, and mud. Susan at age fourteen (I was twelve) spent the summer

VICTORIA LANDIS

perfecting her tanning-under-any-circumstance methods.
Of course, that was relevant to her life. By eighth grade,
she was five-foot-eight, 36-24-36, with long light-brown
hair and a dark tan. Va-va-voom. The daily late-
afternoon scene on our back porch was Susan holding
court to at least six hormone-crazed neighborhood boys
on their bicycles. By contrast that same year, I had the
shape of a ten-year-old boy. So I climbed trees and built
forts.

The biggest problem with the hand-me-down box was
who the clothes were handed down from. My parents'
best friends had two daughters a few years older than us.
We liked their mom a lot, but she had the most hideous
taste. We were no position to be picky. Our family had
six children and not a huge income. We were very used
to just making do, but the prospect of wearing those
clothes made us crazy. Instinctively, even I, the clueless,
knew showing up at school in them would cause
permanent ostracization, they were that bad. In a small
town like ours, you'd never escape the torment. It would
follow you like stink on a skunk all the way through high
school and perhaps beyond.

We knew this because of many legendary examples that
had filtered down through the kid-dom hierarchy. My
schoolmate, 'Lizzy' had an older sister, 'Debbie', who was
in high school and quite developed, and her mother
wouldn't let her wear a bra, shave her armpits or legs, or
use deodorant. Poor Debbie, I'd never met her, and still
I knew, through small town gossip, what a misfit she was
and how all the other girls made fun of her. Whispers
circulated through seventh grade—"Lizzy's mom makes
her sister wear an undershirt!" I worried for Lizzy.

Would she meet the same fate?

Not being in the kid-loop, my mother didn't believe any of it. Clothes were clothes. You were lucky if you had any. She was born during the depression and grew up eating ketchup sandwiches, fried baloney, and cutting out cardboard to line her shoes when the soles wore out. Her father taught her how to catch eels in the river and bring them home for dinner. It's hard to argue with a woman who knows what nothing really is.

But we argued anyway. Mom would scour the neighborhood and march my sister back to stand beside me. As each item came out of the hand-me-down box, a chorus of groans or moans accompanied it. Nasty plaid skirts in mustards and olives. Dresses with squared-off flaps on the neckline with weird nautical appliqués. Homemade sweaters stretched out in all the wrong places. Dorky pinafores. Susan cried real tears, begging mom not to make her wear any of it. I should probably also explain that, back in the Stone Age, girls were not allowed to wear pants to school. Ever. The boys could not wear jeans, and no one could wear sneakers, except for in gym class. It was a huge victory in my eighth-grade that we petitioned and won the right for girls to wear culottes, but they had to be no more than two inches above the knee.

Eventually, we'd wear poor Mom out. I like to think she felt sorry for us, because every year, we'd wind up keeping only one or two of the things from the box, and the rest she'd put in the church donation bin. She taught me how to sew that year, and it was one of the best things I ever learned. I bought Vogue when I could save enough money for it, and made replicas of what I saw. I still do. Only now, what I sew looks like couture.

So, if during your back-to-school shopping, your daughter complains, think about my poor mother, and smile. As for me, I have three boys. One of them cared a little, but by and large, they wore whatever I threw at them. What did they care? Mud, blood, and grass stains look good on everything.

MY DEAR OLD DAD

We only get one father—biologically speaking. But a dad? That's a different story. For some people, Dad *is* the one who contributed his DNA to you. For others, it's the guy who volunteered to step up and be the dad. I am thanking all dads, whether they're blood-related or not. And as a tribute, here's to them and their foibles.

There are a few things I know for sure about dads. They like sports, especially football and—when Mom's not in the room—cheerleaders. They relish a cold beer after mowing the lawn. They make the best tree forts. They believe winking at you erases a clumsy remark. They have deep, meaningful conversations with the family dog, but can't cough up a word when asked by Mom to help explain the birds and the bees to their kids. They love steak. They wear T-shirts from their high school or college days until they disintegrate. They tell the same corny jokes year after year and laugh harder each time, ignoring Mom's eye-rolling. They adore their children.

My dad passed away almost twenty years ago. I question both his and my mother's (very much alive) sanity. They *decided* to have a big family, wanted all six of us. I've raised three children and can't imagine having had three more. I don't know how my parents didn't succumb to the temptation to *lose* one or two of us. In my dad's wake, he left a legacy of events and stories that still entertain us. Tales about Hawaii after World War II, college pranks, and how he won my mother over from some other guy.

Dad loved to dance. When I was little, sometimes I'd wake up at night and hear music. I'd sneak downstairs and find my parents on the sun porch doing a wild, swinging jitterbug to big band music. They were laughing, smiling—no—*beaming* ear to ear.

Dad was cheap. He thought nothing should cost more than fifty dollars—ever. No matter how much time had passed since his find-a-nickel-and-see-a-movie childhood. He'd tip waiters and valets with quarters. As we grew older, we realized Mom always tucked extra cash in her purse for surreptitious purposes. He did get a little better with the tipping thing, but we all were prepared to leave a sweater on a chair as an excuse to run back to the table. He loved cute waitresses, and back in the days before political correctness (think Mad Men era), he'd pinch their bottoms and laugh, embarrassing us. Dad was a charmer, though, and the waitresses never looked angry. Really. I guess some people can pull off anything. My middle son inherited that gene. He'd never pinch anyone, but boy, one smile and whammo—he's got the popular vote.

My dad's favorite drink was the Manhattan. Four parts rye whiskey to one part sweet vermouth with a dash of bitters and a Maraschino cherry. It's etched into my brain because Dad taught me to make them when I was ten. These days, that would probably be considered child abuse. Heck, *my* kids didn't learn bartending skills until they were at least twelve. Kidding. While Mom was busy preparing dinner for eight, I'd fill the cocktail shaker with Manhattan ingredients and frost a martini glass in the freezer for him. When he came home from work, he'd sit at the counter and do the crossword puzzle, sipping the drink I'd served and talking to Mom.

But here's the endearing part, something I didn't realize until many years later. He'd pluck me up and onto his lap and challenge me with some of the crossword clues. No matter what I'd answered, if it was the right amount of letters, he praised me and filled it in. (In ink. He and Mom always did their crosswords in pen.) After a few answers, I'd get bored, jump down, and go find a sibling to pester. Now, as an avid puzzle doer, I can only imagine what a pain in the rear it was to work around and ink over those incorrect answers.

Before the Internet, or even the concept of a home computer, dads relied on nudie magazines. Keeping them hidden from the wives and children was a big challenge. We kids always found the stash, however. We never let on, and we never told our moms. It was our only source of sex education. What we didn't know was that all the moms knew exactly where they were also. Yeesch. Everybody just pretended they didn't know diddly. As it turned out, to share the financial burden of keeping up with the latest issues, Dad had an exchange program going with the Episcopal minister (father of five) next door. They traded copies back and forth for years. I *told* you he was cheap.

I miss him.

I hope you have a dad in your life. He may not be the biological contributor, but love is not measured by DNA. Treasure every bad joke, every inappropriate or clunky comment, every moment they choose to spend with you. Appreciate the efforts made to cheer you on, lift you up, and lessen the pain, even if they don't work. He cares enough to try, and it hurts him more than you know to see you go through life's inevitable adversities. And don't *ever* let him be all alone on Father's Day.

THE E.R.—TIMING IS EVERYTHING

Ah, the Emergency Room. The last option for after-hours care. Nights. Weekends. Holidays.

Why is it most emergencies (the ones I've been party to, at any rate) happen after the doctor's office closes?

I grew up in a family with six children. Very active children. We had one of those old-fashioned family doctors who knew us well. And probably wished he didn't. He'd extend his office hours a bit for us if need be, say, on a Tuesday. But even back in the good old sixties and seventies, expecting Dr. Hamilton to open up at ten PM on Thursday, or a Sunday afternoon, or a holiday for a high fever or a couple of stitches was lunacy. He kept two phone numbers. We didn't have the private one.

As a result, we spent lots of time in the E.R. The Saturday I raced my new bike downhill with no hands, hit a bump, and went (as my dad would say) ass-over-teakettle? Emergency Room. When my sister shoved (on a Sunday-during a football game no less) a tiny Lego so far up her nose even tweezers couldn't reach? Emergency Room. My brother cut his chin open at nine PM? Emergency Room.

Other brother stepped on old, nasty, rusty nail in the woods. (On New Years' Day. More football.)

Another one hit a wasps' nest in the same woods.

Same sister stuffed a pebble up her nose. It went farther than the Lego ever dreamed of. (For the record, my mother swears that this sister has the highest IQ of all of us. If that's true, it answers a whole lot of questions for me.)

Same brother cut chin open a second time. On the same concrete step.

I could go on for days. Broken collarbone from a fall off a bunk bed. Broken arm from a fall off the top of a slide. Baseball bat split a lip (accident). Pretended to play golf with a stick and whacked a gash into brother's head (maybe not an accident—never been proved).

But the topper of all them is when my father cut into my mother's knee with the hacksaw on a Sunday. They were do-it-yourselfers, redoing the kitchen. Chances were there was a football game on at the time, distracting him. Dad wanted the sink reinstalled by dinnertime, so he made Mom drive herself, bleeding, to the Emergency Room. (None of us kids were of driving age yet.) I'm sure he expected dinner on time that night, too.

I suppose you've gathered that my parents were football fanatics. If you suffered an injury during football, it had to be pretty bad before they'd acquiesce to missing the game. If it only needed a few stitches, Mom would douse it with Mercurochrome and use a butterfly bandage until after football or the next day. If the bone wasn't sticking out of your arm, it could wait an hour or two. If you absolutely HAD to go for medical help, the two of them did a verbal tousle over who went the last time and whose turn it was now.

Mom usually won out by using the food argument. Dad couldn't boil water. Mom would lay it on thick—"I was just about to start the pot roast." (Dad LOVED pot roast.) "I suppose I can put in back in the frig. It always takes so long in the Emergency Room. By the time I get back, I guess I'll just scramble some eggs for dinner and make the pot roast tomorrow. Oh. But you're going out of town tomorrow. What a shame."

To be fair, there were countless times Dad was at work or away on a trip when Mom had to juggle it all. Including the stormy night she went into labor with my youngest sibling. Dad was out of town, and the back door fell in—literally came off the hinges. But that's another story.

WHAT I DID LAST SUMMER

Growing up, we knew what to expect on the first day of school. The teacher, smiling, assigned a one-page paper. Everyone's title was the same—What I Did Last Summer.

In our teeny town of five-thousand people, every kid in grammar school knew, or knew of, each other. We knew who the rich kids were, and who the poor kids were. We knew whose dad drank too much and couldn't keep a job. We knew whose mother didn't like somebody else's mother. Why someone's effeminate older brother escaped to New York. Whose sister got whisked away to spend the remainder of the school year with an aunt in Europe because she'd canoodled with the police chief's son. There are few secrets in a small town.

For my neighbor, 'Francie Jones', writing about summer break filled her with delight. She always went to a snooty tennis sleep-away camp for the first month. Then her family would take off for Australia, Europe, or Tahiti. She'd come back with great stories and pictures, samples of exotic foods, clothes and jewelry. And an attitude.

Francie's parents were rich. Her oldest brother attended the most exclusive boarding school in New England. When Francie's family threw a party, they brought in caterers. Francie's mother had a full-time maid even though there were but three children in the household and her mother didn't work.

My family wasn't poor, but we didn't go to camp or take vacations. My dad had seen other countries in WWII, but aside from that, it was a big deal if my parents took the train to New York, an hour away. As a family we never went further than my cousins' houses two towns over. Our summers entailed beach days, building forts in the woods, and late nights under floodlights playing Volleyball, Spud, and Red Rover.

It was a blast. We loved it. I never felt deprived. But when Francie returned from her exotic locales, I felt something I couldn't put words to until years later. Inferior, lesser, inadequate, insignificant. She had that effect on all the normal kids in the neighborhood. When she told her stories, it seemed like she thought she did us a favor, instead of sharing an experience.

Looking back, it wasn't her fault. Her parents had a snotty attitude toward our parents. Francie's destiny was to denigrate others. We knew our parents would never receive an invite to one of the Jones' fancy parties. Mrs. Jones went so far once as to do a *favor* for my friend's mom. She would *allow* her to work as a waitress for one of her parties. Maybe Mrs. Jones meant well, but apparently the way she asked went over like Great-Aunt Edna, after way too much punch at a bridal shower, admitting she still gave Great-Uncle Al a BJ now and then.

So it may have been inevitable that several of us girls, a few days before seventh grade started, pre-wrote Francie's summer essay for her. At 'Judy's' house, because she had the newest full set of the Encyclopedia

Britannica, we searched for an obscure country. To this day I remember arcane facts from our research, not that we bothered using any real facts. We biked to the county library and spent precious coins to make copies at ten cents apiece. On the first day of school, we passed— with surreptitious skill Mata Hari would envy—the copies to our friends. I didn't save it, and I sure don't remember the exact content, but it went something like this:

I, Francesca Jones, have just had the most fabulous summer ever known to man. My really rich family went to the delightful country of Borneo. My mother smeared mud all over her body and wore a skirt made of leaves. The women there don't wear anything on top, so my mom's saggy boobs kept banging on her fat stomach as she danced with the natives.

My two older brothers, Tad and Chip, learned to pick their noses with bones instead of their fingers, which is bad manners in Borneo. Tad also made good friends with the witch doctor's son, and they slept in the same sleeping bag the whole time.

My dad liked the food the best. He asked for seconds when they made grubs. He said he liked the fact that all men in the village had lots of wives. The chief gave my dad a girl to be his honorary wife while we were there. She got to sleep in my parent's hut. My mom got mad about it, but dad said it was important not to insult the chief.

As for me, Francesca, I had all the boys in the village following me everywhere I went, except of course, for the witch doctor's son. And the girls painted me with honey, then put me in the middle of a circle and threw feathers on me. They said it was something they didn't do often. It was a rare honor and I'm so proud they did it to me.

When we got home, my parents told me not to talk about our trip. I think they don't want other families to get jealous of all the fun we had. But I HAD to tell you all.

If Francie ever saw our fake essay, she didn't let on. Do I regret what we did? Sure. Middle school girls can be awful. I felt guilty for years and grateful we weren't caught. At the start of eighth grade, however, Francie's essay—for the first time ever—talked about the few weeks she'd spent at home that summer, instead of the vacation to Italy.

CULTURE CLASH

One person's junk is another person's cultural treasure. Just like with beauty, it's in the eye of the beholder.

Why do some see a neon painting of Elvis on black velvet and swoon, while others cringe and scramble for sunglasses? Why does one art dealer gush over an Andy Warhol when another says it's just a soup can cartoon?

My father was a time bomb in a formal setting. The more Manhattans he drank, the more honest he became. My guess is that's true of many of us. It explains why, at some of the cultural receptions I've attended, the curators and critics drink fancy water, not alcohol. They can't all have been raised in upper-crust families. Which means they've been tutored in upper-crustiness. And just like Eliza Doolittle, it's not possible to expunge all of the plebian tastes from those with humbler beginnings. If they let slip what they really thought, they might lose their jobs.

Back to Dad. If gussied up in a suit, plopped into a swanky art setting with a string quartet playing in the background, then voilá—Mr. Debonair at your service. A natural extension of the Rat Pack. A regular Prince Charming. I use Dad as an example because nearly everyone I know (I'm hopelessly middle-class) has similar stories about their fathers. Guys who, to the unendurable horror of their teenage progeny, wore black socks with sandals, plaid shorts that exposed their knobby knees, and stained fishing hats to the town's Fourth of July picnics. They hung out together at pool parties and barbeques, smoking cigars when their wives weren't paying attention. They made us kids pull their fingers, and asked time and time again if we wanted to see where the horse bit them. Then they'd laugh like they'd invented funny. These same men could don a suit and fake their way amongst the hoity-toities. Until the first drink kicked in. A zebra can only camouflage his stripes for so long.

In the beginning of an art gallery evening, Dad's comments about the displayed items were few, but polite. Two hours and three Manhattans later, there he was in front of a canvas with a bewildered expression, head tilted sideways, saying, "I don't get it. It's just a (expletive) black dot on a white canvas. Who couldn't do that? I wouldn't give you five dollars for it." (For the record, it wasn't the bad word that starts with F. Dad never used it. A rather dubious distinction, but one Mom was proud of.) At that point, knowing the comments would certainly get louder, Mom would make him say his goodbyes and hustle him home.

Dad loved kitsch. He didn't know it *was* kitsch, only that he liked it. Once Mom didn't get him out of an auction in time, and for years, a garish Spanish toreador—we nicknamed him Juan—hung above the fireplace challenging all comers. I got the impression Mom felt about Juan the same way Ralphie's mother felt about the fishnet-stockinged leg lamp in the front window in *A Christmas Story*.

I appreciate when people air their true opinions. Being

an artist and writer myself, it can hurt, but it tells me something valuable. Something my friends won't because they don't want to offend. Since a few friends are artists as well, I know this is not the case for most of them. When a person criticizes a project you've spent a great deal of time and effort on, it's as though they're telling you your newborn baby is ugly. And just as in a certain Seinfeld episode, sometimes babies *really are* ugly. Parents (artists and authors) are the last to know. Unlike the parents—who can afford to be oblivious to such a truth, after all, they're not trying to *sell* junior—the artists and authors are in major league doo-doo if they keep their heads in the sand.

It works the opposite way as well. At one party, an artist of local renown had a few too many. His artwork wasn't my cup of tea, but he had his fans. He'd gotten several terrific reviews on his one-man shows. I felt a solidarity with my father when I viewed this artist's work, and it took effort not to tilt my head and say, *huh?* So imagine my delight—which I managed to conceal despite two glasses of wine—when said artist confided he knew he was a hack. He pulled me aside. "I have perpetrated the biggest hoax," he said in conspiratorial-toned vodka breath. "I can't paint for shit. My stuff sucks. And all these fools think my work is good. The whole business is so full of crap. Can you believe it?" Seems if enough high-falutin' sounding rhetoric gets spouted, you can make people think the way you want them to. I'd heard him expound about his work, and I'll give him his due. He was extremely talented in the baloney department. Spewing sophisticated gobbledygook designed to make you feel so intellectually inferior that you wouldn't dare challenge it for fear of looking stupid or provincial—that was the man's true gift. Now that I think about it, I should hire him to write gobbledygook for me.

My preference is for art to at least appear as though it took some effort to accomplish. But I've learned a couple of things. I wrap my comments in pretty pink paper before I voice them and I never drink Manhattans. They are dangerous and worse than truth serum.

VICTORIA LANDIS

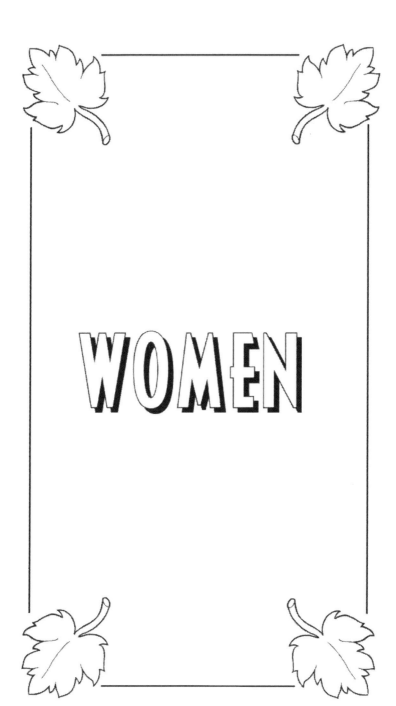

WOMEN

CLEVER GIRL

Beyoncé's Super Bowl outfit a few years back apparently caused some people's brains to short-circuit. I don't mean the PETA folks. We expect them to protest whenever a celebrity wears python, iguana, and cow. I'd be shocked if they hadn't. No, no. I'm referring to the tittering of those who took offense at the *skimpiness* of her outfit.

Their reason was—she wore it during half-time of one of the most-watched events of the year. And families—*children*, for corn's sake—were watching. Gasp. The horror. Really? Unless it was the first-time foray for these protected children up and out of their cable and Internet-free underground bunker, all we can conjure as a reaction to their parents' lament is a huge, collective *HUH*?

So, allow me to get this straight. The violence of three-hundred pounds of muscle slamming into same doesn't register as wrong for children to see? The team cheerleaders' teensy outfits never caught your attention? Your kids never saw a movie? You've never taken them to a pool or the beach? How about dinnertime TV ads for adult diapers or boner pills? The garbage that's plastered along the check-out line in the grocery store? None of this stuff ever gave you an uncomfortable moment with your progeny?

Now that I've shot that argument all to heck, I think we

can see what was behind the grousing. What else could it be but a subversive plot? (Isn't it always?) But whose? Who stood to gain most by distracting Americans from the important issues of the day? The Democrats? The Republicans? Castro? The orange-tinged Speaker of the House at the time sure needed some distractions. Launching protests, however inane, ensured that visual images of the subject popped up everywhere. *Hey, wait a gosh-darn minute.* Now that I put it that way, maybe it was Beyoncé's PR team itself behind the excited frenzy.

That's got to be it. Her designer used not just one, but three types of animals to create an outfit. A grievous sin with zero chance of being missed by people who kicked up a fuss when Obama swatted a fly. It thereby guaranteed headlines on every news and entertainment site for weeks afterward. Which then exposed even those who left the room at half-time to the dangerous influence of flirtatious black lace attached to tiny patches of leather and lots of cleavage. Voilá—instant outrage.

Between the costume brouhaha and the whipped up controversy about the national anthem at the inaugural, Beyoncé started 2013 with a monster lead over any other celebrity in the coveted *No, no, look at ME* category. Don't misunderstand me. I'm in awe of the superstar's savvy. I'm straining my brain to somehow replicate the formula for my writing. Unfortunately, there's no interest in what writers do or don't wear. Delve into your memory and try to conjure one instance when you've seen tabloid headlines about a best-selling author's cleavage. Or a beer belly hanging over a male writer's swim trunks. Or an author neglecting to put on underwear—which is far more likely because, hands down, we have more *absent-minded professor* types in our talent pool. Nobody cares. Seriously, an author could show up in Lady Gaga's egg wearing only Saran Wrap, and it wouldn't nudge an adorable kitten video from its slot on the local news channel. Authors can choose to write something dirty for shock value's sake, but forevermore they will be judged—and harshly—by that drivel, instead of their best efforts. Besides, the *Fifty Shades of Grey* lady already milked the last ounce from that cash cow. (On a side note, if you'd like to read *good* erotica, look up Anaïs Nin.)

Ah, well. I'll keep pondering. If you get any brain flashes, do let me know. In the meantime, I'll keep an eye on the queen of self-promotion, because even superstar Beyoncé couldn't afford the publicity that outfit got her. Well played, young lady. Well played, indeed.

THE HONEY-DO LIST

The jokes about never actually finishing the Honey-Do List are ubiquitous. As soon as one project gets done, another surfaces. But is the never-ending chores list nothing more than a clever and diabolical plot on the part of women? Does the poor average guy stumble mindlessly through his weekends checking off items on a list penned by his mate—in hopes of finishing enough tasks in a given time frame, therefore earning a couple of hours of peace? Hours when he can veg out on the sofa watching a ball game undisturbed? He'll have a beer in one hand, and the other hand absently scratching a nether-region. His faithful dog will rest beside him, chewing on heaven knows what—but all past indicators will point to the likelihood it'll be some essential part of an eighth-grade science project that rolls under the table. (Cue the late night panic-filled run to the hardware store and banging on the door begging to be let in as they're closing.)

But we digress. There is a man who is writing a book about the ways women control men. (I've promised not to reveal a name just yet.) One chapter is dedicated to the Honey-Do List. Are we women that ingenious? What I have a hard time believing is that any women have time to even think about diabolical plotting, much less carry out evil schemes. Real life women are not like the ones in soap-operas and chick flicks. Most women I know feel lucky if they are organized enough to make a grocery list, then actually remember to bring it to the store with them. Lord knows I don't plan that far in advance.

My exes never had Honey-Do Lists. Of course, none of my exes were the handyman type to start with, and in general, it was less annoying and less expensive to just call somebody who knew *how* to fix whatever needed fixing. However, it was pointed out to me by a well-meaning male friend that I may be the exception that proves the rule, evidenced by the difficult, twisted path I've had to navigate in life. Translation? I'm nowhere near clever enough to pull off a plot. I didn't take it personally. It's true. I've simply never been the sort of individual who would expend the energy needed to manipulate others. Perhaps had I been a bit more adept at manipulation, my twisted path wouldn't have taken the shape of a Barrel of Monkeys dumped into the middle of a pile of Pick-Up Sticks. I should have conducted exhaustive research to discover what my exes *were* good at, then given them lists of tasks to accomplish using those skills. Apparently, it was my duty as a female. I failed, and voilá—divorce. But I wonder, is it really a failure if you're not aware that you're supposed to be doing something? Who hands out the *How to Manipulate Men* manual, and why did they skip me? For the record, two of my exes were very good at manipulating *me*.

The idea being promoted as the reason females are behind all this diabolical-ness, is that *women think* by keeping men engaged in busy work—albeit busy work that *does* maintain and augment the home resale value— the wife always knows where her husband is. Meaning keep him occupied, and he won't fool around? I think that's what the general drift is. Idle hands are the devil's workshop? As though a person who wasn't constantly working on something wouldn't have the personal fortitude to act in an honorable manner when left to their own devices. No free will at all. Not currently re-staining the deck? Feel the chill wind of temptation go through you, making you go to the racetrack and bet your whole paycheck. Putting off replacing that toilet flapper? Beware, the devil is salivating right over your shoulder and impelling you to hang out in a bar trying to pick up other women.

I'm sorry. I simply can't buy into this guy's theory. Women asking men to do things to maintain a home isn't about control. It's a quality of life issue. And since when did home repairs and chores that need to be done for the benefit of everyone in the family become a male vs. female thing? If they have the skills, women do plenty of these things, too. Maybe women, in general, derive more comfort from knowing the laundry room won't flood because the washer hoses were changed out on schedule. Perhaps the fact that access to the attic has been denied to rats and squirrels so they can no longer chew on wires and nest up there helps her to sleep better? And, Mr. Ways-Women-Control-Men-Writer, do you know what happens when people sleep better? (Especially women.) They tend to be happier. And when women are happier, they want more nookie. Which usually makes men happier. See? The circle of life, again.

I've learned an awful lot on my expedition down the twisted path. One of the takeaways is—no matter how busy someone is, if they want to fool around, they'll find a way to do it—with or without a Honey-Do List. There is no controlling someone else's free will, and I believe most women know it. So there.

GREAT MOMENTS IN WOMEN'S HISTORY—PANTYHOSE

Once upon a time, women wore dresses every day. When it was cold, since they pretty much were forbidden to wear pants, they wore stockings to keep their legs warm. But not until the mid-1500s when the knitting machine was invented. I don't know what the ladies did to mitigate the cruel winter winds sailing under their skirts before that. Maybe nothing. Women dropped dead at pathetically early ages back then—getting a bone-deep chill couldn't have helped. Had I lived in the cold climates at that time, I would have been one of those women who masqueraded as a man—just so I could wear pants. And the wool stockings. You see, only men wore the stockings at first. With their pantaloons. There are many masterpiece paintings showing noblemen turning a finely-shaped ankle toward the portrait painter. Perhaps to lure a new wife before she also froze to death.

The stockings were knitted from wool or cotton. Wool was warm, but scratchy as heck. Both fibers tended to stretch with wear. The darn things kept falling down, no matter how well-matched they were to the shape of the legs. For those of you who are ridiculously young, you should know the natural fibers that are knitted or woven into fabrics are not elastic. Clothing that can stretch out and snap back wasn't invented until the 1950s, and it took until the 1980s for it to be a common thing. At first, there were ties looped into the tops of stockings. The ties also stretched out, and much time was wasted in constantly re-tying them.

Until some genius invented the garter. Garters were attached to a belt that sat above the hip bones so it couldn't slip down. And while men tend to think garters were/are sexy on women, women hated them. The garters, I mean. Well, I'm sure many of the women were not so delighted with their men either—as both bathing and tooth brushing were rare occurrences. Come to think of it, dropping dead early might have been a pleasant option for those women.

Everything changed in the twentieth century as hemlines rose. The female leg had more exposure than ever, and a man named Wallace Carothers at Dupont figured out how to make nylon. From coal tar, water, and alcohol. Can't imagine how he landed on that combination, but it sure seems like an accident that occurred while trying to do something else—probably illegal. Nylon was sheer and let the essence of the leg show through. Very sexy. Very sexy because the nylon hid just enough of real legs.

Real legs have birthmarks and freckles, cuts and scars, insect bites and rashes, veins that protrude, and lumps and bumps of all kinds. In short, real legs aren't perfect. Nylons made them look like they were. That's why when, after World War II, they were first offered for sale again at a San Francisco department store, ten-thousand women mobbed the place.

And then came pantyhose. Although garter belts were considered sexy, they were really annoying to wear. I know because as recently as my teen years, we had to wear garters to hold up our stockings. Lest you think I'm a hundred years old, that was in the 1970s. Back to pantyhose. All the wonderfulness of nylon stockings that made legs look perfect combined with the comfort of no garter belt. In addition, they did add a layer of warmth for the artificially frigid air of the modern-day office. They were amazing. We *loved* them.

So now we get to the crux of my point. I don't watch much television, but I perused the channels last weekend while folding laundry and caught the lady from *Millionaire Matchmaker* just as she was telling the eligible women to wear short dresses and get rid of their pantyhose and go bare-legged. (Note—said matchmaker was wearing pants.)

WHAT? I don't know where I've been or how I've missed it, but bare legs are now the 'thing'. Are they crazy? Unless the woman is under twenty-one and absolutely *nothing* has happened to her yet, no one's legs can withstand that kind of scrutiny.

It opened my eyes. Suddenly, everywhere I went, women had bare legs. Apparently, this has been going on for years, and it somehow slipped my notice. (This confirms that I will not *ever* bat for the other team.) And let me tell you—seeing a bare foot in high heels is not attractive. I don't care what fashion *experts* say. It looks horrible. Little veins protrude from the pressure of standing at an unnatural angle. Uneven skin tones. Discolorations. Yuck. This seems to be just another modern-day retelling of *The Emperor's New Clothes*. Some fools declare it's chic to go without the sheer veiling of nylon, and all the lemmings play follow the leader and jump off the cliff.

We have come full circle. Women are wearing dresses with the cruel cold wind sailing up under their skirts, and all the bumps and bruises of their bare legs are on display. Humans are hilarious.

KEEPING UP WITH WHAT'S HOT

You've got to keep up with what's hot. Or what? I don't know—I've never done it. Or cared. Until this year, I didn't realize I was being unpatriotic by not updating my clothes.

By and large, boys and men don't concern themselves with what's hot or trendy. They do what they can to insure they don't look like total dorks, but this year's shoes versus last year's? Not a chance. I suppose in a world where a man can wear a twenty-year-old tuxedo and no one is the wiser, they've learned there are no consequences for them. Lucky things.

The same doesn't hold true for women's fashion, and the female gender does care. Some—not so much, and some—more than should be legal. The latest news in hair, make-up, fashion, accessories filter into women's daily lives, constantly urging them to update, update, update. Spend, spend, spend. Imagine how disastrous our recession would have been if every woman simply stopped buying all clothes, shoes, purses, and makeup? It's enough to drive spikes of cold terror into the heart of Madison Avenue. Wall Street? Phooey. We know who really drives the economy.

I fall into the kinda-care-a-little category. I am always a couple of steps behind the fashion world. Maybe several. Well, okay, years behind. I find a style that works for me and I tend to stick with it. However, when my boys (who didn't notice I'd painted the living room, cut off my long hair, or euthanized the fish—long story there) complained about what I wore to their school events, I knew the jig was up. My clothing had to be hopelessly out of date for them to give a darn. My oldest said I embarrassed him in front of his friends. Still I wondered, as I examined my reflection one day, what was so awful? Besides jeans, my standard casual outfit was a cotton skirt and a tucked in T-shirt. It wasn't as though I'd donned plaid culottes, a polka-dotted cowl-necked sweater, tasseled knee socks, clogs, and a name tag that said, *Hi, I'm David's mom.*"

Fashion is so cyclical. The silliest things keep returning. I can see the designers racking their brains for ideas. Suddenly, one cries, "I've got it. When *was* the last time bubble hems were popular? The eighties? Great. Hmmm, twenty years, that's enough time. Let's bring 'em back!" Some young salesgirl tried to get me to buy one for a Bar-Mitzvah last year. I laughed and told her they looked ridiculous the first time around, I wasn't falling for it again.

We all wore bell bottoms in high school. Then I about fell over when my boys' girlfriends showed up in them. Baby doll tops were big then, too. They came back, and they still made even skinny girls look like they're pregnant. In 1992, I bought a lovely little black dress made of silk. It had shoulder pads. I wore it for a few years, then forgot about it as newer things came into my life. I cleaned out my closet about six months ago and sighed with affection when I found it. It was such a pretty dress, but even I recognized that shoulder pads were long past chic. So it went into the charity pile. And wouldn't you know? Just last week on the Today Show, some fashion *expert* was on, explaining to Hoda and Kathy Lee how shoulder pads were the latest thing. How wonderful it made the model look, she claimed. Made her seem taller, more confident, yada, yada, yada. Yeesch. I nearly cried for my little black dress. It's back in style. Stupid fashion industry. They love to keep people like me squinting into the sun, with a big fat—*huh?*—look on our faces.

On the other end of my spectrum, are the women who really and truly live by what's hot right now. They shop for the latest in everything. Imagine knowing by sight if the pair of Manolo Blahniks hurrying past is actually this year's or last year's. Whether the lavender trench with the pleats in back is Dolce & Gabbana, Stella McCartney, or DKNY? My hat's off to anyone who keeps up with it. I can't imagine the homework involved. It's daunting.

Then there are the women who care and want the latest, but they can't afford it. They'll sacrifice food and gas money if need be. That's dedication that needs to be recognized. A friend of a friend has over fifty designer purses. Real ones, not knock-offs. Her husband is out of work, they're behind in their mortgage, and do you know what gift her friends are pooling money for, for her birthday? Yup, a fifteen-hundred dollar handbag. Another woman buys four-hundred dollar jeans, but says she can't afford a new dishwasher. Can't say I understand it, but they're taking one for Team America.

Women are wacky when it comes to clothes, and thank goodness. We should all stand and salute women for supporting our economy. Keep buying, ladies. The way back to solvency for America may be along a path littered with spandex.

HUMAN NATURE

THE SKY IS FALLING
(From 2012)

What's new for the New Year? Well, for starters, we didn't die. We're all still here, and you're reading this. The Mayans—or rather the wacky world-is-going-to-end people who completely misunderstood the Mayan calendar—were proven inaccurate. December 21st in my house only meant the next day was our traditional sugar cookie painting day that required a whole lot of dough rolling and baking. So we baked, on the off chance we might actually wake up on the 22nd after all with fifteen people coming over, expecting to paint icing on cookies. And you don't want to tick off people after telling them they would get homemade from-scratch cookies. People really, really, like cookies.

If the movie *2012* taught us anything other than John Cusack is still quite good-looking, it's that a full-scale disaster of the world falling apart wouldn't be much fun. The thought of looming disaster got me thinking about how people over the ages have been misled into believing in crazy predictions. Why does anyone buy into them? I suppose, in the days before our information-saturated high-tech wizardry, folks believed it because they weren't as well educated as they are now. Yet when the Y2K scare—and now the Mayan calendar—menaced, millions of people not only bought in, but doubled down. Survivalists dug bunkers, stocked them with Spam, Twinkies, water, and guns. Why? Maybe they never learned to read? Or analyze? Maybe they paid more attention to the girls in front of them than the lessons from the science teacher? Were they dropped as babies? Maybe they never got over the childhood fun of building forts, playing war, and just like to pretend they're a combination of GI Joe and Daniel Boone?

As far back as ancient times, respected soothsayers and oracles declared the end was near. Final battles between good and evil would eclipse the world. The sun would go black. The stars would disappear. The land would sink into the sea. The story of Chicken Little evolved from that vein. Curiously enough, Chicken Little might also explain why humans in a hyper-information age believe in bizarre non-scientific nonsense. They want to. The tricky part is—they don't *know* they want to. It's that sub-conscious psychology thing. Harold Camping was wrong about his end-of-the-world predictions several times. In each instance, he said he calculated wrong, and it was really going to happen on *this* date (fill in the blank). His followers kept believing. Some sold their homes and gave away all their possessions. Others stood on street corners with signs imploring the passers-by to change their ways asap, because time was quickly running out, and boy, wouldn't *they* be sorry?

Let's try this. Get one person to run down the street screaming there's an alien spacecraft that crashed a couple miles outside of town, and it's a guarantee at least a few other people will not only join in, they'll text everyone they know while they're doing it. It'll go viral in an hour. When nothing is found, someone will claim the government came and removed the evidence with light-speed precision—because they'll have been tracking this particular craft, and bingo. Instant conspiracy/cover up theory. People will take close-up shots of possible markings in the dirt or grass. The photos hit the Internet. Someone doctors them to enhance the markings and sends them back out, creating more controversy because now somebody else sees the two versions of the photos and declares it only proves the government tried to hide the evidence. Now there are bloggers demanding answers, demanding the *truth* about the crash. The American people deserve to know! (About something I invented.) Can't you see it happening?

Why? It's a heck of a lot more intriguing and exciting than dealing with their mundane life of going to work, coming home, doing the dishes, and sitting on the sofa watching reality shows that everybody knows aren't remotely related to reality.

Which brings me to the Zombie Apocalypse. It started with *Night of the Living Dead* in 1968. Long dismissed as no more than a cult classic, sometime in the last decade zombies became hip. Maybe because all the pretty, sparkly vampires were tiring of the constant paparazzi and snapped at the annoying questions about their sex lives and how they could have babies. Zombies apparently want and need the attention, whereas the vampires don't. I heard they might all move to France where they have paparazzi-restriction laws so they can raise their children out of the glare of the public spotlight.

Anyway, in case you didn't know, there is a Zombie Apocalypse coming. The dead, for no apparent reason, will rise from their graves and try to eat the rest of us. I did some research on this, as I found it confusing that dead people would want to eat anything. I mean, they're dead. Technically, they don't *need* anything, right? Turns out, I wasn't the only one asking tough, in-depth questions. I found a blog that addressed this very issue. The zombies want to eat because the virus that reanimates them activates their brains—or at least the part of their brains that haven't rotted, 'cause they sure don't seem like the sharpest knives in the drawer. So, what's left of their brains tell them to eat, but their internal organs don't work, which means they can't process any of it, much less poop it out. According to the zombie-expert blogger, eventually, their bodies will rupture/explode from all the food.

Strangely, although the virus doesn't activate anything else, they have the ability to move their arms and legs so they can wander around in a clumsy fashion that even a toddler could outrun. I have so many questions. If zombies are so slow and uncoordinated, why is anyone afraid of them? And why, if they're already dead, will shooting them stop them? How do they remove the coffin lid while six feet of dirt is sitting on it? How do they tunnel upward to the surface? If they're six-feet down, how do they contract the virus to begin with? Why bother to eat humans, who fight back, when they could simply stumble into a grocery store and eat things that won't run away? Instead of retreating to a bunker, why don't we sit on the front porch throwing opened cans of Spam for them until they explode? That sounds like a whole lot more fun. Imagine the YouTube videos.

It is, of course, starting in Florida, based on several

suspicious incidents in the recent past. A peculiar rash in a Hollywood high school. The naked face-eating guy in Miami. We'll be ready for 'em. We can't dig bunkers because of the low water table, but we'll leave a trail of sugar cookies to lure the undead into a big cage. Everybody, even zombies, loves sugar cookies.

BE KIND TO YOUR INTERIOR DESIGNER
(It isn't as easy as it looks.)

Once upon a time, I did interior design. I was in my twenties and full of inspiration and bright ideas. I managed to work my way up to some pretty fancy projects. But then I got married, had children, and took time off. When I needed to go back to the world of paid working people, I chose not to return to interior design. Here's why.

Clients. There are several types. Those who know what they want, those who don't know but trust you to guide them and get them a great result, and those who haven't a clue what they like, don't trust anyone, and second guess your every move. The last category also tends to use their hired help—including designers—as excuses and scapegoats.

The jobs for the clients in the first two categories usually go very well. It's a win-win for everybody. It's the third category that'll make you want to hang yourself by the drapery cords. I suppose had I stayed in that line of work, I'd have gotten a lot better at spotting and avoiding them.

The goofiest things happened in this industry. One inebriated client chased after a delivery man with a cocktail sword. Another made the plumber take a shower in the new shower stall to test out the hot water safety gizmo. One contractor knocked down the wrong wall with a sledge hammer, then quit when we raised a fuss. An inexperienced delivery driver backed up the wrong way and launched the back of the truck into a reflecting pool.

I lost one job because the woman asked me to include an expensive hand-painted screen in the design and keep it a secret, telling me it was a surprise for her husband. When the screen appeared in his living room, he had a fit and started yelling at his wife in front of me. She then turned, and pointing at me, said, "It's her fault. I told her not to include it, but she insisted you'd learn to like it, and we should buy it anyway." Ooh. Backstab. Ouch.

Another couple couldn't figure what they did or didn't like. Every move I made, they brought in other people to see if *they* liked it. This was after they'd approved everything. When the painter finished one wall in the bedroom, the client made him stop and wait while the client fetched the doorman from downstairs. He hustled the doorman into the apartment and asked him if he like the color, which was a pale sage green. The doorman said, "No. Not my kind of color. I like blue." The client turned to me and said, "What do you think about blue?" My eyes glazed over. We'd already been through every paint chip known to man, and I thought the color issue had been finally settled.

The same couple invited their poodle clipper (no, I am not exaggerating) home to tell them what she thought of the wallpaper in the den. The poodle clipper didn't like the wallpaper. The woman wore heavy-blue eyeshadow, purple fake fingernails, a leopard print blouse, and bright

neon-green pants. Why would anyone want to know
what suited her taste? I don't know.

Regarding the same couple—yes, it was a job from h-e-
double toothpicks. The wife's mother didn't like the
chandelier the wife and I spent four shopping trips to
find. The wife loved it, had to have it. Clapped and
squealed with glee as the electrician connected it and
then flipped the switch. Her mother said it was too
small. Down it came, and back it went.

I lost another job because of a hunky tile installer, 'Joe'.
I'd done maybe five jobs with him with no problems
whatsoever. Joe was very good-looking and very
muscular. The clients were a married couple with a few
kids. The wife was a stay-at-home mom. As the tile job
progressed, I stopped by daily to check on the work, to
make sure things were up to snuff. It was a large job
with some intricate patterns in the entry. I noticed the
wife wearing less and less around the house as the job
went on, until all she wore was a skimpy bikini. When I
left that day, they both still had clothes on—she lying by
the pool, and he laying tile in the front hall. I remember
thinking, *oh, boy, there's trouble*, but I couldn't imagine she'd
do more than flirt. She did. The husband came home
early and caught Joe and his wife doing things they
shouldn't have been doing. He fired me. Like I could
have stopped them.

On top of silly clients, your interior designer has to deal
with factories that don't notify them when something's
back ordered even though they said they would, so the
designer believes things are on schedule. Sewing
workrooms can misread dimensions and produce

draperies for midget houses. I once had to send back an order for full-length, ten-foot long draperies. They'd made them four-feet long despite the confirmation they'd sent me with the correct measurements. Which meant re-ordering and waiting all over again for the fabric, and arguing with the sewing people as to why they shouldn't be paid. And then being yelled at by the client for holding up the job.

So, if you have, or are contemplating using, a designer, do both of you a huge favor. Once you establish that this professional does indeed know what they're doing, and that you like the projects they've done before—let them do it. If you have a phone call with your designer and he or she sounds somewhat distracted, be nice. It may be they've just gotten off a call from a woman who claims they're at fault for the client's cat ripping the new silk chairs to shreds. Or, if the next time you see your designer and there's a faint glimmer of lunacy in their eyes, try to understand that perhaps the gardener's girlfriend's manicurist has just decided that pink ruffles are the way to go for the bed skirt.

TROUBLES IN THE FIRST WORLD

Thank goodness 2013 is over. It feels like I held my breath the entire year. I'm not normally the least bit superstitious, but in January of 2013, a television 'expert' put the idea in my head that, because of some hodge-podge figuring in the numerology of 2013, it spelled trouble, the Big Trouble in River City kind, the worst year *ever*, for all of us.

Near as I can tell, while there were tragedies and mayhem in the world in the last twelve months, it didn't measure up anywhere near what I'd consider the worst year. But what do I know from tragedy? So, I did some investigating—a plethora of issues made headlines that I cannot believe I missed. Lamentations abounded. Tweets flew like the carrier pigeons of old, and the true hardships wrought tears of compassion from dedicated followers. I am, of course, talking about those horrible, heart-wrenching—**First World Problems**.

Yes, these tribulations are experienced only by well-to-do citizens of insanely privileged countries. Their pleas for understanding and help cannot go ignored any longer. Please forgive me if what I'm about to tell you ruins your optimism for the new year, but I feel it is of the utmost importance to shed light on these land mines of modern life.

The following unfortunate souls:

- Had to get out of their car and physically walk into a bank because they wanted to withdraw more than $500.00.
- Had a backache from sleeping eleven hours straight.
- Had so many clothes, the closet rod was pulling away from the wall.
- Had to walk the entire way in the airport because the moving sidewalk was out of order.
- Went shopping and couldn't fit all the food into the fridge.
- Forgot to charge the electric toothbrush and had to manually move the brush up and down.
- Didn't like flying commercial with both ski boots and golf clubs.
- Hated that her father made her go on (yet another) Bahamas cruise for spring break, instead of to Mexico like she wanted.
- Lived so close to work, the car heater didn't warm the car before arriving at work.
- Had no taco delivery available in town.
- Had a backache from sitting on their butt all day long.
- Couldn't figure out how to clap at the golf tournament while holding wine.

All this misery completely sent their lives into such disarray, while they somehow missed the tornado, hurricane, flood, earthquake, and bombing victims around them. Fortunately, I have the solution. In order to rescue the First World Problems people from their prison of stress, we invent a time machine. Every time one of our pampered poppets needs a wake-up call to snap them back into the world of actual human issues, we will rocket them to fun times in the past.

Now, plenty of epic droughts and famines killed millions in the past. Earthquakes and floods wiped out more. But my vote for worst year for humankind is 1918. The Spanish Flu killed twenty to forty million people that year, or approximately one fifth of the world's population. It killed half of our soldiers fighting in World War I. And it had hellish effects. Imagine our poppets faced with watching people come down with fever, fatigue, and headaches. Then, within a few hours, the sick turned blue. Yes, really blue, so much so the medical reports said sometimes they couldn't discern the patient's skin color. (Can you imagine the throaty valley-girl-inflectioned Tweets that would instigate? *OMG. This is really gross.*) The ensuing coughs sometimes tore the victims' abdominal muscles. Then the fun started. Foamy blood oozed from noses and mouths, and sometimes, the ears. Victims vomited and lost bowel control at the same time. (*Can't* SOMEBODY *put, like, a curtain or something around them so I don't have to watch? And, OMG, what is that smell?*) Patients could die within hours of exhibiting their first symptom. (*I just sneezed. I feel hot, and not, like, a good hot, either. Okay, I totally get it. Take me back now. Please?*)

Yep. A little exposure to actual calamity is all that's needed to whup our first world complainers' behinds back into the fold of reality. If you don't like my choice of 1918, then how about 1932? That was the year Josef Stalin forced starvation on millions of Ukrainians. Or maybe the drought in China that started in 1876, lasted until 1879, and killed over nine million?

Or, if we can't perfect my time machine, let's just cut off their electricity and water for a month (in tandem with freezing their bank accounts and credit cards) and see if they can activate the dead-zones of their brains to survive it. I know, I know, but this is tough love. It's the only way to cure the inordinate stress they're feeling from the mundane. We must save them, before they infect more people and make the Spanish Flu look like a day at a dubious gene pool. If we don't, we might become those roly-poly helpless humans from *WALL-E*.

SOCKS AND CROCS

Young people—watch out! What you think makes you look awesome today will undoubtedly make you look embarrassingly dorky in twenty years. If you're smart, start planning now the ingenious ways you'll torture your future teenagers with the evidence.

Never is anything more difficult—clothing wise—than the hot season. It's tough to project sublime cool when fabrics stick to beads of sweat trickling in rivulets down your body. I think that's why so many people opt out of giving a darn about what they wear when the sun's blazing. So, summer fashions are always a huge challenge. Especially for the designers. I mean, how many ways can you redesign a beach cover up or a sundress? A bathing suit? I saw one last week that had a zillion straps crisscrossing the woman's body leaving tiny odd squares and triangles of skin exposed. That's great if you want your tan lines to resemble a cubist painting. Getting in and out of that suit would probably do me in. I owned a racer-back tank once, and I dislocated a shoulder from *that*. I'd need Carson Kressley's emergency response team for extrication from the complicated one.

Intrepid reporter that I am, I have traipsed all over the Internet (so you don't have to) searching and searching for—the things you don't want to wear this summer. No matter which snooty-hooty fashionista tells you to do it.

But before we get to that, I'd like to revisit the worst perennial summer goof up. Socks with sandals. Even back in the fifties, it wasn't a good look. Nightmarish flashbacks flood my brain at the mere mention of it. My dad and all the other neighborhood dads, standing around the barbeque grill wearing fringed straw Panama hats, open shirts, those horrible too-short shorts, and socks. With sandals. Black work socks. Or white gym socks. And leather sandals.

Year after year, wherever you go on vacation, you'll still see the stubborn middle-aged man scuffling around in white gym socks—with some sort of sandals. He's easy to recognize because he also comes with the obligatory contingent of, A—a mortified wife—who stays a few feet away from him at all times, the better to not allow strangers to think she is with him and, B—mortified, sighing teenagers—who trail behind by at least thirty feet lest anyone know they breathe the same air as dorky dad (yet hovering close enough to ask for money when necessary).

Now, since the advent of the sandal's next best thing—Crocs—we have another problem. Quite possibly worse. Socks and Crocs. Yes, as though the neon rubber clogs weren't awful enough, people are enhancing the effect with socks. One of the most disturbing photos I've seen in ages was a rather large woman wearing a tiny orange spandex skirt with a bikini top and lime-green Crocs—with pink lacy anklets. I wish I could 'unsee' it, but it's burned into my retinas.

We should start a Pinterest page for 'SS' (socks & sandals) sightings. Extra kudos for anyone with a picture of the elusive SpongeBob-red-and-blue-stripes-at-the-top variety of mid-calf white gym socks. I saw an argyle pair with black rubber slip-on sandals posted recently. A matching set of aloha-wear flowered shorts and shirt completed that outfit.

I did once ask a man why he wore socks with his sandals. It was when I lived on Oahu, and we'd struck up a conversation with a tourist couple who seemed very nice, despite his obvious fashion handicap. "Because my feet sweat," he said. "And then they smell." His practical answer surprised me.

Maybe that's the difference between men and women. Well, most women. We'll assume the one in the orange skirt mentioned above is an aberration—for our collective sanity as well as my pithy discussion. A normal woman could have sweat pouring off her feet, leaving a trail of salty puddles behind her, and she still wouldn't wear something willfully embarrassing like socks with her sandals. Practicality be damned.

At this juncture I must point out something my trusty assistant brought to my attention. We have a scape goat. This entire phenomenon is the fault of the Japanese. Their men *and* women of stature centuries ago wore socks and sandals as part of the formal style for special ceremonial occasions. It's part of their culture's history. Very honorable. Unlike us. Think about this now—our epidemic of dads rocking the sock look seemed to mushroom in the fifties. We sent US Army guys to occupy Japan after WWII. And they came back with this ridiculous trend. The Japanese probably never expected their secret plan to dorkify the USA to work so well. Bet they're enjoying it, though.

IF YOUR WALLS COULD TALK

Summer seems like a good time to fix up the house. Well, for us in South Florida, let's qualify that. The *inside* of the house. Our regular afternoon monsoons aren't exactly conducive to outdoor maintenance chores. I know. I've tried to outsmart the weather and failed spectacularly. Years ago, my oldest built a wood play structure (a fort!) for my youngest on a June weekend. Then he vamoosed back to UCF for his summer classes, of course leaving behind the obligatory college-kid debris field. Usually, it's outdated notebooks and textbooks, stained clothes, dirty dishes, and an array of things I'm loathe to gaze upon—much less touch without gloves, but with a construction project, it was tools, wood scraps, and plenty of screws to puncture brand new lawn mower tires.

My job was simple. Get it painted before it started to rot—about ten minutes in our climate. My son used pressure-treated posts, but apparently our neighborhood big box depot store's *experts* never heard of treated plywood, so it became my problem to coat both sides of the fort's floor asap. The first afternoon I tried, the sun was out, and I didn't see anything resembling a storm cloud. Thought I was safe. Silly me. I hadn't lived in South Florida long enough to know better. I'd barely gotten the plywood halfway painted when a menacing cloud swooped in and drenched everything. I ran into the house and watched the paint literally cascading down from the platform like a milky waterfall. The second and third attempts were no more successful. Finally, I decided that older son could just replace the flipping plywood when it rotted.

So—moving indoors to the fun of home improvement projects. I am, in my faux painting day job, a person who actually knows how to do a lot of repairs. I've had to fix botched jobs more times than I care to count. What cracks me up is how inventive people can be when they're too careless to do something the right way. In taking down or opening up walls, I've found masking tape holding the wall together instead of drywall tape, *and* no drywall screws in that section. Masking tape? How lazy do you have to be to put up a wall with masking tape? The lure of not having to run to the store and buy the right thing outweighs the risk of your boards separating and having to do it all over again?

I can just imagine the previous homeowners' domestic bickering that caused such idiocy. There's a section of wallboard missing from a long ago leak repair. The wife nags the husband ad nauseam to patch the wall already so she can hang one of those hideous over-sized *glamour* shots of her and her sisters. The kind that were so popular in the 90s that are now laughable as Throwback Thursday pictures on Facebook? Stashed away in the garage behind a year's worth of old magazines, he finds the drywall piece the plumber had cut out. It fits. He tapes it in place with the masking tape, smothers the edges with some old spackle compound, and settles back into the sofa to watch the big game. Fast forward a few years, and the new homeowner wants her walls faux finished. Mr. Lazy's handiwork now becomes my issue, because I need a smooth wall to work on. Arrgghhh.

Fantasies of hunting him down fill my head as I scrape away his ineptitude.

I'm a bit of a home repair archeologist. I've found some remarkably clever *fixes* under the drywall mud. And some nasty surprises behind the walls. Here we go. Under the mud, used as something to patch a hole. Are you ready? Tin can lids. Poster board stapled into place. Window screening. A chunk of a two-by-four. Paper plate. Plastic plate. (Both in the same house.) Plastic sheeting. A blank CD.

And behind the walls? A bad report card from 1985. Love letters. A McDonald's bag with cheeseburger and fries remains inside. Beer cans, some still filled with beer. Cigarette butts. A screwdriver. A hammer. A comb. A plastic Little Tykes toy. A TV remote. And a pair of black lacy unmentionables. Wouldn't you love to know the story behind that little discovery?

We can't blame the homeowners for all of these, however. I've been on jobsites where the homeowner ticked off the people working there. The workers don't like it when they are treated as less than human. (One homeowner wouldn't let anyone use the bathroom. We had to drive to the nearest supermarket. I wish I was kidding.) So sealing stuff, especially stuff that will attract vermin, inside the walls is a common way to exact revenge on a homeowner who's a jerk. I remove it when I see it, but I can't be everywhere, folks. So, be nice to those who work for you. Or you may never figure out why the bugs just *love* you to pieces.

STUPID HUMAN TRICKS

A portion of our population will always be a constant source of amusement for the rest of us. We've all heard wacky emergency room and strange circumstances stories. Here's a round-up of some more, so you can start the new year feeling darned good about how much smarter your family is than these folks.

Fashion First

A woman who, for years, wore five-inch heels during most of her awake hours, one morning found her ankles permanently locked into that stilted position. Ouch.

A man died in a car accident when the young woman driver couldn't hit the brake well enough because of her platform shoes. Someone should have told her about the existence of 'driving' shoes. They're loafer-ish comfy things, and once you arrive at your destination, you switch to your fancy-schmancy shoes.

A would-be robber wearing the very-baggy style pants, placed his gun in his waistband, but the gun slipped out and hit the sidewalk. He suffered a bullet wound in his groin.

Dance legend Isadora Duncan died because her long, flowing scarf got tangled in the rear wheel of the Bugati she rode in. The scarf strangled her.

Basic Chemistry

A man who needed an oxygen tank and mask also

loved cigars. One day, he lifted his mask for a drag from the stogie, accidentally dropped a burning ember into the tank, and caused an explosion. He died from his injuries. Compressed oxygen plus fire equals—Boom! Every time.

Another guy felt his toupee sliding off while in a nightclub. He found a bathroom and reglued it, apparently using too much. He lit a cigarette while waiting for it to set, and . . . Boom! Again. Too bad nobody forwarded the memo about how bald guys are sexy now.

Under The Influence

Standing up during a roller coaster ride to do *the wave*, a young man was killed when his head hit a crossbeam.

Thrill seeking teenagers climbed on top of a subway car and *surfed*. They were supposed to jump off when the train approached a tunnel and its low ceiling, but estimated the timing wrong.

Spring breakers jumped from the second floor motel balcony into the pool. One guy didn't look first and landed on a girl on a float.

A swim in a dark canal at night. The poor kid was drinking, but said that wasn't why he did it. He'd done it before. Lots of times. This time, an alligator took off his arm.

Thinking he'd share the fun with his beloved pet, a man blew pot smoke into his cat's ear and got the cat high. Instead of chowing down three bags of Friskies, then taking a nap, the cat went bonkers, knocked over the lit candles in the room and set the house on fire.

Temper, Temper

Two truckers got into a fight. One thrust a knife into the other's truck tire. The pressurized air from the hole in the tire made the knife fly out of the tire and hit the first guy in the neck.

When a man attempting to rob a vending machine couldn't get the money out of it, he rocked it more and more violently—until it fell over on top of him.

A golfer, angry about his game, flung his club. It hit a tree, broke, and half bounced right back at him, causing a stab wound.

Not Heeding The Directions

A man emptied two bottles of drain cleaner into his clogged toilet, then fell unconscious from the fumes.

A woman insisted her husband set up the shade umbrella during their day at the beach, despite the strong wind. Not wanting to listen to her complaints, he did. While he was away for a moment buying drinks for them, the wind tore the umbrella out of the sand, and the sharp end of the pole hit his wife in the chest.

The new toaster came with wood tongs for removing bread, etc. The impatient buyer didn't read the accompanying literature that warned of electrocution, and please unplug. Said buyer suffered burns and shock after using metal tongs. She later told the doctor she assumed all tongs were safe, since the manufacturer included a set.

Just Plain Stupid

Having made his own bungee cord, a man

miscalculated the stretch factor and hit the concrete below the overpass he jumped from.

The beeping distress call from an electronic pet made a woman attend to the fake pet and veer off the road while she was driving. She sustained life-threatening injuries.

A woman snorkeling in three feet of water panicked when water leaked into her mask. Instead of standing up and removing the mask, she drowned.

After setting thin bamboo stakes into the ground for her vegetable vines to climb as they grew, a woman began to weed the garden. As she bent to grab a weed, she impaled her eye on one of the stakes.

Terribly afraid of being burgled, a man set up a series of low wires across his front door. The smoke alarm happened to go off that night, and he broke his jaw and collarbone when he forgot about and tripped on the wire in his haste to get out.

There you go. Now, don't you feel downright superior and ready to start this New Year? But if you text and drive, you may find yourself on this list next year. Always follow this basic rule of thumb—a bellwether test, if you will. If a teenage boy thinks it's a good idea, you might want to re-evaluate. Have a wonderful and *safe* 2010!

BE KIND TO YOUR WAIT STAFF

August is our last gasp of summer before getting back to the old grind. Before the damp chills of autumn and winter leech deep into our bones, and the leaden gray skies . . . Oh, wait. We're in South Florida. Forget that part. But the mentality of summer vacation from school stays with us forever, and returning to work after time off has the same feeling as returning to school in the fall. To make reality worse, showing up at the office where everyone has Instagrammed hundreds of *hey-look-what-really-awesome-stuff-I-did-this-summer-and-you-didn't* pictures to Facebook, Twittered the minutest details, and already pretty much driven their co-workers loopy with it all, is nearly as dreadful as the one-thousandth snapshot of an adorable baby cuddled with a puppy. Or an adorable puppy wearing a sweater. Or an adorable sweater stretched inappropriately across *someone*'s Uncle Jim, who *so* should have known better than to drink beer, Tequila, and red wine with two equally toasted old ladies in the clothing-exchange booth at the Fireman's Fair, then invade the kids' amusements, later posting said photo with the caption, *Bounce House Pouncers*. But I digress.

The mere thought of facing the office show-off's superior summer photos (she probably doesn't even *have* an inappropriate uncle) is enough to dream of absconding to the islands for a permanent vacation, taking our chances with the locals. After all, on our last trip, Josie, Brigitta, and Juan *loved* having us at the all-inclusive resort, didn't they? Uh, hate to break it to you, but—not so much. In the midst of our fun, it's easy to forget that the people who make vacations enjoyable for us—are *working.*

Whether it's a Motel 6 or a Caribbean mega-resort, room maids, bartenders, and wait staff have to be pleasant to us or their caboose gets cooked. Derailed. Banished. Pleasant, no matter how some order them around as though they were personal servants. Smiling, despite the measly dollar tips. Nodding in empathy as some complain how the traveling to the vacation spot was horrendous. And laughing at not-funny jokes when the rest of the party is rolling their eyes.

You are making a huge mistake if you delude yourself into thinking, *Wow! I am really rocking it with these people. They love me!* They are not your new BFFs. You might *think* they are, but (trust me on this) they are so totally not. While all the folks stuck in dead-end resort service jobs probably dream of revenge from time to time, let's zero in on food service. The dubious honor of serving food to our fellow humans. Ever wonder why, sometimes, one person's order takes an eternity longer than everyone else's at the table? Ever gotten an ice-cold baked potato? A strange residue at the bottom of your glass?

While I personally never (No, really. I believe in Karma.) did anything awful to the crummiest customers, I sure witnessed others who did. How to exact revenge and not get in trouble is the driving factor for many. I'm not saying it's right, or that I approve of such tactics, but boy, sometimes it's fun to watch.

Contrary to urban legend, spitting into a customer's food before serving it is quite rare. I never saw anyone do it. No, no. Most wait staff seek a higher form of self-expression—a retribution that satisfies the creative muse dancing in their heads. Take, for example, the waitress at a convention luncheon who *accidentally* tripped while delivering a tray of rubber-chicken entrees to one of her five—yes, five—tables of ten. That's fifty hung-over, hungry mouths to satisfy. Her tormentor was a loud woman who apparently thought the waitress' only job was to adhere to her every whim. Immediately. The waitress aimed for the woman's lap, but—in a spark of luck that probably can never be replicated—one of the flattened, grilled chicken breasts took flight and landed *plop* on the woman's head like a bad toupee. I kid you not. If I put that in a book, I'd get howling complaints telling me it couldn't happen. The waitress said the best part was, as she apologized profusely and lifted the chicken from its new perch, the other nine at the table exploded with laughter. Which made the rude woman go along and laugh as well, or risk looking like the sour lemon she was.

Substituting real coffee instead of requested decaf. Serving the dregs of a soup pot instead of ladling a portion from the new one. Using *fish* ice instead of the machine ice. Rinsing slimy vegetables off and throwing them into salads. Replacing a dropped fork with a used one wiped with a used napkin. How to make sure this doesn't happen to you? Easy. Just be nice. As for the office show-off and her spectacular summer? Wanna bet she unknowingly ate some nasty things?

HIGH SCHOOL NEVER ENDS

My youngest started his senior year of high school a couple weeks ago, and the inevitable happened. Emerging from the cobwebs encasing the ancient memories of my senior year was a movie reel of people and events from that time. It escaped the padded cell where I so carefully stowed it and creaked its geriatric way into my frontal cortex.

Then a sixty-something man who works in an upper-level position at a Fortune 500 company made a comment that threw the memory reel into high-gear. When finished discussing a situation at work that showcased some serious pettiness among his colleagues, he shook his head in resignation and added, "High school never ends."

That was enough to launch a nightly parade of people I haven't seen in thirty-seven years marching into my dreams. Oy. During the day, though, I'm now assigning archetypes to people, based on the classic types we all knew in high school. And it's been fun.

While having lunch with a friend, I observed a group of women at a nearby table. Fair warning—if you're within my hearing range, I *will* use whatever I hear at some time in the future. Nothing is sacred. I change the names and places to preserve anonymity, but if you're spilling personal info loud enough for me to hear it at the next table or behind you in line, well, you should know better.

It's surprising how many people do what my grandmother called 'airing your laundry in public.'

Back to the ladies who lunched. They looked to be in their late fifties. Figuring out who was who proved to be easy, because—*high school never ends.* The players were—the sweet and wouldn't-hurt-a-flea one, the brash know-it-all, the fluffy cheerleader, and the nerdy girl. And yes, I'm aware that lots of cheerleaders are smart, brilliant even. But stereotypes develop for a reason.

"My granddaughter did her first back flip," Fluffy Cheerleader said, the remnants of *rah-rah-rah* still evident in her voice. "She's just like me. Isn't that something?"

"Goodness," Wouldn't-Hurt-A-Flea said, "How wonderful. Maybe she'll become—"

Know-It-All rolled her eyes. "All kids can bounce."

"My grandson can name the last ten presidents," Nerdy Girl said.

Wouldn't-Hurt-A-Flea smiled. "That's amazing. You both are so—"

"Yeah, but what about the Vice-Presidents?" Know-It-All said. "That would be something to brag about."

"They're only five," Fluffy Cheerleader said. "At their age, I didn't know there *was* a president."

"Are you sure you could name one now?" Nerdy Girl said.

"That's not—" Wouldn't-Hurt-A-Flea almost said.

"How about Secretary of State?" Know-It-All asked. "He know any of those?"

"Nobody pays attention to that kind of stuff," Fluffy Cheerleader said. "Besides, I'm sure even the President doesn't call his secretary that anymore. They're admins now."

Tiddy Boom.

A few days later, I stood in line to buy movie tickets behind two couples in their thirties. That alone betrays my age because my kids never stand in line for movie tickets. They pull up the theater app on their smart phones, buy the tickets online, then pick them up from an automated box at the theater. I suppose I could get with the program, buy a fancy phone, and learn to app my way through life. But think of the interactions I'd no longer have. I have met the most interesting people while standing in lines, some of whom became good friends. Others became quite *colorful* characters in my stories. Which segues us nicely back to the thirty-something couples ahead of me at the theater.

We had a female terminal flirt, a buttoned-up good girl, a buffed ex-athlete male, and the guy who tries to make everything a joke. Terminal Flirt wore a revealing white gauzy top over a black bra two sizes too small and kept invading the personal space of Buttoned-Up Girl's boyfriend, the Everything's A Joke Guy. Buffed Guy, Terminal Flirt's date, seemed to not notice what she was up to. Probably because he continually scanned the area. Looking for what, I'm not sure, but I followed his gaze once and it appeared to focus on an Angelina Jolie look-alike. Buttoned-Up Girl was visibly upset with Terminal Flirt's advances. She locked her arm around Joke Guy and kept nudging him backward, away from Terminal Flirt. Eventually, she backed the two of them right into me. She turned around and seemed absolutely shocked that there was a person behind them in line. Joke Guy laughed an apology. Hard to describe, but some people can actually laugh while they're talking. Why didn't I execute the customary *I'll keep backing up, too, to avoid you backing into me*? First, there was a gaggle of senior-citizen women behind me whose feet seemed planted into the concrete. They weren't budging, no how, no way. They'd staked their claim in line, and the only movement was forward. A herd of rhinos could've marauded through, and the women wouldn't have given an inch of territory.

Second, I didn't attempt the customary retreat because I was too busy observing Buffed Guy. He stood taller than anyone else in line. His face had that Dudley Do-Right chiseled quality, and as he scanned the crowd, he looked like he was posing for a spot on Mount Rushmore. Okay. As much as I hate to admit it, he *was* a hunk, and I enjoyed the view.

Here's the kicker. The senior women's conversation began to register in my brain. They were clucking and disapproving of Terminal Flirt's outfit. Clucking and disapproving of Buttoned-Up Girl's outfit, too. And making quiet comments about Buffed Guy and his possible abilities. Because—*high school never ends.*

THE IDES OF MARCH

What is it about people that, even when we're warned, we think we know better? We ignore sage advice and assume said sages are unaware of how much more attuned we are to the situation. Or, we've been drinking, and the warnings fall on seriously disabled and deaf ears.

I'm referring to one of the earliest and most classic examples of the *Hah! – Why should I listen to you?* hubris syndrome. Julius Caesar. The man was cautioned in multiple ways. There was ominous, fearsome thunder. Calpurnia, his wife, had dreams of him being murdered. And the soothsayer in the street practically tackled him and said, "Beware the Ides of March." Yet, Caesar dismissed all this and went ahead with his plans. For those of you who don't already know—spoiler alert—he was murdered on March fifteenth, the Ides of March.

I am guilty of hubris syndrome as well. I read William Shakespeare's *Julius Caesar* in high school. Okay, well, like ninety-nine percent of my class, I read the Cliff Notes. The most dramatic takeaway, other than *Et tu, Brute?*, I got from the play was the soothsayer's warning. It's really the only scene I remember some thirty-odd years later. So, wouldn't I know to acknowledge a harbinger of doom from that?

Apparently not. My first ex-husband (there were several, and the stories won't fit in this space) was my boyfriend in high school. His birthday was March fifteenth.

Looking back, that really said it all. I chose to ignore the signs and warnings (subtle little things like kissing his cousin at a party), kept dating him, and to prove I was an ignoramus, I married him. Three years later, loaded with so many hurts and prickly issues, I left him. What made me think there'd be any other outcome? Beats the heck out of me.

So, I got to thinking about human behavior, and I think it comes down to ego and or wimpiness—heaven forbid if someone believes we're weak-kneed. We can't let anyone think maybe we made a bad decision—they might think less of us. In the classic babysitter horror movies, everyone screams at her to not open the closet. The boogeyman is in the closet. We know it. She knows it. Yet, instead of running out the front door for her life, there she is, always clad in nothing but underwear or a see-through T-shirt for some bizarro reason, biting her lip, staring at the closet. She's supposedly the smart girl, the valedictorian of her class. Yes. She does it. She opens it, and we all make fun of her and imagine just how stupid the entire graduating class of I. M. Amoron High must be.

We'd never do something so ridiculous. But we do. All the time. I can't tell you how many women and men went ahead with a wedding even though they felt something was *off* about it. They dismissed the feeling as nerves, called themselves silly, and said *I do*. Some wind up divorcing. Some just live with the mistake and start collecting things. Like glass paperweights, shoes, watersport equipment, bimbos, and boy toys.

How about when we go to dinner at someone's house?

Say a friend or a relative that would take great offense if we wheedled our way out of it. It's a known fact old Aunt Gracie has filthy personal habits and allows her cats to walk all over the kitchen counters. You've seen her merely rinse out a used glass and place it back in the cabinet, instead of actually washing it with soap. The dangling sleeve of her gingham smock keeps dragging into the food, the cat hair, the dirty dishes, and then back into the food she's preparing.

After she refuses to let us treat her to dinner in a restaurant (*Why, I wouldn't hear of it!*), we sit at her table, inwardly cringing, and making pleasant conversation, hoping the whole time the chicken wasn't kept at room temperature for too long before cooking, and that there's Alka-Seltzer at home. We smile, and we eat because it's the polite thing to do. Praying to the gods of Campylobacter and Salmonella to please, please, show mercy and spare us just this one time.

Now that I've made myself quite nauseous, what about politics? Don't worry, no specifics here—especially with our current climate. How many times have we held our collective noses and voted for the seemingly least loathsome on the ballot, even though we're pretty sure there's something darned shady about them? Mind you, I have no solution for this, short of telling you that if you're smart and have a clean record, maybe you should run for office?

Ask any guy who joined a fraternity if he ever did something he knew to be incredibly idiotic, but went ahead with it anyway to avoid the verbal abuse *not* doing it would send his way.

For all our frank American talk about tough love and tough penalties, we really are a nation of wussies. And I mean that in a good way. We are, by and large, nice people at the heart of it all. We don't want to purposely hurt each other's feelings. And that makes us do things like ignore the soothsayer, overlook dirty cooking surfaces, and forget about the last time a friend's idea got us in trouble. Pass the Pepto-Bismol, please.

WEDDINGS

WEDDINGS ARE FUN—
FOR THE SPECTATORS

I know all about *getting* married. It's the *staying* married that makes me flamboozled. So I'll stick to the beginnings.

If you're about to be married, congratulations. If you're knee deep in the preparations, God bless you. Keep the girlfriends close and the vodka closer. The best advice I can dispense after so many years is—whatever you think is vitally important for the happiest day of your life probably isn't.

You need a bride, a groom, a witness, and someone to officiate. Beyond that, it's all balsamic dressing. But there will be flowers and ribbons, rubber chicken and bullet-proof rolls, mini quiches and cake, bad Champagne toasts and drunk attendants.

People become crazed fools around a wedding. A choice you wouldn't spend two seconds on any other time will bedevil you and keep you awake at night. Will the pink Jordan almonds appear too Easter egg-ish? If the ring boy carries a lacy white pillow up the aisle, will he really be traumatized later in life as his father claims? Ah, all that is nothing compared to what happens when a real disaster strikes on your day. I don't mean earthquakes and tornadoes.

From all the weddings I've had and attended, here are

some mistakes to avoid—to prevent the burning of all pictures and video tapes later on. I'm withholding the names to protect the embarrassed and the silly.

1. Do not drink a lot the day before the wedding. Schedule bachelor/bachelorette parties so you have at least one day of rest before the big day. A toasted, but lovely, bride-to-be *rode the pole* (stripper pole—she'd taken lessons) at her party, went crazy and missed a move, then got married the next day with a huge purple contusion on her forehead. Make-up can't cover everything. Not to mention she had a killer hangover and looked like she'd keel over any second at the ceremony. Her eyes did that constant *I really can't keep focused* blinking thing. She had to run to the bathroom to throw up twice at her reception.

Unwilling to claim responsibility for her own actions, she blamed her maid-of-honor—her best friend since grade school—for not preventing her from making an ass of herself. Two years later, they still don't speak. She also blamed the very expensive photographer she *absolutely had to have* do her wedding because he was the best, for the fact she appeared to be hungover in every shot. Lawsuits followed.

2. Resist the urge to sing to your new spouse at the reception. I've seen this more than once, but the funniest example was a wedding I attended in Hawaii. The bride decided (spontaneously, I hope) to grab the microphone and croon *The Wind Beneath My Wings* to her new husband. She knew the complete song and sang it in its entirety, humming during the interludes, even imitating the hummy sounds at the end like Bette Midler.

I am one of four people who know how it ended, because in the space of a few minutes, her dreadful, whiny singing emptied the room of one hundred and fifty guests. Folks drifted away, decided they needed to use the phone to check in with babysitters (no cell phones back then), get a breath of air, refresh their drinks, or make a trip to the bathroom. *Her own parents* took a powder. The poor groom must have loved her. He stayed and listened, a stiff smile plastered on his face, nodding along with the music. Now that's a guy who'll stand behind you. I stayed because it was like a car pile-up. I couldn't not watch. And the writer in me loves that sort of thing.

3. If you host an outdoor reception, have a pest control company inspect the area for red ants and other insects. It was a spectacular day in June. The ceremony, blessedly brief, held under a huge oak tree. A massive white tent beckoned in a field a hundred feet away. The clink of glasses and china, and aromas promising Italian food wafted over the guests. We walked to the tent. The women in heels tried to keep their balance on the lumpy ground. A dance floor, full bar, and tables set for ten awaited us. The music began, Champagne and crudité were served. Guests found their way to their assigned tables.

It started with a little boy who'd been stomping on the grass next to the dance floor. His screams brought people running. But soon, many others were yelping their own discomfort. Red ants swarmed out of their nests, up the legs of the tables and the guests. Within minutes, the bitten had run to their cars, stripped all the clothing they dared, and were shaking, inspecting, and picking the annoying tiny devils from their shoes, socks, and dainties.

4. Don't wear a dress resembling a parade float—with everything ever invented on it. Princess Diana got away with it, you won't. Ruffles, bows, embroidery, lace, flowers, sashes, puffy sleeves, and sheer organza layers are all beautiful things. Pick two. Ever hear the expression, *the dress wore her?* At a wedding in Texas, the bride wore a billowing gown festooned with all of the above mentioned goodies. When she walked up the aisle, even the men in the church raised their eyebrows. And men don't normally notice anything about dresses.

She was a plus-sized girl, very pretty. I've seen many plus-sized women, in gorgeous, flattering gowns, who radiated beauty and sophistication on their wedding day. This misguided girl wasn't one of them. Gee-gaws and fussy add-ons decorated every inch of her gown. Even her veil was bedecked with frilly stuff. She looked like a giant, chaotic, walking wedding cake. As she passed each pew, the rear view sent many guests into sputtering, but controlled, hysterics. The finishing touch? Her dress had an enormous satin bow placed in the unfortunate position of right on her ass.

MAYBE ELOPING WOULD BE SMARTER

Wedding guests. Two words that strike terror in the heart of anyone paying attention. Distant cousins show up in white. Gassy people who forget to take their Beano. Super-loud whisperers. Chain smokers hacking up a lung. The lady who, trying to go unnoticed, takes several interminable tortured minutes to unwrap a candy mint while the entire audience frowns. The bad, but very bold, dancer who dominates the dance floor and scares everyone else back to the bar. (A quick note—unless you look like Angelina Jolie, Megan Fox, or Halle Berry, you *do not* look sexy dancing the Macarena.) The guy who requests so many songs, he's changed the wedding couple's complete play list. The woman who insists on singing with the band. Eccentric aunties and uncles reveal horrifyingly embarrassing stories to your boss. Expect an old codger wearing shorts with suspenders, black socks, and tasseled loafers. An elderly woman in a miniskirt. (If the wedding's in Boca, she'll also have huge fake boobs.) Teenagers. Toddlers. Babies screaming. Oh, the humanity!

Alas, my dear engaged couple, the afore-mentioned are the *normal* guests. The ones we see at nearly every wedding or bar mitzvah since human suffering began. But what about the ones you didn't see coming? The really crazy folks who, when they show up, no one admits to inviting. How do you avoid *them*?

Much is revealed by how someone lives. Not where, necessarily. Unless, of course, your goal is to invite only the well-heeled—thus insuring a substantial wedding present haul. Perhaps that is your focus, and if it is, there's a whole 'nuther column of advice for you. My intent today is pure concern for your happiness. I want you to avoid inadvertently inviting even more insanity into your special day.

At the risk of sounding cynical—I know, it's a tad late for that—it might be best to get a background check for some on the invite lists that you don't know well. Failing that, if you haven't seen or spoken to a potential invitee in a few years, at the minimum, do an Internet search on their name and see what rises from the deep. Also type in their home address on Google Maps, hit satellite view, and you can witness for yourself just how eccentric old Uncle Joe has really become. If the cute cottage with the pretty rose bushes you remember visiting as a child (when Aunt Bertha was still alive) now displays a prominent collection of fifty-gallon drums, a cache of camouflaged sheds, and multiple *Beware of Dog* signs, you may want to reconsider. Because now Uncle Joe will be the one talking nonstop, scaring the bejeesus out of people while exhorting them to stockpile weapons, Spam, and Twinkies, then head to the hills to escape the Black Hawk helicopters.

What about the sweet little old lady who babysat you? Don't be lulled by your innocent memories. Investigate. Old Mrs. Finkle could now be a shuffling human nightmare. And by shuffling, I'm not talking a walker with tennis balls. I mean a gambling fiend. She's deep into the casinos and lost her pension money. She'll hit up the other guests for money to finance the next bus trip to the Hard Rock. Of course, she'll say she needs the money to feed her cat, Mittens, pay her electric bill, or fix her glasses. I've seen it. Almost gave her a twenty myself until the mother of the groom swooped in to the rescue and whisked me away.

But the eccentricities are not exclusive to the older folks. No, no, no. There's a fresh crop of crazy coming along, proudly hoisting the banner high. Haven't seen a college friend in a few years? What if she now runs a pole-dancing studio? And has a few too many? And decides the poles holding up your big white tent are the perfect venue to advertise her services? And—cringe—follows the trend of not wearing undies? I wish I was making this up.

Then there was the thirty-something man who made it his mission to sleep with a bridesmaid. Never mind they were all married. When it looked like he'd finally succeed, he and the woman in question were discovered. The ensuing fist fight brought the police and totally killed everyone's party buzz.

So, if one of your parents offers you a lump sum to elope or have a tiny wedding, it may be because they know the potential guest list better than you. Think about it.

WEAR BEIGE AND KEEP YOUR MOUTH SHUT

In the movie *Monster-In-Law*, Jane Fonda's character went to her son's wedding wearing white. Most people would think, I expect, that the mother of any groom could never be so insensitive to her future daughter-in-law. Don't we wish.

Actually, part of me doesn't wish because then there wouldn't be any instances to poke fun at. Weddings are fraught with emotion. Everyone involved, it seems, has to put their nickel in. Aunts, uncles, and cousins no one's heard from in years crawl from the shadowy recesses of outer Podunk. They offer uninvited advice, ask for favors, and make demands. The bridal couple's parents' old college roommates and their coterie of dysfunctional children inevitably get tossed into the soup, too.

Next thing she knows, the bride's been told her menu is too ethnic or bland, her music too contemporary, her music isn't modern enough, her colors are garish, her colors are subtle, and her invitations either look cheap, or she overspent. The groom should kiss her on the cheek, tell her to do whatever she wants, and bow the heck out of the decisions. If he's smart, as she makes each final choice, he will execute the time-honored groom's serious nod of agreement and say, "Excellent choice. I like it, too."

Warring factions soon battle for dominance in the seating chart and a coveted spot at the rehearsal dinner. A guest the bride's never met reveals he has a rare allergy to perfume. Every perfume. Could the bride please inform all attending not to wear any? The groom's grandmother's cousin, who's one-hundred and five, decides she'll risk the trip away from assisted living, but her nursing aide must be next to her wheelchair every moment to monitor the oxygen tank and handle a possible incontinence problem. Meanwhile, the list of foods taken off the menu because of allergies has grown. The wedding *feast* will now feature only a tray of baby carrots and the ubiquitous rubber chicken filets—plain. The tarragon-wine sauce was axed.

At this point, our beleaguered bride is ready to jump ship, elope in Vegas, or yank out sections of her hair, if she hasn't started doing so already. Her own mother has succumbed to the insanity and retreated to the sanctity of Elizabeth Arden's red door. This weary bride needs a friend. The mother of the groom is in a unique position to endear herself to the bride and the bride's mother. She can do as her son does as described above, or better yet—she can keep her mouth shut.

I haven't been the mother of the groom yet. In my mind, it seems like a simple thing to do. Smile and nod approvingly. Guess it's harder than it appears.

The doting mama of an only child, Annabelle wanted total involvement in her son's nuptials. Both sets of parents lived in the same city, so Annabelle assumed it wouldn't be a problem for her to accompany the bride, Veronica, and her mom as they visited the various vendors. I suppose for a woman who has daughters—plural—maybe that might be okay. But Veronica was an only child as well. And *her* mother wasn't about to relinquish one precious iota of control.

Veronica cringed behind a practiced smile as she told Annabelle how thoughtful it was she wanted to help. Annabelle arrived at the florist's shop an hour earlier than planned. When Veronica and her mother stepped into the place, Annabelle and the florist sat at the planning desk surrounded by loose photos and albums.

"There you are." Annabelle jumped from her seat, flushed with enthusiasm, and ushered them to the desk. "We've got it all figured out. Wait 'til you see." Oblivious to the shock on their faces, Annabelle showed them the bride's and bridesmaid's bouquets, the boutonnieres for the groom and groomsmen, the arrangements for the church *and* the reception. She'd chosen yellow roses and voluminous clouds of baby's breath. Never mind the wedding's colors were blues and greens, and Veronica disliked both roses and baby's breath.

The order was discreetly changed, and Annabelle banished from all future planning. The relationship between Veronica and Annabelle, while a tinge frosty at the wedding, developed into a massive ice age. Now Annabelle has great difficulty securing time with her two grandchildren.

Another groom's mom, Beth, fancied herself quite the singer. Amateurs singing at weddings is the stuff of legends. Rarely does it go well. You might as well do the proverbial dance-on-the-table-wearing-a-lampshade. No one ever forgets either performance, and now with YouTube, an embarrassing lapse of discernment could wind up on the *Today Show*.

Beth sent subtle signals throughout the planning period to probe how the bridal couple felt about her singing *Only You*. The idea was rejected. At the wedding, however, Beth had one too many Pinot Noir's, and asked the band if they knew *Only You*. They did. She belted out the song, much to her family's horror. She went off-key and slurred a few words. Her voice cracked at the high notes. She used great sweeping gestures to emphasize the emotion of the song and knocked over the pianist's water glass.

Her dignity was rescued by her husband, a vice-president at a Fortune 500 company. He hurriedly offered twenty-dollar bills to the teenagers who'd captured her solo on their cell phones, and watched them delete it. Word was he had political aspirations, and that episode wouldn't have done much for the campaign.

Then there was Sylvia. Sylvia wore fire-engine-Scarlett-O'hara red satin and five-inch red stilettos to her son's wedding. She was single. She was stacked. The dress was low, low cut. One unfortunate twist or tug, and there was a serious risk of a major wardrobe malfunction. It was hard *not* to stare at her instead of the bride. In addition, she wailed through the entire ceremony.

That's why women need friends who will tell them the truth. Poor Sylvia apparently didn't have any who were brave enough to tell her she was a wee bit—maybe just a hair—over the top. Good friends save us from ourselves when we need it most. The best advice ever? Wear beige and keep your mouth shut.

HONEYMOON

Honeymoons are supposed to be fun. The stress of planning and carrying out the myriad wedding details simply melt away the moment the bridal couple board the plane or cruise ship. Or that's the fantasy, in any case. In the course of erasing their pre-nuptual wear and tear, some go overboard. Not really. Well, some literally *do* go overboard. Then there are denials, investigations, and maybe a lengthy trial. But I'm talking about the innocent people who go a little nuts to try and make things fun and exciting for their new spousal unit.

Curb your enthusiasm is a great watch phrase for newlyweds. Every one of us knows of someone who came back from a honeymoon in a cast, with a chipped tooth, covered with hives, or talking annulment. You might not have gotten the full story of what happened, but you sense there's a doozy just waiting to be told.

While you're waiting for your friend to 'fess up, here are a few tidbits to hold you over.

Lizzy loved gummy candy and chocolate. So her new hubby searched for and found red gummy hearts that were dipped in chocolate. To surprise her, when they arrived at their chosen bed and breakfast on a lesser-known Caribbean island, he hid the treats in one of her bags. She'd find them with his love note when she unpacked. The moment they checked into their room, she announced they should, before doing anything else, go for a stroll down the gorgeous beach as the sun set. Get the circulation moving after the long plane ride.

It was summer. It was hot. The air conditioning in their room seemed to be on the fritz. On their way out, they spoke to the manager who said they'd have the A/C looked at right away. Lizzy and spouse had their romantic stroll, went straight to dinner, then returned to the B and B.

We think humans own the world, but in reality, ants do. In a wine-induced amorous fog, the couple opened their room door to find it still stiflingly hot. But they were in the mood. First things first, then they'd go lodge their displeasure. With a gallant sweep of his arm, hubby pushed her bags to the floor, then placed her on the bed. It took a minute until they realized they were not alone. It started with the tickle of teensy feet. Then little pinching bites. Then the horrible sensation of bugs crawling everywhere. They jumped from the bed screaming, and hubby dove for the light switch. The bed had dark brown stains covered with swarming ants.

Hubby had put the candy in the one bag that was netted. The chocolate melted from the heat and seeped into the bedspread. Apparently, the B and B's exterminator was on the fritz, too.

Men seem to just love the idea of having a hot tub in the hotel room. It's a symbol of sorts for them, I think. A code for—*I'm going to get wildly, out of the ordinary lucky if I have this.* Honestly, I don't know too many women who think of stewing in boiling chlorinated water as an aphrodisiac. It smells. It dries out your skin. It's humid.

If you've just spent two hours getting your hair done to perfection, so your new husband will think you're sexy, going in the hot tub will wilt it until it resembles a wet mop head. Then all your make-up oozes down your face.

Joe wanted a hot tub in the room for his Las Vegas honeymoon with Cheryl. She didn't care a whit either way, so she went along with it to make him happy. They were too tired to try it out the first night. Cheryl had spent major bucks and time on her hair for the wedding, and wanted the glossy locks looks to last for more than a day. Thus, the second night passed with the newlyweds engaged in more conventional entanglements.

On the third night, Joe insisted. Cheryl's hair had lost its wedding day allure. Since she needed to wash, dry, and restyle anyway, she agreed. Men should learn from this. Want her to go snorkeling with you? Wait until she announces she needs to wash her hair. You'll get yes at three times the rate of when her hair looks great.

Joe hit the switch. Bubbles erupted and sloshed over the edge of the raised tub. They opened champagne. Cheryl slid into the tub with a provocative smile for Joe. After some silly he-man posturing with the champagne glass in hand, Joe ran across the slick marble floor and, as he approached the step to the churning waters, slipped in a puddle and flew headfirst into the tub side. The glass hit the floor and shattered, Joe collapsed, and Cheryl screamed.

Joe was lucky he didn't break his neck, but he did spend the remainder of the honeymoon in one of those stiff white collars. He no longer thinks hot tubs are such a big deal.

One more from the Caribbean. Although most staff at resorts are trustworthy, why serve up temptation? Anxious to please his new bride, Steve bought her a diamond bracelet she'd been admiring in the hotel gift boutique. While on the beach in the afternoon, Steve made arrangements with the waiter delivering drinks to the private cabanas. He ordered fancy rum cocktails in coconuts with the tops lopped off. He gave the bracelet to the man and asked that he drop it into her drink. To make sure she got the right coconut, they agreed the one with the bracelet would get an extra paper umbrella.

Someone else delivered the refreshments about ten minutes later. Hers indeed had two umbrellas. Steve encouraged his wife to guzzle her drink while nervously scanning up and down the beach for the man he'd entrusted. She had no desire to hurry, though. Steve stood, hand shading his eyes, and searched again. When she asked if something was amiss, he smiled, but his panic grew. Finally, he lost patience, grabbed her coconut, spilled the contents onto the sand, and did a frantic finger comb for the bracelet—which, of course, wasn't there.

People have crashed through windows while in an amorous mood. Jewelry attached to kites has sunk to the bottom of the sea. Honeymooning campers have forgotten to set the brakes and caused the camper to roll down the mountain. If your friends return and the only thing they kvetch about is the slow room service, hand them this.

MODERN LIFE

FACEBOOK FOR OLD FOGIES

Every young adult child fears it. The looming threat of their parents becoming active on Facebook. The squeamish wincing brought on by clicking the 'Accept Friend Request' button—allowing your parent or one of their buddies to become your *friend*. Or the *ick* factor that drapes your personal space like a shroud when your friends begin to LOL with your parents. But I'm here to say—buck up, you wimps. That's absolutely petty patooties compared to what your poor parental units are braving.

Oh, the nightmare of Facebook for aging folks. Zuckerberg has no idea what the heck he's unleashed. He's too young to know. Unlike the teenagers and twenty-somethings who are in the process of creating their lives and have few, if any, skeletons, we-the-middle-aged are hiding from decades of social blunders, bad decisions, and ex-lovers. And wouldn't you know? People who can't remember diddly about their own awkward moments seem to recall with crackling-sharp crystal 3D clarity the office Christmas party where you had one too many martinis and got caught in the copy room with the boss's gawky nephew, making out like lust-crazed eighth-graders. Okay, maybe it was two too many martinis.

The point is—so many people from your past that you'd deleted from the memory banks find you and request friend status. You hardly knew them way back when, but you grant the request because you don't want to hurt their feelings. The first couple of postings on your wall are innocuous enough, so you're lulled into thinking, *no harm done.*

Stay tuned for phase two. A cruel invasion—old photos. Just when you think you're safe, some nimrod from your seventh grade homeroom forty years ago posts class pictures. Of course, the post-er only shows the ones making him/her look amazing, while the rest of us post-ees seem like serious contenders for the Ultimate Dork competition. A side note for anyone under thirty—when we were 'tweens, the term *supermodel* hadn't been coined yet, and if you wanted straight hair you had to iron it on your mom's ironing board. No one ever heard of conditioners for hair. Hair dryers were bubble things our moms perched on a table, then sat with a head full of rollers under it while reading *The Saturday Evening Post* or *McCall's* magazines. None of us kids knew how to apply makeup, fewer than that were even allowed to wear it. We weren't allowed to pluck our eyebrows or shave our legs. And for some inexplicable reason, clogs became an acceptable shoe choice. They looked especially fetching with knee socks. Pantyhose hadn't been invented. We wore multi-colored fishnet stockings held up by garter belts on our hairy legs. I kid you not. It was the Stone Age.

Some photos of those days surfaced in my house recently. It was the early seventies, and our mothers sent us to class in clothes wild enough to make today's kids think we'd enrolled in clown school. Obnoxious color combinations—like bark-at-the-moon lime green and maroon. Plaid pants, narrow-striped pants, wide-striped pants. Blazing orange and rust chevron-patterned shirts paired with (you guessed it) striped skirts and orange socks. Perhaps our mothers did more than just 'sample' some of those Valium pills that seemed to rock the world of mommies everywhere at that time. *Mother's little helper* did a number on millions of pre-teens' social lives.

It's doubtful the fashions of any recent decade will go down making Baby Boomers cringe more than the seventies. Is it any wonder so many Boomers needed therapy? But I have a solution for my fellow red-faced victims. Learn how to manipulate. Simply scan the offending pictures and save them to your computer. Then open them in the photo-fixing program of your choice. Get rid of the pesky braces. Erase the zits. Smooth the complexion. Whiten the teeth. And re-color the clothing. Re-write your history. But the question is—leave everyone else in the picture the same? Or fix everyone else except the meanie who showed the world the day you spilled onto your lap, and everyone laughed because it looked like you'd peed your pants. Posted it with a big LOL they did, a smiley face, and a jovial note—*remember this?* If you do post your new version, being sure to tag everyone in the picture. Voilá. Revenge served very cold, indeed.

Once the reservoir of embarrassing pictures is exhausted, political ads and diatribes soon appear from the newly added friend. You politely ask them to refrain from posting them. The crazy-train of misinformation continues. You ask again. They persist but, with time, it does wither into nothingness. No doubt others have told them to cool it. Whew. Almost had to 'unfriend' someone. Or is it 'defriend'?

With the political attacks on the wane, the mind-numbing idiocy of cartoon birds, farm, or fish games begin their assault. Grown adults broadcast that they've acquired enough feed corn to buy another chicken? So and So earned forty extra *gems* that look like the cheap plastic baubles sold for preschoolers? What are we? Five years old again? What is the allure that compels a fifty-year-old to immerse themselves into an inane game? It's almost as if they get deeply involved in order to be too busy to deal with real life and its real problems.

Hey—wait a minute. That's it! Well put me into a Hollywood Square and call me Dr. Joyce Brothers. It *is* the way they're avoiding their own lives. Okay, now that I get it, I'm totally cool with it. Conceal the college tuition bills. Forget about the underwater mortgage. Deflect the haunting specter of five-figure credit card balances. Carry on, noble Boomers, carry on.

THE GOOD OLD DAYS

Whenever I think of September, several songs always come to mind. One of them is *Try to Remember* from the off-Broadway show, The Fantasticks, in 1960. Sung by Jerry Orbach, it brought bittersweet sentiment about days gone by. *Try to remember the kind of September . . .*

My dad was born in 1923. To him, the good old days were the 40s—after he came home from the war. The end of rationing, the Rat Pack, Big Band music, the GI Bill. A cute little Cape Cod style house with a big old honking homemade brick barbeque in back—right out of an *I Love Lucy* episode. And everything cost either fifty cents or fifty dollars.

Dad spent a lot of time trying to convince his children that the world we were growing up in was rapidly swirling down a giant toilet. Drugs. Free love. Raucous rock music drove him nuts, never mind that *his* mother thought Big Band swing and the Jitterbug was the certain undoing of good girls. My mom was great at Jitterbugging, so I guess that cements that argument. (Kidding, Mom.) I might should mention here that my grandmother had a few scandalous years when she got her freak on, too. She and her sisters, while in their twenties, flirted with being Flappers in the twenties. *Her* mother was horrified.

Back to poor Dad's lament. Males in the 60s and 70s grew long hair and put it in *ponytails*, for God's sake. Of course, men, including our founding fathers, wore their hair long and tied back with ribbons or covered by a powdered fancy-schmancy white wig for a good part of our history. That was different, he said. How—we don't know, that's when he'd clam up, while my mom snickered. Onward . . . Woodstock. Women burning their bras. Manners stopped existing. (That wasn't true, as every kid we knew had mothers who'd punish bad manners. Heck, back then, your neighbor's mom was allowed to discipline you if you were rude, but Dad was on a roll . . .) The era made no sense to him, although he didn't complain about the breasts said bra-burning exposed.

My dad wasn't alone. Ever since man began writing stories, the scribes of any particular age wrote about how society was going to hell. The ancient Greeks and Romans. Old English texts and poems describe the people's sad state. Charles Dickens did. Ditto Mark Twain. Fast forward to today, and—believe it nor not—even the scions of the gaming industry are complaining that things aren't like they used to be. Doesn't anyone believe the best days are yet to come? Sigh.

It's hard to fathom, but thirty years from now, 2013 is going to be lots of people's 'good old days'. How much weirder will life have to get in order for that to happen? Let's examine what they'll be nostalgically pining for in 2043.

In our *golden age* in 2013, you can't swing a cat (an expression, by the way, from the good old days of the naval world in the 1600s) without seeing or hearing about fictional gorgeous, sparkly vampires who date and mate with real humans. We've got zombies, tons of 'em—everywhere you look. They are neither gorgeous nor sparkly, but that hasn't stopped regular people from jumping their bones in the movies. As a result, we've got actual people, *right now*—in this incredible age of information explosion—who believe the creepy, crepe-y creatures exist.

I'm thinking that one hundred years from now, they'll label this era as The Idiot Decades. The time when the result of humans outwitting natural selection came into evidence. Due to protecting dim bulbs and fools, who in the past would have been left behind as bait or tribute, or been caught and consumed by wild animals, or accidentally killed themselves out of stupidity, we are living with brain-dead morons among us. Hey, wait— zombies *are real?*

In the good old days, when people were easily taken in by legends and myths, it was because they had either no education or were limited by available knowledge at that time. We have the unique situation—for the first time in human history—where great, accurate knowledge is everywhere and *free*. In 2043, I'll look back on this time and cringe from embarrassment. I'm cringing now, just imagining the gobstopped looks of my great-grandchildren when I'm asked to explain dimwits who stockpiled weapons and food for the Zombie Apocalypse. Or politicians sexting. Or the super-goofy looking men's suits with short shorts that were shown this year. Or dog wedding attendants. Or dog weddings. Lip tattoos that look like sores (*Really?*). Or reality television shows that aren't the least bit real, whose stars are more recognized than the Speaker of the House. Dear Lord, I'm praying for better times.

THERE'S AN APP FOR THAT

Explaining the world as it was—even ten years ago—to a young teenager is not easy. Their minds can't fathom the foreign notion that a phone didn't have a touch screen with pictures flying across it with the casual sweep of a finger. Go back further, and they look at you as though you came in riding a dinosaur when you tell them that, once upon a time at Grandma's house, everyone shared a phone, and it was tethered to the wall by a long, curly cord. I don't dare explain about the rotary dial. They already think I'm old as George Washington's teeth, the round phone dial might convince them I helped build the pyramids.

Most kids have iPhones now and all the attending accoutrements. Including apps. (That's short for applications—for those of you who've dug yourselves a comfy little cave under a big 'ol rock.) Lots of my fellow dinosaur-era friends are also crazy hyper-happy over smart phones and showing off the hippest apps, too. The convenience of having instant information at their fingertips is changing society in ways we never imagined. No one uses a phone book anymore. Few ask for restaurant recommendations. We don't have to remember who starred in a movie, to pick up the kids or the dry cleaning, or even who gave us what for Christmas.

There's an app for that. There's an app for every blessed freaking thing we could ever have or want to do.

Americans are more tethered to their phones than at any time in its history, but now the cords are invisible. It would be so nice to have a real conversation again, without the constant interruption of cute little bleeps indicating an app performing a task or the arrival of a text. Without my friend holding up a finger and saying, "Just a sec," as she checks the message, giggles, then furiously works the keys for her return text. The evil part of me wishes for a solar burst that will interrupt wireless communications for a week—long enough for people to shake off the fog of dependence and regain some perspective. Especially since a new study confirmed that the more people depend on devices, the weaker their brains become, and the more likely they'll be to have lazy-brain-caused dementia. And I really don't want to be in the lonely position of being the last of my generation with intact marbles in my head. Then again, I'd finally be a shoo-in to win a Scrabble championship.

But apps are influencing a prominent sub-culture, too. An essential part of us. The indomitable entrepreneurial American spirit—present ever since the first colonists mixed alcohol and tree sap, slapped a spiffy and misleading label on it, called it miracle medicine, and sold it for the equivalent of a week's pay. It's as American as pretending to sing the national anthem—which, by the way, is totally not our fault. The song is impossible for average people. Those of us who fake it are doing the rest of you a huge favor. The point was, we are nothing if not shameless opportunists.

So, creating an app is the latest way to make it big. The new get-rich-quick thing. It's replacing the once ubiquitous *Invest in Real Estate—Become a Millionaire!*

seminars taught by cheesy Ron Burgundy look-alikes in Holiday Inn meeting rooms with tables in the back that are laden with cheap cookies, how-to books, and CDs for sale. If it wasn't the lure of real estate tycooning that drew wannabe gazillionaires, then it was another *can't miss* opportunity—writing a screenplay. But step aside, oh magic money magnets of the past, for here come the apps.

Seems everywhere I go, people talk about new apps, free apps, updates for old apps, and of course, their no-way-it-can-fail ideas for more apps. Being the curious and investigative type (with a healthy dose of I-just-can't-resist), of course I needed to check into this phenomenon.

Within minutes, I found myself immersed in articles and blogs about how to create an app. How to price an app. How to market an app. And the inevitable—how to hire the right people to make your app actually happen. How now, cash cow. With a literal million apps out there and floods of them entering the market yearly, I suspect the real money in apps is in charging earnest folks who believe their idea will not just fly, but soar above the others. Charges range from three to ten thousand for preparing a simple app and fifty to one-hundred and fifty thousand for a complex one. Holy crackers. Don't know if that includes the spiffy and misleading label. I may have to hang up my dinosaur saddle, tether myself to a smart phone, and enroll in a tech school.

UP, UP, AND GOODBYE—REASONS AUNT MAISIE WON'T FLY

Having nearly completed the summer vacation season, my aunt announced the other day that she and her favorite thing in the world were history. She would no longer fly. Anywhere. Via plane or broom. (Kidding. Although she was, by all reports, quite bewitching in her prime.)

Aunt Maisie is in her seventies. She looks like a grandma. No Botox. No hair dye. No artificially enhanced body parts that appear to be likely places to stash contraband. Yet almost every time the woman flies anywhere, the TSA agents pull her aside for an extra check. We haven't figured out why they seem to think she's a danger to the rest of us. I flew with her once a couple years ago, and they flagged her again while I waltzed through with no problem. Perhaps they misinterpret that mischievous sparkle in her eyes as something sinister and suspect she's smuggling homemade apple muffins.

The woman took her first airplane ride in 1963. She wore a tweed suit, stockings, spectator pumps, and a pillbox hat. Oh, and gloves. How do I know? Her brother took a picture of her doing the Queen's wave in front of the portable stairway leading to the fuselage. Airplane travel was a big deal then. Dressing up for it was expected. Others on the flight felt sick and used the complimentary barf bags, but not Aunt Maisie. She reveled in every bump and shudder as the plane encountered turbulence, staring out the window with a map in her hands and marveling at the world below her.

After that first trip, Aunt Maisie was a fanatic. She'd go to anyone's wedding if it meant flying there. Heck, she'd attend the grand opening of a Waffle House in Stumptoe, Arkansas if it involved boarding a glistening metal tube of enchantment.

It took the family a little while to decipher her acceptance pattern. How was it she couldn't arrange her time to attend cousin Rachel's wedding—only an hour's drive away—yet she RSVP'd with exclamation points for a casual friend's grandson's wedding in Omaha? Of course, that may have had more to do with being a passenger in my father's car than with not flying. Dad was known to *hug* the right side of the road. At sixty miles an hour on winding two-lane hilly highways, I can't tell you how many times he came within an inch of destroying a mail box with the protruding side-view mirror. We kids learned early to claim the left side or the middle seats and to simply keep our eyes shut if we lost the battle and wound up on the right. Those were the days before seat belts were mandatory. I don't mean wearing them. I mean the cars didn't *have* any.

Back to Aunt Maisie. The years went on and everything improved on airplanes. Including the food. (I know, I know, you think I'm telling fairy tales, but it's true.) When the first jumbo jets came out with the double decks, piano bars, and lounges, Aunt Maisie was front and center. She saved her splurge money and wrote to Pan Am requesting a first-class ticket on the maiden 747

flight from JFK to London. She didn't get it, but
managed to secure one soon after.

She feasted on beef tenderloin and Champagne. The
lounge upstairs offered free cigarettes and snifters of
brandy. She brought us plastic flight wings, swizzle
sticks, and matchbooks and told us all about it. Which
was the only way we'd ever know about such things. It
sounded magical. We never flew anywhere—too many
kids. Even if we had, I'm sure it would have been in
steerage class—did the plane have an underbelly where
poor folks huddled, drinking water, eating hard bread
crusts, and sharing tattered inflight magazines?

Flashing forward to the post-9/11 airport scene, Aunt
Maisie went right on flitting around the country. She
endured the interminable security lines. Her patriotic
sense of duty carried her through the trials of shoe
removal and pat-downs. Then the airlines began
restricting the number of bags she could take, and
charged for the ones she did. The free use of pillows and
blankets was gone. So was the gourmet food.

Aunt Maisie's final straw came last week. Her trip from
Florida to New York took sixteen hours. She'd arrived at
the airport two hours early. She was ready, no way
would she get flagged this time. Her one bag, a carry-on,
had the required three-ounce or less toiletries—in re-
sealable clear bags. She wore no jewelry. After an hour
in line, she made it to the security check. She had her
trusty Keds untied and ready to remove. Placing her
carry-on, purse, and sneakers into bins on the conveyor
belt, she then stepped through the metal detector. It
didn't beep. Breathing a sigh of relief, she went to collect

her things.

But one of the men approached her, explaining that he needed to use the wand on her. She padded over to the side with him in her fluffy white tennis socks, asking why since she (for once) hadn't set off the alarm. It was just a routine random selection, he said.

When she arrived at her gate, the young woman at the counter announced that the flight was delayed, but didn't say why. Aunt Maisie waited, reading a mystery paperback. Ten minutes after the flight's scheduled departure time, they announced they now waited for new equipment. That meant a new plane. Fifty weary people joined the growing line at the gate counter demanding a transfer to another flight, an upgrade using their frequent flyer miles, or just to vent their frustration. Businessmen pummeled their smart phones, and college students slept using their backpacks as pillows. Toddlers ran amuck and tripped over the students.

Finally in the air, the flight had to land in Jacksonville because a woman's water broke, and she went into labor. Soon after they escorted the woman off, bound for a local hospital, a hellacious thunderstorm dropped hailstones the size of golf balls. People were hungry and thirsty. Babies cried. Tea-cup purse puppies whined. Couples got into heated arguments. The teensy bathroom toilets overflowed. The storm passed, but the plane needed serious cleaning. They had to deplane. Three hours later, they took off for JFK.

They reached cruising altitude and out came lap-tops, cell phones, and iPads. Food service began. Remembering the glory days of air travel, Aunt Maisie refused on principle to pay for anything extra. The only free beverage was water, the *food* was hard pretzels. She'd finished the novel. She recalled when wonderful selections of the most current magazine issues were available in a rack near the stewardess' work station. No more. Fishing around in the seat pocket in front of her, she came up with a used tissue and a ragged inflight magazine with a sticky candy wrapper stuck to the cover. Water. Hardened bread. Tattered magazine. She sighed as she realized she now traveled in steerage.

Aunt Maisie's thinking of buying a convertible and learning to drive.

MIDDLE-AGE CRAZIES

Finding themselves single in middle age comes as a shock to many people. We expect to be married forever and—whammo. One, or both, of the partners canoodles with someone else. Or all those years of living with his overpowering mother finally take their toll, and you go to the store for milk, take a detour at the casino, and never return. It's either that, or you're afraid you'll make oleander tea for Mama and wind up in an orange jumpsuit trying to make nice with a woman named Rhonda with beefier arms than Schwarzenegger. (PSA: Every part of the oleander is very toxic and potentially lethal, so DO NOT do that.) It happens. Especially in Florida. We set a very high bar for the rest of the nation when it comes to stupid criminals.

Perhaps the stressful years of raising teenagers wears your soul down to a sad little nub, and you just can't muster the energy for anything else. Or you both would rather not talk because it always leads to an immature fight about whose turn it is to do something. You'll know when it has reached the ridiculous phase when even the family dog does an eye roll and runs for cover. And down the tubes the relationship goes. Happens every day. You're left out to dry in the humid Florida air, with the sun glaring at you, and it feels as if there's no shade or sunscreen for many miles.

Suddenly, you're up there in the decades count, all alone with no conscious recollection of how, exactly, your aloneness occurred. But cheer up. Don't despair. Being older and single these days is way better than it was even ten years ago. Because now—there are dating sites. And even if you don't find *the one*, or *any one,* the entertainment value of stories you'll garner is priceless.

Out here in middle-aged single world, stories about dating are valuable because they make you a sought-after dinner guest. There is no telling the level of crazy you'll find while meeting someone who really seemed quite sane via messaging.

A potential date told me he'd wear a green shirt. When I spotted him at Starbucks—wait, let's back up for a moment to share another PSA. One—use your own transportation to the rendezvous site. Two—always let a friend know who you are meeting, when, and where. Three—meet for coffee or tea during daylight in a public place. So, upon arrival, I scanned the place for the guy whose pictures I saw on the dating site. There was only one man wearing a green shirt. And he had to be at least seventy. Not that there's anything wrong with that, but I specifically set my matches' age limit at ten years my senior. And seventy-something was *way* over my set parameters. This man in green didn't look anything like the guy, but out of stupid curiosity, I went ahead and approached anyway. "Are you Stan?" He nodded. I'm sure my disappointment showed. Right off the bat— he'd lied to me. I asked him why he'd lied—didn't he know the moment I saw him, I'd discern that he wasn't in his fifties, as advertised? He attempted an impish grin and said he'd hoped I'd find him so cute and irresistible that I'd overlook the age difference.

Now, if you're going to try to charm someone out of being annoyed with you for lying, wouldn't you do your best to *look* charming? This guy had long, wiry gray hairs growing from his ears, his nose, and from several moles on his face. Must we go back to the films they showed us in health class? Personal grooming, people.

I went to buy a coffee (to go), and he tailed me like a bruised puppy to the counter. He told me he was rich— he'd give me a credit card. He said he drove a Mercedes—did I want to see it? It was right there in the parking lot. With a frozen smile, I politely refused while the girl behind the counter rolled her eyes. As a last ditch effort, he whispered, "I have good stuff. Let's go to my place and I'll show you. I promise you won't be disappointed." He elaborated further, but this is a mostly G-Rated column.

Ew.

ELEVEN, ELEVEN

November is the eleventh month. November 11, 2011—11-11-11—is causing a stir of activity in the ceremonies world. People want important occasions to happen that day. Weddings. Bar-Mitzvahs. Anniversary parties. Proposals. C-sections. Choosing a pet. Buying a new car. Even divorce decrees. The populace has gone eleven crazy.

Numerologists tend to hold the number eleven in high regard. I didn't know why, so donned my Sherlock cap and investigated. What I found out is fascinating, bizarre, and downright silly in some instances. From Harold Camping and his May 2011 major rapture failure to innocuous beauticians dabbling in numbers reading on the side, numerology is a seriously goofy subject—ergo—perfect for me.

I went online for more information. In numerology, letters are assigned a numerical value. Your name could be evaluated by adding just the consonants, which tells you what lesson you're supposed to learn. The vowels added tell you something else, and adding every letter means something else again. It's confusing. One site said to add your middle name, others not to. What frizzled my brain cells was the fact that if my parents had picked another name, my whole life's purpose would have been different? What if they'd spelled it differently? Same name, radically different mission? I hoofed it to my local hair salon, always a reliable source for cosmic experts, and found a nail tech who not only spoke English well, but did indeed do numerology on the side. As luck would have it, the owner wasn't in, so we didn't have to meet at the coffee place at the end of the strip mall—where she said she normally does this, and not to worry, the stylists were cool with her doing numbers in the salon, and she'd done all of theirs—for my analysis.

She also did astrological charts, but she wanted several hundred dollars for that. I'm no fool. I said I'd think about the chart, then handed her the thirty-dollar fee to do a quick number assessment for me. She balked at the idea of a receipt. I hope my accountant will accept my hand-written one on an index card as a legitimate research expense.

Then we got serious. She smiled knowingly at my questions, as if she was a guru at a remote mountaintop, and I had just clawed my way up to see her. The answer was, although my parents didn't know it, they'd settled on my name and its spelling because of vibrations from the Universe. It wasn't random, it was destined. I totally agreed about my parents not knowing they'd done that, especially my dad who, after fathering six of us and consequently working long hours out of town to keep us in Kraft Mac 'n Cheese and new Keds, rarely got our first names right—much less any secondary ones.

First, she added up the letters of my full birth name, telling me the online site was mistaken about the importance of separating the consonants and vowels. That was a relief to me, as I asked what happens when someone uses a *y* as a vowel? Like my friend Cynthia? Cocking her head and frowning at me, she then figured the values of my middle and last names. My first name equaled forty-three. Add the four and the three, and the result is seven. Her eyebrows rose. My middle name became a three, and my last name a five. For the final result, she added seven, plus three, plus five, equaling fifteen. She grinned, as she added the one and the five and wrote a large six on the page and circled it. The Cheshire Cat bemused smile returned.

I leaned forward in my chair, waiting for her wisdom. "Your birth name number," she said, her navy-blue painted acrylic nails tapping the laminate desk surface, "indicates your expression of destiny—what you must learn in this lifetime." *This* lifetime? The idea that I might get a couple of do-overs for the bone-headed mistakes I'd made intrigued me. "Um," I asked, "how many do I get?" Again with the mysterious smile. She may as well have called me *grasshopper*. "You hate to argue," she continued. "You are loving and need balance in your life." I nodded, conceding those points. "Your problem is you have spent your life sacrificing your potential in order to keep the peace and prevent discord. Unpleasant confrontations upset you greatly, and you'll do almost anything to avoid them. Your lesson is to keep the balance you need, but stand up for yourself."

Yikes. She'd pegged me. Only after I'd turned the magic corner of middle age had I realized I'd been a doormat all my life. Maybe there was something to this. But what about the *master number* eleven thing? I'd almost forgotten. "I was born on the eleventh of the month," I said. "Eleven is supposed to be special. Why?"

She rolled her eyes. "There's *so* much to explain, I

wouldn't know where to begin. The important thing to remember is it means duality. A ying-yang kind of thing. It can be really good or really bad." That didn't help. Why would anyone want to be married on a date that could go either way? I guess my concern showed, because she took pity on me. She cut her eyes toward the others in the salon and lowered her voice. "It may mean you are a Light Worker." She consulted the numbers she'd done for my birth date. "You have psychic abilities you haven't tapped. Do some research." At that point, her next nail appointment arrived, so we finished up.

I liked the sound of being a Light Worker, whatever that was. I left feeling special and one-hundred dollars poorer—the down payment on my astrological chart.

POKEMON VERSUS HISTORY

Sorry, kids. School is back in session, and the *Pokemon Go* diversions—like walking into cars and stumbling down ravines to find dead bodies—must take a back seat. At least we hope they will. Wouldn't be a problem, though, if school was more fun, huh? Lucky for you, I'm here to make you realize that ridiculous human antics are not new at all, and that makes learning way more entertaining. We humans have done idiotic things from the get-go. In all honesty, it's a wonder we've survived this long. If you promise to behave, I'll tell you some fun history stories.

Mankind hasn't always behaved well. Well, okay, it has rarely behaved well. "A person is smart," Agent K tells Edwards in *Men in Black*. "*People*—are dumb, panicky, dangerous animals, and you know it."

I wonder how much intellectual progress mankind has *actually* made since we began forming languages and cultures. Oh, sure, we've got geniuses in every fields making amazing discoveries to help us along. But I fear they are a minority. The Flat Earth Society is a real group. With a real web page. There are those who still believe in theories from the middle-ages. And some who believe the years 614-911 didn't really exist, for heaven's sake. Yes, I am right there with you mouthing a giant *say wwhaaattt?*

Some other amusing beliefs are—and I'm finding this to

be quite the subject, so I promise to dedicate a whole column to whacko theories soon—the earth is hollow and populated by magical creatures, the moon is actually a hologram and doesn't exist, and the Denver airport is evil.

An impressive (but depressing) percentage of the remaining lot of us regular people are reactionary, stubborn, and ego-driven hot messes. (I refer you to the sadly appropriate quote from Agent K above.)

As children, we don't take it well when someone plays in our sandbox without permission. We don't like when someone ridicules us, and we lash out at them. Our parents, and our communities-at-large, are supposed to guide us past those immature impulses, by their words and their examples, until as adults, we have the grace and strength to rise above petty disputes.

Alas, some of the folks who don't ever outgrow their childhood impulses rise to power, where they can cause all kinds of chaos. Again, luckily for us, sometimes those stories make for fascinating stories. I mean, they're funny *now*. I'm sure the poor people who got killed or lost everything they had didn't find it the least bit amusing at the time. But, I digress.

In 1859, the United States and Great Britain nearly had a major battle over a pig. An American farmer shot a British-owned boar that was uprooting his potato crop. That led to a ridiculous escalation thanks to a US army captain and a British naval officer who got into a tug-of-war of massive egos.

Fifty people died in Bulgaria in 1925, when a Greek soldier crossed the border while chasing his dog and was shot. Already angry from long-held hostilities between the two countries, the Greeks invaded Bulgaria and occupied several villages before the League of Nations stepped in and stopped them from shelling the city of Petrich.

El Salvador and Honduras played a (supposedly) friendly game of football in 1969. Not a metaphor, a real game. El Salvador lost. They were sore losers, to say the least, and declared war. The war lasted for one-hundred hours—yes, hours, not days—until the Organization of American States intervened. Three-thousand people died. So lock up your guns first before your Thanksgiving touch football game with the in-laws.

Please keep these poor souls in mind when you choose to play *Pokemon Go* instead of studying history. I totally understand why you might want to escape into that world, but we really need you to be 'edumacated'.

OFF TO THE RACES

Humans are competitive. About everything, but especially sports. We are also quite inventive. So when some of us are no longer willing or capable of exerting *ourselves,* we find surrogates to compete for us. Who, or what, are those surrogates? Well, in the 'good' old days, slaves and prisoners were fodder for such *amusements.* In modern times, forcing others to run, fight, or die for our entertainment pleasure is, apparently, frowned upon. Sigh. So what's a rabidly competitive society full of obese couch potatoes supposed to do?

Entrance, stage right, our animal friends. Seems as though they're game to do anything for us. Some actually know we're using them to amuse ourselves. Dolphins and elephants come to mind. And the penguins from *Madagascar.* But others are thrust into situations that have to be bewildering to them. It's beyond bewildering to me.

Take, for example, the Crisfield Crab Races in Maryland. Officially called the Crisfield National Hard Crab Derby, it happens annually over Labor Day Weekend. So, sorry to say, if you're just reading about it now in October, you've missed your chance. It's a crab-themed festival with cooking, rides, crafts, fireworks, beauty queens, a parade, arm wrestling, and racing crabs. A much-needed aside here—somebody please clarify for me just what sort of young woman wants to wear the label *Crab* Queen? Or Queen of the Crabs? I think even the pushy mothers from *Toddlers and Tiaras* would have enough sense not to allow their daughters anywhere near such a moniker. That is a title that will follow you for the rest of your life. What if she decided to become an X-rated film star? Her chances would be torpedoed from the get-go.

Back to Crisfield's celebration of the crustacean. As much as I studied the web page, I did not see colored racing stripes or painted flames of glory on their backs, only boring chalky white numbers. Not very exciting. And, although it paints a picture in your head of crabs doing their darnedest to inch along a track, carefully staying in their designated lane, that isn't at all what happens. The pictures I saw show a multi-laned board all right—but one end was hiked up to an almost forty-five degree angle with little 'starting gates' at the top. Once the gates open, the crusty critters kind of slide, more than race, down. I for one, am outraged. The good folks in Crisfield could learn a thing or two by paying attention to the other absurd animal races.

There's hamster racing—in little cars no less—in the UK. It started in 2001, when a hoof and mouth disease put the kibosh on some of England's horse races. They keep World Records and everything. (See? I told you we were inventive . . .) There's even *professional* Hamster Racing now, covered by BBC London, *The Sun*, and *The Daily Mail*. Bookmakers take bets on it.

There are races for cows. For cockroaches. Rabbits. Lizards. Buffalo. Ostriches. Snails. Sheep. Cane toads. Camels. And pigs. Yikes.

As much as I would like to enlighten you about all of

these wonders, my space is limited. So I will wrap up with what seems to be the biggest misnomer here: Snail Races. The World Championships are hosted by our buddies, the Brits. Placed in the center of a fourteen-inch circle, the first snail to touch the outer circle line wins. In what has to be the most sleep-inducing event in the sports universe, it takes the average snails almost four minutes. Ah, but a snail named Archie in 1995 won it in just two minutes. Those spectators assuming they had plenty of time for a bathroom break must have been majorly bummed at missing that finish.

CHRISTMAS

MURPHY'S CHRISTMAS TREES

Gosh, it all seems so simple. Buy a tree. Put it in a stand. Add water. Decorate.

Not.

Murphy's Law dictates that whenever it is the absolute worst time for something to go kaflooey, that's when it'll happen. Take the above mentioned instructions for Christmas trees, for example. Don't I wish it worked like that. Alas, there is no lack of whacky ways for things to go wrong.

First, a little background. You should know where my compulsions came from. As a child in New Jersey, I was always so proud of my mother's holiday efforts, especially when it came to Christmas. We lived in a huge old house. Mom had two trees. One humongous twelve-foot Frasier or Noble fir for the formal living room, and a more modest and homey Douglas fir for the bay window of the dining room. That tradition started because Mom loved to decorate the living room tree in a precise way. Miniature, slow-action lights that winked on and off in a subtle way, not the flashing annoying kind. Garlands of small beads hung in looping, calculated patterns. Ornaments that coordinated with the color scheme. Two strands of tinsel draped at perfect intervals on the branch tips to give a low-key shimmering overall effect. It belonged in a frou-frou magazine.

But my mother had six children, all of whom inherited serious artistic genes and stubborn-as-heck personalities, a frighteningly intolerable combination. (I really don't know how she managed to restrain the temptation to *accidentally* lose one or two of us.) We made homemade ornaments, and we wanted to help decorate the tree. Mom, being an amazing child rearing wizard, came up with the dining room tree solution. That tree was ours to do with as we pleased. We labored over hand-strung popcorn and cranberry garlands for it. Blanketed with construction-paper chains, painted hard-dough 'cookie' shapes, twirling stars made from straws and obscene amounts of glitter, real candy canes, and pretty much anything else we could paint or glitterize. Pine cones, acorns, toilet paper rolls, old earrings, Silly Putty eggs— nothing found lying about was safe from our creative fervor. One year, Dad found his WWII service medals hung by chains made from every last paper clip in his desk. My father was much like the dad in *A Christmas Story*. He rolled his eyes a lot and hid behind a newspaper.

My older sister started the Christmas tree disaster saga. She'd moved out, had an apartment in the next town, and done her own version of Mom's living room tree. It was beautiful. Then on Christmas Eve, her tree fell down. Stand and all, it just keeled over like a belle-of-the-ball fainting because the attention was too much for her delicate constitution. I felt awful for my sister, but at the same time, a kind of superiority. *That* could never happen to me. She must have screwed up somewhere.

I lived on Oahu for many years, and in the very first year came my initiation into the tree mishap club. Being horribly homesick, I opted for a version of our homey-warmy dining room tree. I strung the real popcorn and cranberries and hung the real candy canes, but upgraded the ornaments a bit. It looked great. Unfortunately, I hadn't given a moment's thought to how the tropical climate would affect my holiday accoutrements. It's cold in New Jersey in the winter, and it never occurred to me that maybe things wouldn't work in the same ways.

Although I lived on the ninth floor of my apartment building, I woke up one morning and while drinking coffee and admiring my lovely tree, realized it was teeming with ants. An emergency run to the store and two entire cans of Raid later, my poor tree, stripped of anything remotely edible, looked like a refugee from the Island of Misfits. The Raid left discolored pitting on the ornaments and lights, the needles drooped, and instead of a fragrant evergreen aroma, it stunk of insecticide.

A couple of years later, I tried candy canes again. This time, I was sure I'd outfoxed the ants—the candy canes were individually wrapped. I'd moved to a mountainside of the Manoa valley. The moisture in the air there was so intense that mold grew on your shoe leather within days. De-humidifiers, while de rigueur, only kept it from raining indoors. It never occurred to me what extreme humidity could do to confections. Woke up one morning to see pink puddles of candy on the floor. The humidity melted the sugar, which leaked through the wrappers. And, of course, the pink puddles of goo were crawling with my nemesis—ants.

Fast forward. I'd moved back to the mainland. To Atlanta, where my family had relocated. Georgia boasts a proud collection of insects that survive the winter as well, but by then, I was an expert at bug-control. You should see the three-inch Hawaiian cockroaches with attitude. They wear Ray-Bans, flip you the bird, and laugh if you miss. Oh, I forgot. They can also fly and will launch an air attack right at your face. They are fast, but I am a Ninja-level killer. So, bugs didn't bug me in Atlanta.

By then we'd all had our tree foibles and follies. Crooked trunks. Split trunks. Ant nests *inside* the danged trunk itself. One was infected by beetles. Dried out needles. More trees falling over—including mine (Wicked crooked trunk. As a side note, never go tree shopping after drinking tequila). We had to attach guide wires to the wall to keep it from reoccurring.

Mom, not wanting to be outdone by her childrens' disasters, took the Lifetime Achievement Grand Prize. On Christmas Eve—when else?—she awoke to a terrible crashing and smashing. Running toward her family room, she stopped short at the doorway. The entire room's drywall ceiling had let go and come crashing down. Lamps, pictures, shelves, curios, and the Christmas tree all smashed to smithereens. What were the odds of that? Murphy just adores my family.

WHAT I WANT FOR CHRISTMAS

It's Christmas time? Boy, that was a speedy twelve months. Seems like I just finished the last update of the continuing saga of my family's decorating disasters. What happened to Hanukah? It got royally gipped this year, coinciding with Thanksgiving like that. Wonder how many enterprising folks tried making a turbriska instead of a turducken? That would be latkes wrapped by brisket and stuffed into a turkey—something I made up. Or at least, I thought I did. There are over a hundred thousand recipes and articles about turducken on the Internet, but nada for my turbriska. There *are*, however, four entries for tur-briska-fil. Gefilte fish inside brisket inside turkey. And I thought my concoction was awful. There was even a quote in the tur-briska-fil entry from a guy named Howard—"It's not as good as it sounds." Well, Howard, it sounds putrid. No offense.

Having brisket and latkes with my turkey so did not work for me, not to mention *nobody* actually had gifts ready and wrapped for the first night of Hanukah. Okay, the overachiever moms did, but they don't count. I'm glad this is coming out after the weirdo combo holiday, because one of those supermoms would no doubt demand my recipe for turbriska. I'd be forced to create a diversion while I got my neighbors' dog to eat a piece of paper I'll say was the only copy. Then I'd owe my neighbors cookies. Again. I bribe people with cookies. Not just any cookies work, though. Homemade, from scratch, using the best ingredients I can find, cookies. You can get amazing results if you put in the effort. Works like a charm.

So, it's now the Christmas shopping season. What's new for the 2013 holiday spend-a-thon besides scheduling conflicts? Gift suggestions galore get thrown at us from every morning show, news publication, and blog, but the fussy queen bee of Christmas sales pitches is the Neiman Marcus catalog of ridiculous presents. Perusing through, it occurred to me there should be a wish list. Oh, not the wish list they think we want. The wish list that would be so amazing that everyone, rich or poor, would want to buy the stuff.

Over the years Neiman's has featured camels and personal submarines. His and hers hot air balloons. Python accessories. Lots of really ugly, really expensive women's clothing—modeled by anorexic young women who look like they'd just as soon bite you. Not that I blame them. Starving women are not known for their sweet dispositions for a reason. (I would *so* give them cookies.)

One year Neiman Marcus had a $100,000.00 hen house. Yes. You read that right. 100K for chickens in your backyard. And the chickens weren't included. They have quarter-million-dollar cars. Private Boeing jets. $1400.00 face cream. A life-size edible gingerbread house. And it goes on and on. And on.

This year, there's a 201-inch outdoor movie/television entertainment system that rises from an underground bunker in your yard. Depending on your choice of options, it's an outlay of a mere 1.5 to 2.6 million. Guarantee you nobody in South Florida buys it. With the wind and rain we get? That thing would short circuit before you could say Category One. Or the ants would nest inside all the intricate underground workings. Or the iguanas and geckos would take turns pooping on it.

About my aforementioned wish list. I'd want:

The Long-Promised Jetsons-style Flying Car.

A Kickstand for Humans. It would be made from that new compositey-graphitey metal and extend from the size of a cane to something we could lay back against while waiting in line for the new iPhone or a theme park ride and playing *Fruit Ninja*.

A Lawn Roomba. The cute little thing would tool around outside and cut the grass and remember where the ding-blasted sprinkler heads are so I wouldn't have to replace one every freaking time the yard guys come. I mean, really. It just isn't that hard.

And speaking of lawn maintenance, I would pay big bucks to anyone who could invent a Silent Leaf Blower. Well okay, fine, you'd get cookies. But you'd sell a gazillion of them, so there'd be money, too.

Oh. And World Peace.

I saw a mention that the *Wall Street Journal* once reported that in a decade of offering gifts worth over a million dollars, Neiman's have only sold one? Apparently, no one's been able to confirm this. Can't say it's a surprise, though. If you or I had that much money, would we really waste it on something 'bespoke'? *Bespoke* is a term they throw out there to make people who aren't from old and very classy families desperately want to buy the bespoke item so the old and classies will accept them. Sorry, new money people. The old monies don't want you in their club.

But never you mind. You can be in my club. We have way better stuff. And I have really, really good cookies.

HOLIDAY DINNER DECORATING

My parents bought a big house when I was little. Huge, actually. It was on the run-down side—over one hundred years old and poorly maintained for most of those years. So Mom and Dad spent every weekend for a decade repairing and decorating. The result was a super family-friendly home where lots of people could gather. And, oh boy, did they.

Our dining room was around eighteen by twenty. As a result, our house became the go-to site for holiday events. Sit down dinners for the entire family weren't unusual. It wasn't until later in my life that I realized how that impacted all of us. It shapes your sensibilities as far as taking life as it comes, and it totally warps your sense of humor. Whenever you gather aunts, uncles, cousins, and assorted hanger-on-ers, good stories happen.

Everyone, it seems, has the one loud-mouth uncle who knows *everything*. The elderly auntie who drinks too much. The brash young nephew who just outperformed every other cousin in every category known to man. The cousin who lives in mysterious circumstances.

I can't use real names, of course, without fear of banishment—although there were times when banishment seemed like a welcome alternative—but we had a certain relative who could always be relied upon to cause conflict at the family holiday dinner. We'll call her

Aunt Ida. Think Baroness Von Schrader (only stuffier and more rigid) in *The Sound of Music* and you'll have the right image in mind, including the pinned-up blonde beehive. Aunt Ida's children were grown. I knew their names, but never met them. It always seemed strange to me that she spent holidays at our house instead of with her children and their families. Now I know why. Poor thing had a bad case of didactic-expertitis. Her kids didn't want her. Not that I blame them.

My mother is a genius at handling people. Aunt Ida would stand in the kitchen, while drinking martinis, and suggest *much* better ways to do absolutely everything Mom had already finished in preparation for the big meal. Mom would nod and agree, pour Ida another drink, then continue things her own way. We girls—it was the 60s & 70s—helped Mom with all of it, so came into direct smack-down contact with Ida and her authoritarian ways. We also knew that the faster Mom could get the martinis into her, the sooner Ida would be nodding off on the living room sofa instead of bugging us to death. Which was awesome, because Ida never approved of our haircuts, our clothes, or much else about us—except for my youngest sister, who was *perfect*.

One Christmas, after Ida fell asleep on the sofa, one of my younger siblings took the liberty of decorating her. Everyone else was in the kitchen, family room, or dining room, and when my father was given the unpleasant task of waking Ida for dinner—she was *his* aunt, after all—we heard him let out a loud snort of a laugh. "I can't do it," he said, coming back into the kitchen. He turned to the crowd of all of us young cousins and tried his best serious stare-down. "Which one of you kids did that to her?"

Denying everything and adopting our best innocent faces, because we *all* knew exactly who'd done it, we followed the adults into the living room. Ida was snoring away. Remember trolls? The short, plastic dolls with the unruly shock of colorful hair? We had dozens of them—they played the important role of being our Barbies' children. Well, the trolls were gathered on her chest, stomach, and tucked under one hand, while several more stared down at her from their perch on top of the sofa back. GI Joe and one Barbie (wearing her Christmas dress) sat on her shoulder. Leftover tinsel strings flowed from Ida's beehive. Green and red construction paper chains snaked along the length of her body. And an enormous red bow stolen from my brother's new banana-seat bicycle sat on her forehead. Thank God there were no cell phones or Internet back then. No one took any pictures, even with my sister's snappy new Polaroid in the house. They managed to un-decorate her before waking her up, my mother praising the knock-out punch ability of gin the whole time.

During dinner that Christmas, it was hard not to crack up as Ida went on and on with her expert opinions on the world, blissfully ignorant of how ridiculous she'd looked a half hour earlier. Mom jumped up in the middle of the meal and ran into the kitchen yelling, "Oh my God! I forgot about the beets!" Like the house was on fire. Nobody cared about or missed the beets, because Mom was the only one who ate them. Meanwhile, Uncle 'Jim' predictably spilled his wine, Grandmom and Grandpop argued over Grandpop putting little white onions on his plate—they gave him the wind something fierce, cousin 'Ned' licked the sweet potatoes serving spoon, and cousin 'Beth's new boyfriend took way too much gravy.

Flash forward to today. I don't have a huge dining room or house, but I do have a compulsion to host holiday dinners. We've had massive pre-dinner Nerf gun battles, but fortunately, no troll attacks. After growing up in my family, there isn't much that ruffles me, even if the Nerf darts land in the potatoes I'm mashing. No such thing as a stranger in my home on holidays, either. If my boys tell me of a friend with nowhere to be on that day, they're welcome here. But they'd better have a good sense of humor.

WHAT THE WISE MEN STARTED

Christmas shopping tends to make people crazy. Well, crazier. The endless comparing of prices. The mad rush to buy the best deal. Staggering out of bed in the middle of the night while suffering from a turkey hangover to shiver in line with equally grumpy people in the dark? (Some of whom couldn't possibly have bothered to brush their teeth.) Returning gifts after buying them a second time elsewhere. Or worse. Forgetting to return the first ones and finding them still stuffed away in a closet when hiding Easter baskets—knowing the receipts are shredded landfill history.

Even if you shop online, it's a never-ending cavalcade of sale prices, expired coupon codes, discounts, free or not shipping, and out of stock problems. Or you watch your delivery go viral on YouTube as the driver makes a cavalier twenty-foot toss from the truck to your porch with your package marked *FRAGILE* in huge black magic marker letters all over the box. Hint: Never order glass *anything* online. Been there, got way too many damaged T-shirts.

But—why? What for? What's the frenzy all about? Unless the recipients are small children with their heart set on the latest toy, does it matter? Most adults really don't care whether their gift is the *latest* whatever. In fact, in our current digital world, the people who want the newest order it themselves immediately or camp out (in yet another line) for days to get it *NOW*. I submit that most adults would prefer you give them a consumable—chocolates, booze, gourmet fixings—rather than something they'll have to return. The real shame is that odds are they can't stand whatever it is you spent hours choosing for them, and they *want* to return it, but they won't. It'll be relegated to their closet until they go to hide the Easter baskets. Then it'll become a re-gifted item for the next holiday or birthday. Which is not what you intended when you gave all that time and bother obtaining and wrapping the freaking thing. Not to mention the multiple times it had to be reordered and delivered—the box having suspicious dents suggesting it was possibly used as a basketball. (Check the YouTube video.)

And—if your recipients *do* place big emphasis on you providing them with the latest gizmo or fashion accessory, dump them. Now. You don't need the stress they'll bring to your life. You clearly have enough.

I think I've figured it out. Our ridiculous state of affairs is totally not our fault. We've been doomed from the very beginning of this holiday.

See, it's all the fault of those three *wise* men. They see a shining star that bedazzles them, and voilá—suddenly they have to one-up each other. The gift competition began. Precious and rare oils? Really? What, pray-tell, was wrong with bringing something the new family could actually use? Like lots of cloth for diapers? Back then, cloth was a big deal. The normal people had one, maybe two if it was a good crop year, robe/toga thingies to wear. There were no wardrobes. Unless you were Pharaoh's daughter, in which case you probably yawned at the gift of yet another embroidered frock, jewel-encrusted cuff, or glittering headdress.

And not only did those three men start the gift competition thing, they also can be blamed for the obsession of everybody trying to look forever young. I did a little research (literally) and found out that Frankincense and Myrrh were both used by ancient societies as rejuvenating oils. For the face. To ease wrinkles and heal chapped and cracked skin. So basically, they were ensuring that young Mary knew she'd better not show any signs of aging. My guess is the stupid men stopped by Pharaoh's palace on the way and asked his daughter for advice as what to bring as gifts. Only a rich girl would think rejuvenation oils was a great gift for poor people.

When a gift-giving tradition begins like that, who can be surprised it wound up as such a riotous mess? Save yourself a ton of time and trouble. Buy gift cards, weight them down with a bag of chocolates in a big box (so people will pick it up and not think—*oh crud, it's just a gift card*), and wrap it up in gorgeous paper. And you're done. Soooo much easier. You're welcome.

AN ADULT CHARLIE BROWN TREE

Don't know if you've caught wind, but there's a trend to make holiday trees out of something unusual. Unopened wine bottles. Empty wine bottles. Unopened beer cans and bottles. Empty beer cans and bottles. Unopened liquor bottles. Empty liquor bottles. Add a couple strings of white mini-lights, and voilá, your living room now resembles an uber-trendy bar. Or a cruise ship. Aren't *you* just the cat's meow.

Next, by all means, post many, many pictures on Facebook, Instagram, and Pinterest. Because nothing says the holidays like telling the world just how much you are in love with alcohol. Now, I adore my glass (or two) of wine just as much as the next suburban mom. When my boys were teenagers, it was a great way to mellow out when all I wanted to do was wring their hormone-ravaged little necks. I am rather certain, however, that constructing a liquor bottle tree in the house and worshipping it would have *maybe* sent the wrong message to the impressionable minds in my life. And the kids, too.

Back to social media. This intrepid reporter's investigation into alcoholic Christmas trees has revealed some pretty darned interesting phenomenon. It used to be Martha Stewart's exclusive domain to make the rest of us feel like we were born with only thumbs permanently encumbered by Band-Aids. Now we have Pinterest.

Where crafty folks post pictures of their perfectly turned out DIY projects. This is way worse than Martha. It's one thing to be put to shame by comparison to an all-things-domestic diva. It's a totally devastating development to be bested by thousands of amateur crafters, who—if you believe what's presented to you—constructed their masterpiece while working full time, heading the PTA, cooking gourmet quality dinners, and attending daily yoga classes. At least Martha admits that creating her perfections is her full-time job.

Back to the bottle 'trees'. What could possibly go wrong there? I know what would happen in my house. One by one, the bottles would disappear. Oops, forgot to buy wine for our dinner party, I'll just swipe a few from the back. No one will notice. Oops, attending a holiday gala and ran out of time to shop for a hostess gift, I'll grab a few more. After drinking with friends at my own gathering, I'd no doubt hand one to each parting guest. By the time Christmas Eve arrived, my poor 'tree' would look like the glass version of Charlie Brown's. And after having to tangle with Lucy all his life, it's entirely plausible Charlie Brown's adult tree might very well be made of booze.

Not everyone on social media is aware of their own limitations. Some, having forayed into DIY projects for the first time, proudly post their creations, too. So blinded by enthusiasm and adoration, they can't see what the rest of us do. It's very much like when someone doesn't think your baby is the most beautiful in the world. And perhaps the less than wonderful crafters are the real reason we peruse these sites. Somebody else failing to reach perfection makes us feel sooo much better about ourselves.

I saw a bottle tree made from a few dowel rods stuck, at odd angles, into a stump. Yes, a stump. The beer bottles didn't match, still had their labels on, and clearly hadn't been washed first. You'd have to drink a lot of beer before that spectacle looked good to you.

I've also seen trees mounted to the ceiling. Yes, it's different. But, oy, can you imagine how disorienting that would be on Christmas morning while you're nursing a hangover? Both Santa and the kids would be so confused. Sometimes, we should just celebrate normal. And that's a good thing. Right, Martha?

ASSORTED OTHER HOLIDAYS

HENCEFORTH IN JULY...

I love the Fourth of July. It's my favorite holiday. Fireworks reawaken the ooh-ahh childlike wonderment in me. I'm talking about the big displays put on by paid professionals, not the do-it-yourself in the backyard type. I only go to the professional ones now because the backyarders scare the bejeebers out of me.

Any activity that combines lack of visibility at night, relatives and in-laws, massive amounts of alcohol, and gun powder is, in my mind, a fiasco in the making. Throw in drought conditions and you've got a perfect storm. We've all seen news reports on the fifth of July. Tens of thousands suffer injuries, and there are over a thousand house fires and six-hundred highway fatalities every Fourth of July. Yeesch. Consider yourself warned. I'm a mom. Can't turn it off. But—I can't ignore the crazy and silly, either.

Consider Brad, age sixteen, who was caught red-handed with illegal fireworks. His father threatened to take his car (a BMW) away if he bought them again. With the Fourth only two days away, the pressure from Brad's friends was too much. They planned to set off fireworks on the beach, far away from their parents—who planned to watch New York City's display on their sixty-inch flat screen. Knowing they would be infinitely more clever this time, Brad and friends went back to the sleazy guy hawking the super-spectacular illegal-type fireworks from the back of a rusty van out on the highway. You'd think

277

between the bumper sticker on the van that said, *Laws are for fools with bad aim,* the fact the windows were blacked out, and the man's hands lacked a digit or two would have been enough to scare the boys away, but that kind of horse sense apparently doesn't develop in the average American male until later.

Brad's father went out of town, due to return the afternoon of the Fourth. Brad hid the fireworks in a place his mother would never find them. The gas barbecue grill. His father's exclusive domain. Something his mother and even the maid never touched. Murphy's Law loves a *never.* Wouldn't you know the third of July would be the first time his mom decided to grill steaks for dinner? She turned on the gas burners before lifting the lid, and ka-pow. Mom came out of it fine—she'd ducked back into the house for a minute—but the wall behind the grill went up in flames. And, no, the Beamer wasn't taken away. After all, they lived in Boca. Disciplinary threats are not acted upon there. I think it may be a town ordinance.

Some backyarders pass on a tradition of cautious celebration, teaching their offspring to treat fireworks with respect. Imagine Mom and Dad Suburban, both wearing red, white, and blue Ralph Lauren clothing— probably with nautical embellishments of some kind— taking care to instruct little Jimmy and Jenny Suburban on the ins and outs of long-enough fuses, safe storage of matches, and keeping the first-aid kit stocked and handy. They're all wearing shoes. The dog has been sedated and sequestered in a bathroom. The water to the hose is turned on, ready for action with quick squeeze on the trigger. Except for the resemblance to the cast of a

National Lampoon movie, they really aren't funny. Serious suburbanites usually aren't.

Most of the backyard Fourth parties I've had the dubious pleasure of attending didn't indulge in pesky details like the Suburban family did.

My friend and I arrived at one such party around seven o'clock. Adults sat in lawn chairs, manned the barbeque, and played horseshoes and bocce. A hoard of shrieking, unclaimed children ran around barefoot snagging treats from the dessert table on the fly. Big dogs jumped on guests and stole food from plates left in low places. Huge coolers overflowed with iced beers, wine, spiked lemonade, and sodas.

By show time at nine, there'd already been one almost-fistfight between two rather large and unshaved men with intimidating tattoos, and a woman who left in a fit of fury because her husband and her sister had taken a might too long checking out the homeowner's collection of old posters that decorated the spare bedroom.

The host and his best buddy made an attempt at safety and had everyone move their chairs to make room for his fireworks show. Kids sat on blankets. The host lit the initial rocket, then backed up a few yards. The dogs whined and barked. The rocket took off, went about fifty feet in the air, and exploded into a starburst of red and green. People stomped and cheered. The dogs howled and retreated, trampling a blanket full of small children, who screamed. A mom checked the kids, pronounced them sound, and the show went on.

A squirming five-year-old boy couldn't contain himself a moment longer, no doubt a result of having nothing but soda and cookies all day. He began twirling around and around—a game we used to call Dizzy Duck. His father yelled at him to stop, but his mother yelled back saying the poor kid shouldn't have to be made to sit, the child had too much energy—what were they supposed to do? "Well go spin over there," the father said, pointing to an area behind the crowd.

Soon the other children were spinning, running, and tumbling. One dad started lighting sparklers for them. Meanwhile the host continued the fireworks and drank beer. The kids' antics grew wilder, and they strayed from their prescribed territory. The adults seemed glued to their chairs, ignoring the chaos. One of the barefoot munchkins stepped on an expired but still hot sparkler, yelped like a banshee, and stumbled backward—into our host. He was just touching the lighter to a fuse and got knocked over sideways. Sparks ignited the crispy drought-dried grass. Flames erupted. Panic ensued. Dogs went wild. Children screamed. Drunk people staggered from their chairs. No one could locate the hose. A woman threw a pitcher of Sangria on the fire, which flamed higher in appreciation. It ended when the big tattoo guys emptied the coolers, now full of icy water, on the fire.

And that was the year I decided to stick with the professionals.

HALLOWEEN TREATS

How *did* the tradition of knocking on strangers' doors and asking for candy start? Turns out the roots of it took hold over two thousand years ago.

The Celts in Scotland, Ireland, and northern France believed in evil spirits. The Celts knew the weakest link in the space/time continuum (thank goodness for movies like *Back To The Future* which gave me my impressive science knowledge) occurred during Samhain—the end of the Celtic harvest and their year. Apparently the ubiquitous evil spirits spent every second of their other-worldly existence scheming to enter the human realm.

Why? They were jealous. Jealous of those lucky humans and their lavish no-bathing-hence-lice-encrusted, pelt-wearing, and tooth-rotting lifestyle. Well, that and the fact humans were on top of the earth breathing fresh air, while they (the demons) sucked brimstone fumes in the netherworld. They systematically tested the strength of the boundary between the two worlds (much like, I imagine, the crazed penned-in velociraptors in *Jurassic Park*) hoping to find the weak matrix point and break through. Then they set off to the tasks of stealing the harvest, deflowering daughters, and generally scaring the crap out of everyone.

During this matrix weak point known as Samhain, the Celts donned masks when they left the safety of their homes to frighten the evil spirits away. That didn't suffice, because they also began hollowing out turnips, carving scary faces into them, and using them as lanterns to further spook the pesky devils. Evidently, that didn't stop the onslaught either. The Celts had a priest class called the Druids. The priests began the practice of calling on each household October 31-November 1 to collect food and coins. The priests would intercede and pray for the family's deliverance from the troublemaking ghouls and collect a nice remittance which they said they'd give to the spirits in exchange for leaving them in peace.

Here's how I see the whole thing playing out. At first, the priests had great intentions and probably placed the coerced loot on a rock. Not just any old rock mind you—it would have to have been a sacred rock in the middle of a revered burial ground or spiritual site, preferably near an oak tree. (The Druids loved oak trees. Thought they had mystical powers.) Can't you just see them fussing over which rock? Near which oak? Almost coming to fisticuffs over which was most attractive to ghosts? And which animal should be sacrificed? I imagine an old man stroking his scraggly white beard with his long, bony fingers with a thought bubble over his head. Inside the bubble—*Hmmm . . . Sacrifice a bunny? No. Too cute. These are serious demons. Maybe a bull. Yes. A white bull. Wait!* The priest raises an a-ha index finger. *Perhaps a virgin would appease them more. Colin-the-mead-maker's wife just bore him a seventh daughter. Hmmm . . .*

No doubt some lower-ranking priest, anxious to unseat the head priest and take over the big-cheese position, would be talking stink behind the head priest's back.

Taking it upon himself to whip the initiates into a worried frenzy because wasn't it obvious the man was past his prime and clearly couldn't see the omens in front of his face? What if he screwed it up and they all got swallowed by mistake into the netherworld with the spirits? Who would have thought the Druids also invented office politics?

There would have to be ceremonies, too. You couldn't expect any self-respecting ghoul to be attracted by food and coins just lying there. You'd have to entice them. Cleanse the rock. Anoint it with aromatic herbs and oils. Sprinkle the ground with grains. The Druids wore acorn necklaces and danced. Drank lots of wine and repeated chants. A whole lot of fuss and bother went into the show.

Then finally at nightfall—exhausted from all the hullabaloo, like Linus waiting for the Great Pumpkin, they'd duck behind a bigger rock and watch. And watch. At dawn, seeing the food now swarming with ants and the money shining in the rising sun's rays, the priests reclaimed the offering. Not wanting to admit they'd failed, reveal the congealed egg on their face, they kept the goodies and told the townspeople all went as planned. Humanity was safe for another year. Somehow, I doubt they tried this for more than a couple of seasons. That persnickety upstart junior priest probably succeeded in his quest to be head poohbah and convinced the Druid council that since the ghosts hadn't taken the bait and the offering ritual was secret, why not simply skip the hoopla and pocket the contributions. They could save all that time and energy, not to mention Colin-the-mead-maker's daughter (on whom he most likely had a crush), and get a decent night's sleep. The townsfolk would be none the wiser. And he would never look like the failure that his predecessor did, helping him avoid the next upstart who aimed to topple *him* from his lofty position.

There you have it. My version of how trick or treat was born. Give us food and money or the ghosts will get you has morphed into the modern-day model—give me candy and I won't toilet paper your trees.

BAD COSTUMES

Every Halloween, in every town, in every neighborhood, there is an overachiever mom hell-bent on producing the absolute *world's best* costume for her child. And that's terrific. Usually. Unfortunately, some parents miscalculate. I guess, depending on where you live (or what medications you might be on), the unintentional effects of costumes can be either hilarious or disturbing.

One California homeowner opened her door, looked down, and saw a sweet dimpled baby dressed as a boiled red lobster strapped into a twelve-quart pot. A second, smaller pot—marked *butter*—was attached near the bottom and held the collected candy. The parents were watching from behind a tree, laughing hysterically, not knowing the woman called the cops. The article I found never did explain why she dialed 911. You'd think Californians would be more accustomed to unusual costumes. After all, it is the state that made celebrities of tap dancing men in raisin outfits. Perhaps the baby lobster gag is a regional thing, best reserved for Maine? Or Mini Lobster Season? Another couple with triplets decided to turn them into spaghetti and meatballs. They wheeled the toddlers around in a triple-wide stroller. The child in the middle was made the 'spaghetti' by encasing the poor thing in one leg of a large pair of white tights. The children on either side of Mr. Spaghetti Noodle wore big foam half-rounds, painted red and brown. What the trio of costumes resembled most was the apparatus used to conceive them, if you'll pardon my bluntness. And does dressing up your child to resemble a loaded baked potato belong in Idaho—the place where they really *dig* potatoes? What is it with the food costumes, anyway?

My perusal through lists of the worst Halloween costumes for kids treated me to a baby in fishnet stockings held by her mom on a stripper pole. Mom was scantily clad, too. The family that strips together . . . ? Several children wore cardboard toilets—head emerging from the tank—with one boy carrying a handy plunger. It's tough to believe that when those kids' parents asked them what they wanted to be for Halloween, they answered "toilet". I have three sons, and every year in early October, I'd ask them that question. They came up with all sorts of costume ideas I had to veto. Most entailed too much blood and gore. (This was fifteen-to-twenty years ago, before bloodied zombies became so haute couture.) The word, toilet, *never* passed their lips. Not once. Not even as a joke. Although, I'm pretty certain that had they *seen* a walking toilet during their trick or treating, said toilet would have been further embellished with a couple of unwrapped nutty chocolate bars. A few of the boys in the neighborhood (the ones who TP'd everybody's trees) would no doubt have made sure the walking toilet was thoroughly festooned with toilet paper, too.

I saw a picture of a toddler dressed as Hitler—including the little Nazi uniform, black boots, swastika, mustache, and a replica cover of Mein Kampf glued to the front of his trick or treat bag. You have to assume the parents are Neo-Nazis. What else could anyone think? There was a little boy in a giant Trojan wrapper. A boy dressed as a bottle of Jack Daniels, and his sister as pack of Marlboros. Lots of mini Walter Whites from Breaking Bad. Really? A meth dealer? It'll be such a shocker when these kids turn out to be a tad strange, won't it?

Somebody took the time to sew and stuff a big green marijuana leaf for their child to wear. And some poor kid in a fake turban with bombs strapped to his chest. Yup, a suicide bomber costume.

The kicker is—some of those extremely inappropriate costumes were well done. Great details and execution. Especially the marijuana leaf. If only they'd put that much effort into thinking about the effects of the costume on junior. That all his friends will still be making fun of him fifty years in the future for having been a Trojan wrapper, a liquor bottle, or a urinal when he was eight. As much as he might attempt to burn or hide all the evidence, you *know* his crazy parental units will show those pictures every chance they get.

We'll never know what, exactly, is wrong with those parents. But a word to the wise—keep track of the weirdo-costume kids and make sure your child never goes to a sleepover at their house. If you can't figure out why, then maybe you should rethink what you're planning for your progeny's costume.

LEAVE THE POOR GHOSTS
ALONE ALREADY

There are friends of mine who love—and I mean *love*—anything to do with ghosts and paranormal activities. They traipse through graveyards, attend séances, and do whatever they can to insert themselves where a spirit might reveal itself. I don't understand the compulsion.

Do deceased humans exist in spirit form after they die? Some say the spirits with unfinished business stick around, while the other, more well-adjusted ghosties float their merry way to . . . well, wherever they go. So, let me get this straight—the dead people who mucked up their lives, and possibly the lives of their family and friends, are stuck here with the living, trying to set things right? Isn't that kind of a hard row to hoe when almost no one can hear, see, or sense you're there? It must be terribly frustrating. Maybe that's what purgatory really is. Once you're able to make amends, you get to join the good spirits who are having a happy cosmic afterlife. They're probably at some heavenly cocktail party where there's great music (not harp, I'm thinking Marvin Gaye), and everything you say is witty and wonderful, and everybody likes you, and there are comfy clouds to lounge on.

And if you're one of those goodie-two-shoes deceased, you get to tsk-tsk while watching the unfortunate spirit wretches still on earth tying themselves into wispy pretzel knots to get the right human's attention? Maybe the wretches can also hear the heavenly cocktail party going on, but can't access it, and that's part of the purgatory too? Like a glazed donut dangling in front of them— here's what *you'll* have when you atone for the fact you totally screwed up your brother's life by cheating him out of his share of the family business? Or having been extraordinarily mean to the guy who married your mom?

It's just their bum luck that it seems the *only* living people able to discern they're there have nothing to do with clearing their slates. People like a few friends of mine. Enter—the ghost hunters. The few adventuresome folks able to see or hear them and eagerly poke their noses into spirits' private beeswax. That has to add all kinds of major-league stress to the already difficult burden of the reform-school spirits. Why antagonize the poor things by pestering them like that? No wonder there are so many cranky ghosts.

I grew up in a haunted house (yes, really). Unannounced, our neighbor, Mrs. Martin, brought a spirit medium to the door one day. When Mom saw the effeminate little man, and Mrs. Martin introduced him as Sidney Porcelain, she exploded with laughter—thinking it was a joke. This was around 1970 when the phrase *politically correct* was but a demented twinkle in J. Edgar's eye. The medium was from New York and was only visiting that day, so after Mom regained some composure—dignity being out of the question—she let them in.

Following Porcelain through the house, Mom took notes. Ever since my parents bought the big old mansion, Mom had been researching—trying to discover more about its history. This was long before the Internet, and finding any detail took a considerable amount of time. So it was darned impressive when Porcelain spouted arcane facts about the people who'd lived there as he entered each room.

When he left, Mom went a few doors down to see an elderly woman who'd grown up in our house. She refused to talk about it. Said she had bad memories. Mom persisted, though, and got her to at least verify things Porcelain said. Turned out, all of what he'd said was true. Weird stuff. Stuff there was no way he could know by looking it up, even if there was someplace to look it up. Which there wasn't, as Mom knew very well.

Another time, I'll share that part of it. We were a family of eight. Six kids. Life was always noisy and full. The house was rumored to be haunted when my parents bought it—it had been on the market for twenty-five (yes, twenty-plus-five) years because of the supposed ghosts. We kids took our cues from our parents. We paid no attention to the rumors and went on with our serious business of homework, playing, rough-housing, and generally torturing each other. My sister had a tidy little income on the side, charging neighborhood kids a nickel to ride the elevator (it *was* a very cool old house) and a dime to venture onto the third floor to see if they saw the ghosts. My sister told them if they could stay up there for more than a minute, she'd pay them a dime instead. Of course, we'd set up a few dusty dress-forms and fake spider webs, then kept the lights off, so she never did have to pay anyone.

Apparently, the old woman neighbor had ticked off the ghosts somehow. She hated the place. Makes me wonder now why the spirits never bothered us. I guess they liked kids. Or maybe the fact we really weren't trying to mess with them and minded our own beeswax.

BIRDS OF A FEATHER

It's time to talk turkey. Like how much we love to eat it? No. That's a given. How lame it is such a delicious bird that is indigenous to our continent is named for a country straddling Europe and Asia? Well, that is curious, and a truly dorky name, too. Just the sound of the two syllables fits as a descriptor of something or someone that is one step off the sidewalk. But, no— again.

Besides being the feathered feature of our feasts every Thanksgiving, the turkey has more association with people than you've been led to believe. Some of its behaviors mirror ours so much, it makes me wonder if someday anthropologists will find a bizarre common ancestor. Kind of a turkey-man hybrid. Wouldn't that be cool. Maybe this hybrid creature could fly. By the way, contrary to conventional wisdom, turkeys *can* fly. At least the wild ones can, up to fifty-five miles per hour for short distances. They can outrun us, too, capable of up to thirty miles an hour for 100 yards. For the record, that absolutely destroys Usain Bolt's standing. (He could only sustain such speed for twenty meters.) The domesticated birds meant for our dinner tables, though, can't do any of that. They are like the fattened pampered humans in H. G. Wells' *The Time Machine*. Or the plump and coddled humans in *WALL-E*. Eating and napping are their big challenges. Also just like humans—after they eat turkey. Hmmm.

If you squint a bit, the turkey is rather beautiful. The broad spread of tail feathers, the rust and bronze highlighted upper body feathers, the stylish white stripes on the wings. The squinting helps when you get to the head. It has wart-like growths, called carbuncles, all over it. A long red thing dangling from the forehead resembles, in shape and movement, the icky congealed mucus blob swinging from the nose of a sick toddler. That dangly bit is called a snood. As if that weren't gross enough, they also have a wattle—another dangling bit, this one from the chin. And the toms (males) have sharp spurs for fighting. As in one to two-inch spikes. Protruding from the back of their ankles. Do not mess with them. They are powerful. Yes, the American wild turkey is a badass, the Liam Neeson of the bird world.

Studies have shown the toms with longer snoods have more success at mating. Much like their human counterparts, toms most likely give those studies a lot of weight. They probably get envious of each other's snoods. The hens (females) probably snicker at such tom-foolery, then go back to taunting them. It may be difficult to disrespect the males for long, because—also like humans—related toms will band together to approach the females and court them. They have literal wing men. Only one of the toms gets to mate with the female at that time. Don't waste your tears on the others. The whole lot of them are as randy as lust-driven teenagers and mate as often as they can get away with it, with any bird who'll let them. Borrowing from *The Bachelor*, they don't even pair up for a single season.

Turkeys eat insects, seeds, and berries. Even aging, fermented berries. That could explain a lot. Turkeys get beer goggles. Just like us.

TURKEY ON A CASTLE

If you carve your Thanksgiving turkey in a galvanized tub while wearing cargo shorts and sitting on a stool on a flat castle roof, you might be a unique kind of redneck.

For sixteen years, I hosted Thanksgiving dinner, usually for ten to twelve people. I skew toward a medium-formal setting when I host—placemats, napkins, matching silverware, a table centerpiece, but nothing *too* Martha Stewart-y. But last year, I needed a break from the two full days of dawn-to-dusk cleaning, prepping, and cooking. So I made my cancellation announcement to the normal invitees, withstood some loud and withering complaints, and my significant other and I headed south. Since we were lucky enough to be in the Florida Keys, we were invited to partake of the annual feast at the home of an acquaintance of the SO's.

They were so kind to include us, and we gratefully accepted. I brought a big bottle of Pinot Grigio and a from-scratch apple pie. We arrived at three, as requested. They lived in an unusual place. In a fake medieval castle. Yeppers. Had the notched parapet wall at the top and everything. A souvenir shop occupied the ground floor, and although there was no way to tell from the outside, the second floor had four apartments.

We trudged up the exterior stairs, knocked on the first door and found thirteen other people crammed into a teensy apartment without a table. There was a small living area that barely fit a sofa, side chair and the television stand flanked by a miniature kitchen with maybe eight total feet of counter space.

Now, don't get me wrong. I'm not putting my hosts down for being obviously economically challenged. Lots of people are. But imagine our head-scratching, trying to figure out how they planned to feed us. There wasn't space for each of us to actually sit anywhere. I wondered if their good intentions hadn't been thought through.

The tiny kitchen had every available inch covered with various foods in the making, ingredients, dirty prep dishes, and booze bottles, since it also functioned as the bar. I opened my Pinot Grigio, poured a generous amount into a red plastic cup, and asked if I could be of any help in the kitchen. She put me to work making the gravy. While busying myself with my task, I asked the hostess, as nonchalantly as I could, how she planned on serving everyone. "We're eating on the roof," she said.

That inspired one of her kids to show me said roof. We went outside, up another flight of stairs, and a huge open area of flat concrete appeared. The notched walls were high, so no one would ever suspect parties could happen on top of the souvenir shop. Folding chairs lay against the wall, and three silt-encrusted folding tables sat empty in the middle of the space, but far away from and at odd angles to each other. So, you might ask, why wasn't anyone from the crammed apartment hanging out up there?

Wind. It was so windy. How to prevent everything from blowing away? I shook my head, shut my mouth (it's taken years, but I've gotten pretty good at that), and went back downstairs.

Our hosts made enough food for half the town. Two turkeys—one oven-roasted and one deep fried—and an enormous ham simmered in a big pot of Coca-Cola. No, I can't explain that. Three kinds of potatoes. Green beans. Cornbread. Pasta salad. When it was time to eat, we hauled the food to one of the roof tables. The sooty dirt wasn't cleaned off of any of them. The tables weren't repositioned so the guests might feel like they were dining together. No tablecloths or placemats (they'd have blown away). Paper plates and paper towels were weighted down with rocks.

Our host pulled up a stool and put two galvanized tubs on the concrete floor, each holding a turkey. Using an electric knife, he carved them and placed the meat on platters, also set on the floor. Remember, it's outside. Loose dirt abounds. And it's windy.

It was a precarious thing, holding a flimsy paper plate flapping in the wind while trying to plop food on it *and* keep the plastic wrap or foil covering each dish from becoming airborne. In the end, that effort failed, and all that wasn't secured did eventually sail off into another person's backyard celebration.

We ate holding our plates down with one hand. When my SO, seated to my right, had finished his meal, he forgot for a moment and let go of his plate. A gust of wind picked it up and flung it at me. I went home with gravy and potato grease spots all over my shirt.

Thanksgiving is the American holiday. We celebrate it in many ways. There is no right way. And, although it's a ton of work, I am looking forward to my more traditional one again. Indoors.

DIRTY SEXY NEW YEAR
(With apologies to Meghan McCain)

New Year's Eve makes people do things they never imagined they'd do. Is it those treacherous tiny bubbles in the Champagne that makes tossing caution into the Jacuzzi an option? The silly hats? The kazoo-type noisemakers?

Whatever it is warping the normally sensible person on that night, it's fun and fascinating to watch it in progress. Maybe the lapses in judgment come from the euphoria of knowing there's a fresh start in the morning. The slate gets wiped clean. We press the do-over button in our minds. So the logic might follow that we'd better take this last chance on this last night to be mischievous. *Tomorrow, I'll be good as gold. I promise.*

As a teenager, I spent most my New Year's Eves babysitting. A few times the couples came home enrobed in a frosty silence. One occasion in particular stands out. For my benefit, Mr. and Mrs. 'Smith' adopted frozen smiles as they paid me at 2 AM. Terse little comments directed at their spousal unit escaped from those resolute lips. I'm sure they thought I had no clue they were fighting about something, due their convincing cover-up performances, but I could tell. Mr. Smith noticed I'd done all the dishes (even the ones they'd left from lunch) and said, "Thanks. I'll definitely call on you again." From behind clenched teeth, Mrs. Smith muttered, "That what you told Nancy, too?" Mr.

Smith blanched. I pretended I didn't hear Mrs. Smith and hurried out the door.

I grew up in a small town where everybody knew everybody or their relatives. The next day, the gossip flew through the neighborhood. Aunt Bea and Clara from Mayberry had nothing compared to the ladies on our street. Mrs. Jones from next door hustled to our back porch to borrow a cup of flour (excuse) and, once seated at the kitchen table, just about exploded from holding in the scandalous news while hinting I should find something else to do. My mother shooed me away, so I did the time-honored teenager thing and perched on the stairs around the corner to listen. It was about Mr. Smith's flirting with the very married hostess at a New Year's party. Except he didn't just flirt. Things were getting steamy in the coat closet beneath the front staircase when a departing guest went for her coat and got treated to a most revealing view of Mr. Smith and hostess Nancy.

Mom and Mrs. Jones agreed that Mr. Smith was a well-known hound dog, but it could have been the booze. Mom recited a short poem. That was the first time I'd heard of Dorothy Parker and her famous quote about too many martinis and you wind up under the host. I vowed to never drink martinis (but I do, and I love them) and to check out Dorothy Parker on my next trip to the library. And they decided that Nancy-the-hostess probably didn't put up much resistance, on account of her husband being a diabetic. I had no idea what that meant, but I'd find out. For those of you who are younger than we Baby Boomers, this was how we learned about life. The old-fashioned way. Nobody ever told you directly about anything. You had to remember inferences and then ask your friends, or your friends' older siblings, what it meant—and hope they didn't laugh at you for being impossibly lame for not knowing.

Another year, an inebriated Mrs. 'Miller' came in from New Year's party on the arm of her husband. She teetered to the sofa, plopped onto the cushions, then glanced at her cleavage in confusion. Then she put her hand in her bra and pulled out a twenty. "Huh," she said. "Where did that come from?" Her look of magical amazement didn't match her husband's angry face. Again, I left as fast as I could.

Fast forward to adulthood. I always thought dancing on coffee tables and donning lampshades was just in the movies. Nope. People go nuts at New Year's. The challenge is in having fun, but not so much that you're all anybody can talk about for weeks afterward. Mr. and Mrs. 'Anderson' were (are) a lovely, sophisticated couple. Mr. Anderson had a devilish side. One New Year's Eve, the party host convinced him to participate in the stroke of midnight presentation. No one but the two of them knew.

The ball dropped, Auld Lang Syne began to play, and Mrs. Anderson stood in the middle of the exuberant kissing crowd wondering where on earth her husband was. All eyes turned to a commotion at the top of the grand staircase. Father Time (the host in a white robe and long gray beard) and Baby New Year descended the stairs. To Mrs. Anderson's horror, her pot-bellied and hairy husband was Baby New Year. Dressed in nothing but black socks and shoes—the better to show off his bow-legs and knobby knees, a white towel wrapped like a diaper, top hat, and a red satin sash, Mr. Anderson puffed on a cigar, grinning ear to ear, as he made his way to the ground floor. We, the crowd, thought it was great. Hilarious. Mrs. Anderson didn't speak to him for a month.

Probably the weirdest display of the dissolving of the sanity filter happened a few years ago. Fifty or so people, dressed in their finest, had apparently had imbibed enough that forming a raucous conga line around the swimming pool seemed like a nifty idea. Wearing paper hats and sequined tiaras, hoisting drink glasses in one hand while grasping the body in front of them with the other, they staggered and kicked their way around the chaises—to (here's the unbelievable part) Tom Jones' *She's A Lady*. And yes, right about the third time around the pool, several people lost their footing and splashed in, dragging others with them.

All in all, one of the best New Year's parties I've been to.

A CLEAN START

I love writing about January. It's a new year. An arbitrary date that really means nothing, yet it symbolizes a fresh beginning. The chance for everything to be *washed* clean, metaphorically speaking. We've been doing silly things in honor of the New Year, ever since we invented calendars. Why should 2017 be any different? In honor of our being washed clean, starting anew, etc., let's see how many of our planetary roommates celebrate.

First up—Throwing stuff away. In theory, I can see how getting rid of the old to make room for the new became a tradition. Somehow, the Italians embraced the idea a little too fervently, though, and began tossing old furniture out windows. One would imagine copious amounts of wine had something to do with it. Think about it. Okay, Maria and Antonio decide new chairs are in order. They want to get rid of the old nasty ones with the two-hundred-years' worth of wear—sweat, wine, and *god-knows-what-that-is* stains from untold numbers of folks. Yeah, that would skeeve me out, too. Most people would simply carry them out the door. For some reason, on that particular New Year's Eve, Maria and Antonio thought, *Hey, let's toss them from an upstairs window instead. With any luck, we'll accidentally hit that annoying Fabrizio who's been soused and camped out on the sidewalk for two days.* Maybe they eliminated poor old Fabrizio, then all the neighbors agree it was a brilliant *accident?* And it caught on. That's the best I can come up with. Honestly.

Not to be outdone, the South Africans apparently loved the Italian thing, so they go one better and earn bonus execution points for throwing old appliances out the windows. Do *not* get drunk and loiter under windows in Johannesburg, people.

Continuing with the destruction of property (and possibly people), the good citizens of Denmark have a strange belief that throwing old dishes at their friends' front doors will bring luck. To whom, I'm not sure. But offhand, if I woke up on New Year's Day with shattered china littering my stoop and cut marks in my door's paint job, I'd be ticked off, but good.

Thailand has a bizarre way of cleansing for the New Year. They throw buckets of water on anyone, anywhere. Water pistols the size of machine guns and hoses are also employed. And no one is safe. Cars driving by with open windows? Target. Old ladies ambling by on the sidewalk? Target. You're getting doused whether you like it or not. But the next part is the real puzzle. Step two is flinging talc at you until you look like you crawled through a white mud bog. How *did* this start?

In many countries, celebrants visit graveyards. Honoring ancestors. This, I understand. But some carry it too far and actually spend the night sleeping on the graves. I suppose if you've never seen a horror flick, you wouldn't be creeped out by this, but for the rest of us? That would be a big, resounding *hell, no*. One weird moan from a distant animal in the night, and I'd scramble over anything or anyone in my path. I'm pretty sure my ancestors wouldn't approve of my accidentally crunching someone's hand, foot, or head as I escaped.

Now we come to wardrobe choices. Especially in the unmentionables department. Yellow undies are all the rage in Venezuela to bring luck. Red underpants are supposed to bring romantic love in the New Year. And green undies will lead to financial fortune. This might explain quite a bit in my life. I'm not sure I've ever owned private garments in any of those colors. So *that's* what I've been doing wrong. Well, I'm correcting that immediately and will report back to you with my scientific results.

POTPOURRI
FOR $200

THE FUTURE IS SWIFT

Yikes. The end of another year.

They say time flies faster the older we get. Recently, in my day job as a decorative painter, I had a new client who is ninety-nine years old. She's not only got all her marbles, but she's still knocking some others out of the playing circle. She's got game. Had a hip replacement at ninety-six and is planning to redo every room in her condo. Guess she's expecting to be here awhile yet.

I got me to thinking—which, granted, isn't always my best move—what will I be like when I'm ninety-nine? I decided to interview the *me* of the future. It is now 2056.

MN (Me Now): Tell, me, Victoria, what's the secret to your longevity? And may I say you don't look a day over eighty-five?
MA99 (Me at 99): Stretching, dark chocolate, and gin. Not necessarily in that order.
MN: What is your deepest regret?
MA99: None of your blessed business.
MN: I beg to differ, considering, you know, you're *me*.
MA99: You can't handle the truth. Next question.
MN: What, in your opinion, is the greatest innovation in the forty-one years since 2015?
MA99: Have you learned nothing from that critique group of yours? Saying 'in your opinion' is redundant. Of course it's my opinion, what else would it be?

MN: Wow. When did I get so cranky?

MA99: According to your surviving siblings, you came out of the womb being cranky.

MN: Let's move on. Best innovation?

MA99: It's a toss-up between the non-polluting, self-powering, land and water levitation vehicles or the silent leaf blower.

MN: OMG?! Leaf blowers are silent in the future?

MA99 (Rolls her eyes): I was making a false equivalency. The blowers are small potatoes next to the LEVs. That's what we call 'em now—LEVs. They run on either solar panels or water vapor in the air, whichever there is more of at the moment.

MN: So, when my neighbor decides to do his yardwork at 8:00 AM on Sunday morning, the blower's not going to wake me up anymore? That's awesome.

MA99: The LEVs have no tires. No more flats. And anybody can operate one safely, even if they've been drinking, or are on meds, or are high on pot.

MN: What year are the silent blowers invented in? How long do I have to wait?

MA99: I really can't believe you are me. LEVs have solved all road problems. No more accidents. No more road rage. No more DUIs. It's miraculous.

MN: Wait. Are you saying that smoking pot is legal everywhere now? Er, then?

MA99: Sure. But nobody smokes it anymore. It's in pill form over the counter. Like aspirin was—

MN: Was?

MA99: Stop interrupting. I could croak any second. Overdoing alcohol or drugs isn't cool anymore. Only losers and morons do it.

MN: How'd *that* happen?

MA99: The Swift Administration twenty years ago. She made it her top priority.

MN: She? We finally have a woman president?

MA99: They've all been women since. Taylor was the first.

MN: Taylor Swift? Is POTUS?

MA99: Was. Two terms. Both huge landslide victories, too. We were all Swifties then.

MN: Who is the President in 2056?

MA99: Look in the mirror.

MN (In genuine shock.): I am? Seriously? But I've never even run for city council.

MA99: No, of course you're not, dummy. You're ninety-nine. I was just having some fun with you. Dear God, how did I make it to this age? You're so gullible. No wonder no one took me seriously. It's Malia Obama.

MN (Feeling deflated.): Oh. Well, sure. Please tell me that the magic cars—the LEVs—are at least powered by the flux capacitor from *Back to the Future*.

MA99: No.

MN: Rats. Flux capacitor is so much fun to say. What's the best thing about living in the future?

MA99: Silent leaf blowers.

MN: I knew it!

FLOWERY DELUSIONS

In my mind, I've been a marvelous gardener for years. But on occasion, reality lobs a moldy tomato at the fantasy.

My mother kept impressive flower and vegetable gardens in our yard in New Jersey. I spent many hours turning soil and weeding. Not because I was a dutiful child, but because Mom, who had six kids, was a wiz at accomplishing multiple objectives with one act. When we misbehaved, she didn't confine us to our rooms. No, Mom gave us choices. Clean the bathroom or work in the yard. I always chose the outdoor work. (My sister misbehaved enough to draw the hard labor—shoveling dirt into the huge crater that appeared behind the house one morning—a story for another day.) Anyway, by the time I left New Jersey, I thought I knew a thing or two about successful gardening.

My serious delusions began when I moved to Hawaii. New Jersey and Hawaii have nutrient-rich soil in common. In Jersey, the dirt was a natural dark chocolate brown. Loamy. Easy to turn. You can't find better tomatoes or corn than what's grown in Jersey. Their taste is ambrosial. In Hawaii, the soil is volcanic. It's red and packed with everything plants need to thrive. There's a reason Hawaiian pineapples are by far the best in the world.

Early on in my Hawaii experience, I visited friends on the North Shore. They'd just had a massive tree trimmed. It looked like they'd overdone it. The drastic cut left hacked pathetic limbs attached to the trunk. The poor thing would surely croak and go to the big forest in the sky. Concerned, I asked how long, if ever, the tree would take to recover. The man laughed and said, "Oh, about fifteen minutes."

During my twelve years on Oahu, I lived three times in houses with yards. In each, I'd tend what was there and plant new. In Kaimuki, the property had a huge white plumeria tree. To plant another, you cut a small branch, stuck it in the ground, and in no time at all, a tiny tree sprouted more branches, leaves, and flowers. No root toner, no fussing with gradual pot sizes.

Everything planted there flourishes. The bougainvillea went bananas in Hawaii. Every other Saturday, I'd prune back at least three feet of branch growth. The flowers never stopped coming. No matter what I did to them, they always provided a riot of colors. My gosh, I was good. Such a green thumb.

Then I moved to Atlanta, Georgia. They, too, had red soil. But it was hard-packed clay. With almost no nutrients. That didn't discourage *me*, the super-able-to grow-anything-pro.

Home gardening is a huge industry in Atlanta. Garden clubs with coveted memberships abound. A very popular magazine in the south featured tips and stunning photos of area gardens every month. I bought a subscription and devoured the info in each issue. Soon, I knew what to do about the soil conditions. You had to *amend* the clay. So I did. I broke my back turning that thick, heavy, sticky clay. I added the prescribed amounts of top-soil, peat, and sand. Threw in bone meal. Iron-rake-mixed it until my blisters under the leather work gloves exploded, and I couldn't take it anymore.

I envisioned the results. There would be gorgeous drifts of orange day-lilies, purple irises, and golden-ochre yarrow. Amazing shrubs with glossy dark-green leaves and aromatic white blossoms. Brilliant pink clematis vines enveloping my mail box post. My neighbors would ooh and ahh, and bestow compliments.

And I wanted fresh tomatoes in the summer. In the back yard, I prepared a bed with everything a tomato could want. The perfect dirt. I bought tiny tomato seedlings and lovingly placed them into their sanctuary. An article in the magazine suggested hanging red Christmas balls from the plants as soon as they were strong enough to support them, as a deterrent to birds. If they learned the red things weren't food, they'd leave the real tomatoes alone. I suppose I was the only person who read that article, because my family and all my neighbors thought it was hilarious.

By the end of the season, my imagined cascades of flowers were sad bedraggled spikes with an occasional bloom under attack by insects. The green shrub leaves looked dull and brown on the edges, their flowers sparse. My clematis seemed to limp up the mailbox post.

Talk about disappointing. I'd tried so hard to do everything the right way. I'd fertilized with the right types in the right amounts. I'd watered at the right times. I'd pruned and pinched. I'd even talked to my plants.

And my tomatoes? Southern birds were smarter than whoever wrote that stupid article. They never fell for the Christmas ball ruse, waited for the *real* red tomatoes, then had themselves a smorgasbord. I swear one crow actually shot me an eye-roll from his perch on the tomato cage. The neighbor's cat had a blast with his new toys, though. He batted those ornaments for hours on end, which did help with the bird problem, but not enough. My sons still tease me about it.

We had no fresh tomato slices to layer with buffalo mozzarella and balsamic vinegar. No BLT's. No homemade sauce for the freezer. It was so disheartening. How could this happen to me, the *super gardener*? I had to admit I wasn't such a horticultural genius after all.

Now, fifteen years later, I'm blissfully blind to reality again. I gaze out at my newly acquired property in South Florida, and all I see are the beautiful possibilities. A lush, thick green lawn. Gardenias overflowing with showy flowers. Night-blooming jasmine vines. My neighbors see brown crunchy grass, meager shrubs, and some stumps left from Wilma. "Don't worry," I tell them. "Wait 'til you see it this time next year."

ESCAPE FROM HONOLULU

Living on Oahu made it difficult to keep a straight face when I said I needed a break. No one back on the mainland had any sympathy when I explained I hadn't had time off in over fifteen months. Even my mother scoffed.

Where do you go for a respite when you live in paradise? I sunburned on the most beautiful beaches in the world every weekend. I'd chugged up the thousand thigh-burning steps to Diamond Head, cried at the Arizona Memorial, fell in love with red feathers at the Bishop Museum, and nearly drowned body surfing at Makapuu. Those were regular things to do on an average Saturday or Sunday.

So, when my sister in San Francisco decreed she would spend her precious vacation time with me, I had to take the time off, and I needed a plan. Island hopping in the off-season presented the most economical option. I'd been to several outer islands, but not Kauai. When Susan (name changed to protect my ever-taunting older sister) arrived, we headed straight for the inter-island terminal and our puddle jumper of a prop plane.

Susan is a talented natural instigator. As a child, she perfected the art of creating a diversion—doing something to provoke trouble or hilarity, then slipping away undetected, leaving the rest of us to suffer my mother's wrath. Such as the time during dinner she yelled, "Kohoutek!", and pointed out the window. It was 1973, and the comet was big news. While the family strained to see a flash in the sky, she dumped the remainders of her peas and mashed potatoes into my brother's and my milk glasses. Her plate empty, she excused herself and escaped to her room. That is one nasty surprise when you go to finish your milk. Mom punished my brother and me for wasting food.

On Kauai, our first stop the next day was a park on a wind-swept cliff. A few weather beaten, but picturesque, trees grew from the rocks on the cliff. The scene looked like a Japanese wood cut print come to life. We took a few pictures, then Susan declared that a photo with a person in it would better show the scale and magnificence of the scene.

"Go sit under that tree," she said. It's important you understand the dynamics of our relationship. We'd never had one. In school, she was cool, and I was a super-nerd. She ignored me most the time, and when she had paid me any mind it was to humiliate me in front of her cool friends. The fact she wanted to come to Hawaii and spend time with me now blew me away. Of course, if I'd lived in North Dakota, I doubt she'd have gone there.

Being the archetypical younger sibling desperate for acceptance and love, I overrode my better instincts and obeyed her. I stepped past the low railing meant to keep the stupid from venturing too close to the edge, then eased my way downslope to the tree. The sheer drop of the rocky cliff into equally rocky waters about two hundred feet below came into view, and the bitter taste of bile in my mouth made me latch on to the first tree available, not the one she'd indicated. Too bad. It was this tree or no tree. I would only go so far, even for her approval.

I sat and held the tree's gnarled trunk with one hand, waving the other at the camera. Behind me the slope had ten feet of rocky dirt, then the drop-off. She snapped the picture. It was much trickier trying to ascend. My foot slipped on some loose gravel, my feet shot out backward, and I wound up on my stomach seeing my life flash before me as I did a slow slide toward impending doom. My hands scrabbled at pebbles and tufts of grass. Lady luck, however, loves me. My foot hit the base of the tree she'd wanted me to pose by to begin with, and it stopped my slide. Several Mai-Tais later, we decided it was funny.

Kauai's Waimea Canyon is called the Grand Canyon of the Pacific. Susan and I went there the next day and spent some time taking in the view. It was a peaceful morning—sunny, light trade winds, birds chirping their serenity.

The squeal of air-brakes sounded. A charter bus pulled up, parked, and opened its doors. Another bus followed. Japanese tourists spilled out their doors like salmon massing upstream. The de rigueur outfit for touristing Japanese back then *did* consist of aloha shirts from Hilo Hattie's, plaid shorts, either black nylon knee socks or tall white athletic socks and leather sandals, expensive cameras hanging from their necks, and Pan-Am bags on their shoulders. In 1982, Pan-Am still existed.

Ahh, stereotypes develop from truth. I actually love the Japanese. They're good people. But I'd seen a gazillion busses loaded with Japanese tourists all over Oahu and knew what to expect. They're enthusiastic to the point of hysteria. Smiling, happy, and loud. Yes, the people we see in movies as quiet and deferential become boisterous and giddy while on holiday. I'd been caught in a crowd or three of them in Waikiki and it's LOUD.

The swarm moved to the outlook edge, all maneuvering for the best camera angles. It hit me that it was quiet. Just as quiet as it had been before. How odd. Like someone had pulled the sound plug. This huge crowd of tourists hadn't uttered a peep. They signed with their hands at a furious pace. They were deaf.

One man noticed Susan's light-brown hair and handed his camera to a friend to take his picture with her. Then they switched. Then a couple did the same. Susan—the traitor—lost patience and pointed to me across the clearing. I had waist-length blond hair. The Japanese saw me and scrambled my way. Apparently, blonde hair was a huge curiosity to them. Within a few minutes, I'd been jostled back and forth to every person from those busses. They snapped my picture, shook my hand, some touched my hair. All while flashing rapid hand signals to one another. It was dizzying. Susan, now left alone, doubled over with laughter. Some of the tourists bowed as a thank you. Smiling, I bowed back. Then in an instant, the chaotic whirl ended. They were back on the busses and headed down the highway, leaving me feeling like I'd survived a tornado of humanity.

I have pictures buried somewhere of that trip to Kauai. Now, many Mai-Tais later, I realize my sister's devilish streak gave me lots of good stories, and what didn't kill me made me a more entertaining dinner guest.

THE AFTERGLOW

Some years, January seems to stretch out in front of you as a bleak, interminable number of days where life is lackluster and a bit of a grind. Why are some Januarys worse than others? My uber-professional (meaning it sounds reasonable to me) research has resulted in the following—the dismal, life-is-boring factor of any given January is directly proportional to the number of social occasions one attended during the preceding holiday blitz period.

The more parties you attend, the more socializing you do, the faster the exuberant whirl takes you—the more the days afterward seem duller than working a jigsaw puzzle at the old folks home (although my mom swears the Charles Wysocki ones are quite challenging). The real-life post party afterglow, the *denouement*, is somewhat less than what's illustrated in the movies, where after the company has left and the kids are back in school, our heroine looks lovingly at the holiday remains, gently touches the discarded decorations, her dreamy eyes revealing the wonder of life as she hugs herself and imagines what lies ahead in her exciting new year.

No one I've ever met does that. Instead there's an overwhelming amount of chores to attend to. But first, there's the headache from over-indulging. Your head feels like a Macy's parade balloon. You're taking ibuprofen and drinking ginseng tea. Your skinny jeans don't fit because somehow an extra five pounds magically glued themselves to your behind, so you're wearing baggy sweatpants. By the way, our heroine mentioned above didn't gain an ounce during her holidays, even though we saw her dumping extra gravy on her plate, eating pie, and drinking egg nog. On the bright side, eating all the wrong foods has made your skin look like it did in high school (break outs). Everyone knows that having pimples and wrinkles at the same time is very sexy.

Then there's the mess. Decorations need to be boxed and stored. Sparkling confetti glitters from the strangest places, like in the lampshade folds and in the bathroom magazine basket. Pine needles have worked themselves into every minute crevasse of the house. Wax from sputtering, drippy candles covers menorahs, candlesticks, and table tops. Gummy candies are imbedded in the carpet fibers. Sweet potatoes are ground into the tile grout. Crusty mashed potatoes, gravy, and pie remains dot the upholstery, and red wine spills now show up as dark spots on the draperies, tablecloth, and the walls.

Of course, I've only experienced this from the viewpoint of an average person. I love the holidays, and cooking, and entertaining. While the season's churning, I turn a blind eye to the eventual work it all causes. But I realize for the wealthier among us, it's probably a very different experience. They probably use caterers who clean up afterward. They hire decorators to put up and take down the decorations. Their maids do the carpet spotting and tile scrubbing after every gathering. What would that be like? Chances are their jeans get just as tight, though. Or maybe the personal trainer is able to keep them on track through the whole season. That would be an entirely amazing and wonderful way to sail effortlessly along the holiday river of fun. I should have listened to my mother. She told me it was just as easy to fall in love with a rich man as a poor one. In the meantime, I'll keep buying lottery tickets.

Back in the real world, the dog barfs, the kids spill, and there's no servant to call. Is it any wonder we scan the debris trail and want to hibernate, hoping that when we wake up, someone else has noticed the things that need doing and has done them? Now, I have heard of women who have families like that. Their husbands and children actually *see* what's needed. But most of the women I know, and have known, have spousal units that can live in the after-holiday disarray, and it will not register that they're sitting on dried food remnants.

I think this may be why the Young Adult fantasy novels have become so popular with adult women. We want to believe in magical beings. We *need* to believe in them. Curling up with a book about too-good-to-be-true heroes while munching on leftover M&Ms in our sweat pants is way more appealing than facing up to the bleak tasks of January.

BEING A LOCAL AUTHOR

South Florida is known for all sorts of things. Alligators. Big snakes. Small dogs in purses. Canals riddled with guns, knives, and cars. Con men headquarters. And lots of very entertaining other people.

Some of those people are writers. Authors like me. I know quite a few of them. They are dedicated. Serious. This is their story . . .

Yeah, okay. I can't tell their stories. I can only tell mine. As a fourteen-year member of Mystery Writers of America, I've gone from a newbie who didn't know what she didn't know to a respected, well-reviewed author. And along the way, I've met some of the biggest names in the book world. But before I get to the blatant and gratuitous name-dropping portion of my piece, I must tell you about the local authors—what's it's like to be one and know plenty more.

What happens when you start? A whole lot of dancing, as it turns out. When I began writing novels, I was mystified by my family's reaction. Not one of them (and I have a large family) seemed all that interested, and they avoided my attempts to get them to read some of my work. Twisted themselves into verbal pretzels to dodge my pathetic pleas for feedback. I later found out from my sister that they were sure my writing would be horrible, and they wouldn't know what to say to me. Just so happens their feedback wouldn't have been worth much anyway—as I found out later.

Several of my friends, however, were happy to read my stuff. They gave me glowing remarks. Practically cooing their *Oh my God, this is SOOO good. How did you do that?*

Except my writing wasn't sooo good. It *was* pretty darned awful in the beginning. I learned this undeniable and humiliating fact at my first writers' conference, SleuthFest. After sitting in on several workshops and panels, I skulked away hoping no one would notice that my superior look of confidence (I'd been a voracious reader since Dick & Jane had seduced me, so of course—*of course!* I knew how to write fiction.) had withered to an apologetic grin.

And so I discovered that the only way (for me) to get valuable feedback and learn the craft of writing was to be around other writers. My luckiest break was becoming serious about it in South Florida. It's a veritable hotbed of writers. They're everywhere. Joining Mystery Writers was a lucky move because, and I did not know this, mystery writers in general are the most accepting, paying it forward, encouraging, and helpful in the publishing world.

The late, great, *NY Times* bestselling author Barbara Parker was active in the group. The year after I joined, the Florida Chapter decided to do a progressive novel. A spoof noir called *Naked Came the Flamingo*. Barbara Parker was one of the editors, and the novella got its kickoff chapter from another bestseller, Elaine Viets. The PJ Parrish (also *NY Times* bestsellers) team wrote the ending chapter, and everything in between was written by us newbies. It was a lot like herding cats, I'm told. One author wrote a chapter, then passed the whole thing to the next author to write the following chapter. It got slap-me-silly-crazy in a good way, and it was a wonderful experience getting to know the other writers.

Another incredible advantage the local South Florida writer has is the overflowing fruit basket of nut jobs who gravitate here. It's Mecca for the mentally unbalanced. They and their antics supply more material than we can use in a lifetime. Stunts so stupid and bizarro, if we made them up, people would accuse us of stooping to the ridiculous to attract attention. Seriously—a naked man eating the face of another on the side of the freeway? A man shot his roommate for forgetting to buy toilet paper? That's absolute gold. In fact, I've had to modify real events to fit into my books, because I just knew I'd get emails telling me how *that could never happen.* Even though *that* is exactly what happened. Maybe they don't obsess over the local news coverage like we do.

By actively participating and volunteering in my writers' group, I've met some of the biggest names in the industry. Had actual conversations and/or shared a drink at the bar with them. (Yup. Here comes the blatant name-dropping.) Janet Evanovich. Linda Fairstein. Lisa Scottoline. Michael Connelly. David Morrell. Dennis Lehane. Lee Child. In fact, Lee Child went to dinner with me and three of my friends near the Deerfield Pier and picked up the whole check. Super nice guy. I've met Robert Crais, Robert B. Parker, Paul

Levine, Dave Barry, James Patterson, Laura Lippman, Charlaine Harris, Brad Meltzer, Jeffrey Deaver, and Jeff Lindsay.

I think the most rewarding aspect of being a local writer, though, is when people do read my books, they feel comfortable contacting me to tell me they liked them. And they don't act half as surprised the writing's any good as my family did. My mother was shocked. *But, honey, I didn't know it was a REAL book. It was so good!* This from the woman who, in the beginning, told me I should write children's books instead—while practically patting me on the head. Now, she's my biggest fan and tells everyone to buy my books. Only took fourteen years.

WHAT'S BUGGING ME?

I lived in the bug haven of the world, Hawaii, for twelve years. Insects had no seasons. They thrived all year long. And I had many an escapade trying to eradicate the little devils—or at least lure them elsewhere.

Lately, I've noticed that South Florida's bug problem is becoming more and more like the South Pacific's. They don't seem to want to be reverse snowbirds and go away for the winter anymore, and they have definitely adopted the in-your-face attitude of their tropical Pacific cousins.

It makes me wonder if the Hawaiian four-inch cockroaches and seven-inch centipedes decided they missed me, packed tiny suitcases, and stowed away on a cargo ship bound for the Atlantic. Maybe a bad case of Rock Fever finally got to them. That's the label we slapped on someone when they just couldn't take being on an isolated island anymore. It usually happened to the kind of person who liked long car trips. The type who drives straight from Michigan to Florida and sits at the bar on the beach in a flowered shirt animatedly bragging about the trip's gas mileage a half hour after arriving, instead of lying comatose on his hotel bed like a normal person. For happy islanders like me, the three-hour drive around Oahu was exhausting, more than enough car time, and we still needed the naps afterward.

Back to my insect buddies. The cockroaches in Hawaii,

as big as they are, can actually fly. One day, I cornered a fat specimen in my kitchen. Had a slipper (what Hawaiians call flip-flops—pronounced slee-pah) raised and at the ready in my right hand, edging step-by-step closer to him. He was three, maybe three and a half, inches, poised mid-way up the wall on my blue and white checked wallpaper, antennae twitching, staring me down. Daring me to confront him. When I got to within a few feet, the twitching stopped. His wings spread, and he catapulted himself off the wall and straight toward my face. I shrieked, dropped the slipper, and ducked. I swear I heard eensy peals of laughter as he scurried away into a crevice under the baseboard. Maybe he donned a flowered shirt and bellied up to the bug bar to brag about his long journey and scaring me.

They have what we called pineapple bugs in Hawaii. They look like miniature beetles—black, about half the size of a lady bug. Whenever a crop of pineapple was harvested, the growers burned the remnants of the plants to ready the field for the next crop. The smell was divine, like everyone baked a pineapple upside-down cake at the same time. Unfortunately, this produced an incalculable number of whisper-thin black cinders that floated on the air for miles—affectionately known as Hawaiian snow. There was no brushing them off. The moment you touched them, they disintegrated into black dust that stained all fabrics. The second consequence of the field burning was the pineapple bugs apparently didn't care for their homes being torched. They flew en masse toward anything that smelled sweet.

One evening, I was preparing dinner—pork chops with an orange sauce with red and yellow bell peppers. About halfway through cooking, I noticed a little black bug flying around the kitchen and swatted it with a towel. Then there was another. And another, etc., until I looked at the window over the kitchen sink. It was like an Alfred Hitchcock movie. Swarms, literally thousands, of the bugs covered the window screen like I'd pulled a pulsating black shade over it. They were wiggling their way past the screen edges, desperate to get in. Streams of them making it inside. It was a nightmare Alfred would have appreciated. Well, simply close the window, you say? Um. There was no window. Just the screen. Someday, I'll describe that old 1930s sugar plantation single-walled house. That's a column all by itself.

This brings us back to South Florida, where the bugs are keeping up with the Hawaiians lately. My screen cage seems to be an irresistible place for a real diversity of pests. They manage to find and squeeze through the most minute gap or hole, yet none of them ever show any aptitude in finding the clearly-marked exit signs. There are geckos and regular lizards. Ants, bag worms, and an amazing array of spiders. I even had a long black snake hiding in the post holes for the pool's baby fence, which totally creeped me out. Recently, I saw a rather large (for Florida) cockroach in my cage. He had to be a brave one, because usually the lizards eat roaches. But this guy (I'm sorry. I know it could have been female, but I don't know how to differentiate them.) sat sunning himself on the pool railing, where a gecko usually holds court. The gecko was across the way, on the pile of foam noodles, looking a bit put out.

Now this, to me, signifies something has changed big time in insect dynamics here. Why wasn't the gecko stalking the roach? Why was the bug out in broad sunlight? I thought they were supposed to lurk in dark corners. It looked like the roach was lording over the gecko. This is why I think the bravado gene of the Hawaiian cockroach has somehow been introduced into the Florida roaches. Either that, or I've got a blind gecko in residence. But he wasn't wearing dark glasses, so . . .

Incredibly, a day later, while sitting by my pool, I realized a swarm of little black bugs were climbing up and down the screen, outside, near the door. There were so many of them, it reminded me of the pineapple bug night. So I took a closer look. The bustling highway of bugs acted like ants, the way they orchestrated their work. They were moving something downward, toward the cracked place in the dirt where their legions were emanating from, and returning to. And lo and behold, what were they laboring so hard to shuffle along? A cockroach— one that looked very much like the sun-god from the day before. I scanned the area, half expecting that gecko to be nearby with a self-satisfied smirk on his face. Then I called my exterminator man. Sorry, PETA, but I don't want to be afraid of making pork chops ever again.

SOMETHING 'BOUT A BOAT
(With apologies to Jimmy Buffett)

People who own boats are different than you and me. Doesn't matter if it's a mega-yacht or a rowboat. Something invades their brains during boat ownership. Something I call the *frippery slope*. An insistent and annoying (to the rest of us) certitude idles its way into their psyche and whispers to them—much like the Greek sirens calling Jason—*You are now the master of the seas. You are now much, much better, way smarter, and more worldly than any land-based citizens.* Of course, they will never admit this phenomenon exists. But we know.

I have several friends who are serious *boat people*. Not the kind who came over from Cuba during the Mariel boatlift in 1980, although I'm sure they also have many—albeit tragic—stories. No, my boat people are the ones who make you feel like a dork of the greatest magnitude for asking where the bathroom is. They'll roll their eyes so far up their irises disappear, chortle amongst themselves, then—quite condescendingly—say, "You'll find the *head* down the companionway, just past the galley." Well, excuse me for not speaking *boat*.

We—the losers-who-don't-own-a-boat—don't really care whether we learn the terms or use them properly. Or use them at all. Ever. That's a good thing, too. Because, apparently, one of the requisite customs seems to be when a boat person hosts a landlubber is—get them as drunk as possible—as soon as possible—and do it as often as possible. This makes the retention of any nautically-correct terms doubtful at best. Indeed, I believe it is a purposeful part of a vicious cycle. Visit. Become familiar with boat terms. Consume large quantities of alcohol. Forget all boat terms. And repeat as necessary. This ensures your boat friends will always have someone to make fun of. It also ensures I will always have a way to irk the heck out of them. Which I do enjoy tremendously.

Despite their disdain for my non-boat-person status, they tolerate my presence from time to time and share their adventurous tales. Some have sailed the world. Others have braved only the wild and crazy Intracoastal Waterway. But if they own a boat and know the buzz words, they are in the club and entitled to tell stories.

How big the fish really was before it snapped the line is a time-honored one—usually told with the wife pantomiming something much smaller behind the guy. Dolphins playfully following or swimming alongside the boat seems amazingly common. Whales in the distance, at first delighting everyone, then coming too close and causing abject terror that they might tip the boat. Those encounters make !AMAZING! YouTube videos.

Strange global wanderers abound, too. All the boat people who explore other seas have encountered folks who clearly aren't . . . mainstream. An old man, fished out of the Pacific, who claimed he was out for a swim and got towed by a turtle into the middle of nowhere. A lady psychic in Belize who claimed she knew where a boat's previous owners—slain onboard no less—were buried. That freaked out the current owners of said boat, since they had zero clue that anything untoward had happened. They sold the boat as soon as they returned to Florida. No, I'm not allowed to divulge the craft's name. A helpful note, though—if you own a boat with a name that rhymes with *nut*—you might want to skip the trip to Belize. There was a young man hired on as a cabin boy. (I most likely got the nautical term for indentured servant wrong.) He was cute and polite and dabbled in voodoo. Unfortunately, he had no power to control the *spirits* he called upon and claimed they alone were responsible for the owner's daughter's obvious pregnancy. It wasn't him.

What percentage of these tales are true, exaggeration, or outright lies, I can only guess. The comedy of physical errors, however, are well documented. The US Coast Guard reports that South Florida leads the nation in boating accidents. Quite shocking, I know. The most common accidents are collisions with other boats and collisions with fixed objects—like concrete bridge pilings. Those things can just jump right into your path, can't they? A huge percentage of groundings happen, too. I suppose these are the dangers when way too much partying happens and everybody on board passes out? Thank God my boating friends, for all their snooty-hootyness, take driving the darn things seriously.

An intriguing counterpoint to my *frippery slope* syndrome is if the boat owners become non-boat owners again, the sirens apparently stop speaking to them. Within a few months, they are almost normal. They do manage to retain the wordage, but quit the habit of framing every blasted conversation around something nautical. I like that because then I no longer wear the dork mantle for asking where the bathroom is.

THE RUSSIANS ARE COMING

They're wonderfully evil villains in movies. They're young (ish). They're rich beyond comprehension. Their kids are spoiled and invariably wear scary black boots. Technically, however, Russian oligarchs no longer exist.

Oh, there are plenty of Russian billionaires gallivanting around the globe, money spilling out of their pockets, but oligarch-ery is kaput in Moscow, thanks to Vladimir Putin. Which is somewhat amazing, considering the oligarchs from Yeltsin's days are the very men who hand-picked Putin.

But Putin apparently is loyalty-challenged and cracked down on the interfering billionaires who were, in essence, running the country. He made them offers they couldn't refuse—get out of politics and sell much of their holdings back to the government at rock bottom prices. A foolish few did refuse. One had all his businesses confiscated by the state. Another did too, but also went to jail. Putin's finding ways to grab much of their fortunes, and they are *not* happy about it.

Don't waste empathy on them. They still have more money than you and I dare to dream about. But when they're unhappy, they go shopping. See? They're just like you and me. Hoping to fill any gaping chasm of despair or emptiness with things. The difference is you won't see them on a hoarders' show with living rooms piled to the ceiling with unworn clothing or shoes, cheapo knick-knacks, broken furniture and gadgets, and a hundred scrawny cats. No, they're buying sports teams, mega-yachts, tech companies, and media. *Their* cats are tigers on gold leashes. Mostly, though, it's property. Lots of property. The most expensive, especially in London and New York. Russian billionaires and their ridiculously attractive offspring are snapping up the best in the west. The Russian economy isn't so terrific. Putin's taken whatever he wanted from them in the past, so they have to move it as fast as they can without ticking him off.

Dmitry Rybolovlev's daughter bought the priciest apartment in Manhattan, while still in college. Over sixty-seven-hundred square feet for 88 million. Then she needed a refuge—away from the pesky paparazzi. So she bought the island of Skorpios. If that sounds familiar, it should. That's where Jackie Kennedy married Aristotle Onassis, for crying out loud. This rich kid is setting herself up to be a perfect Bond villain. I mean, please, Ekaterina (that's her name), try to look at it from our perspective. At least skip the boots. You're a walking caricature.

Andrey Goncharenko bought the UK's most expensive home, in London for 205 million, then expanded the basement-level indoor swimming pool, added a sauna, steam room, a gym, a beauty salon, yoga studio, two massage rooms, a cinema, wine cellar, and a games room. That way, when he spends a few days a year there, he won't have the hassle of having his chauffer drive him somewhere. Won't have to interact with any non-billionaire peons, either. That is so tiresome, isn't it?

For the rich in Russia who *must* (poor dears) travel amongst the masses, they buy, and are driven in ambulances, sirens blaring, to get around traffic jams.

Roman Abramovich had special lasers installed on his 111 million-dollar yacht—to stop intrusive paparazzi. They scan around the ship for any CCD from a camera—no clue what the heck that is—then fire a bolt of light that zaps the photo being taken.

If this makes you envious, don't be. Russian men have horrible life-expectancy—sixty-four being average, making the Beatles' famous question a moot point. Worse, one in four kick before their double-nickel birthday. The average Russian drinks fifteen half-liters of alcohol a week, not including beer. Beer isn't considered alcohol. They have terrible drinking water, tastes like jet-fuel, I'm told. Sixty-percent smoke. There is no word for 'fun' in Russian. The constant stress of protecting their money and their privacy can't be helping. And McDonalds serves something called McShrimp nowhere else but there.

I'd rather live to one-hundred, and no amount of money could make me eat those shrimp.

MARCH MADNESS

March is a busy month. There's the end of Mardi Gras—the celebration of all things debauchable—to prepare (of course) for the remembrance of a certain Biblical figure who abhorred debauchery. Then the Spring Equinox inspires lunatics all over the globe to spout silly theories and decrees about impending doom and invaders from spectral worlds. Personally, it's one of my preferred times of year, because there's *always* new crazy-people stories emerging from it. My favorite was the guy who made his wife sleep in a tree for a week, believing the escaping spirits would ravage her at night and forget all about ruining his newly planted crops.

There's World Water Day and World Kidney Day. Not sure what they're all about, but it sounds like a World Bean Soup Day ought to be next. Followed by Should Have Taken Beano Day.

March 17th means beer and rivers turn shamrock green, people wear green, and since the St. Patrick's Day revelers give the Mardi Gras-ers a true run for the party animal designation, eventually many celebrants' faces turn a sickly green. Beer consumption must be the reason people think they love St. Patrick. Despite the fact that the *snakes* he supposedly drove out of Ireland were, in fact, the Druid priests, and many historic artifacts and sites were destroyed by the Catholic Church, St. Patrick is heralded as a favorite saint among the Irish. Ask any drinker on a bar stool here in America why they're guzzling green beer and you'll get a dazed smile, a shrug, and a kiss because *one* of you is likely to have some Irish blood.

Pi Day is March 14th. Get it? 3.14? Those of you who flashed on blueberry, apple, and coconut cream pies may be excused if you promise to watch all the *Big Bang Theory* reruns. Wait—what are those aromatic discs floating around in my head now? Key Lime. Strawberry Rhubarb. Pecan. Okay. Never mind. It *is* far more fun to think about eating pie than finding the circumference of it.

The UN French Language Day is the 20th, and International Francophone Day is the 22nd. I didn't see any other countries or languages listed as having their very own day, so why do the French get two? I'm sure they employed two women in their lobbying efforts— Brigitte Bardot and Catherine Deneuve. Men were defenseless against them.

An extremely curious designation is March as Hexagonal Awareness Month. From what sparse intelligence I could gather on the subject, it seems to be the pet project of some math nerds who clearly have *way* too much time on their hands.

Save A Spider Day is March 14th. I didn't know they needed saving. Apparently I exist in a fool's paradise, because I believe there are way too many of them around. A friend told me a spider fact recently—no matter where you stand, you are never more than three feet away from an arachnid friend. This doesn't square at all with Save A Spider Day. If my friend's fact is true, then it should be Save The Humans From Walking Into Webs Day. Because every morning I venture out to the car in the driveway, and the spiders who claim my home as their territory stayed up all night creating ginormous webs across the sidewalk, from the house to the car, from the shrubs to the lawn—in places where I am guaranteed to walk straight through them. I imagine them at 8 AM in a group clutching tiny mugs of coffee, pointing and laughing their bony little legs off. Then, once I am away in my vehicle, they take naps and awaken in time to do it all over again that night. You'd think they'd be bored to tears by now and want to create something significant—like Charlotte did for Wilber. Just my luck I'd get the low-achiever spiders.

My favorite discovery, by far, is National Potato Chip Day on March 14th. I don't know whose idea it was, or how long it's been official, but it's a holiday I can get behind—even more so than the pi that shares the same day. As much as I love the potato chip, I'm aware it is very bad for us. This is a fact. But we don't care—so are liquor, cigarettes, and bacon. The potato chip's popularity led to people around the globe concocting bizarro flavors of them. I, for one, am not the least bit curious about tasting Korea's octopus-flavored chips. Australia has honey-glazed ham and hot dog flavored ones. Hot Chili Squid chips are from Thailand, and England offers Prawn Cocktail ones.

It occurred to me we are not using our brains here. Offering only the foreign flavors might go a long way toward solving America's massive obesity problems.

Can't you see it? Order a cheeseburger and the waiter asks if you want squid chips or broccoli with it. For the first time, broccoli wins. Flavor all our fattiest foods with octopus or seaweed, and our nation gets skinny. Then we export them to China. They'll get our fat, diabetes, and heart disease—and we eliminate the trade deficit.

IT CAME FROM A SWAMP?

With all the icky blue-green algae bloom problems infecting our waterways lately, it reminds me of a supplement promoted a decade or so ago. Yes, a supplement. Like the kind you swallow. Which raises some interesting questions now, considering the experts say our South Florida blue-green algae is toxic to humans.

One of my exes swore by blue-green algae. He used to take capsules filled with it every day. Yes, purposely swallowed them so the algae could roam freely about in his body. He said *they* said it would improve, well, just about everything. He became an ardent pusher of the stuff, trying to make money from his newest fix. He believed in the magical *they* more than anyone I've ever met. Unfortunately, he always embraced – with great enthusiasm – the *they* who espoused the goofiest of things.

Had I known that about him beforehand, I would not have married him. Actually, there were a lot of things that, had I known in advance, would have made me run for the hills faster than you can say *low IQ caused by accumulated brain damage*. A Public-Service Announcement/side note to anyone contemplating marriage – DO NOT marry anyone until you've discovered the answers to the following (Believe me, I wish someone had told me this.):

How many conspiracy theories do they subscribe to, and which ones are they? (Some are screaming-in-all-caps-RED-flags, and you should run even faster than described above. I'll leave it to you to decide which.)

Have they ever watched a show on the History Channel about *ancient aliens*, then spent the next few weeks doing further serious 'research'?

Do they think UFO sightings are real? If so, how do they explain that, since the advent of the camera phone making *everything* that happens documentable, UFO sightings are pretty much non-existent now?

Do they believe zombies exist? The follow up question to this is – what are their plans for when the zombie apocalypse comes? (If you decide to stay with this person, despite this flaw, you'll want the best and most luxurious escape/survival plan possible, right?) While you're at it, can you get them to explain how it is that dead people need to eat anything at all? You'd be doing me a favor – that question's been bothering me for years.

Do they believe any of the Kardashians are famous for a good reason?

And, finally, can they complete more than one sentence without making you think you're being encircled by an intricate knot of word scrambles?

If there's any lesson I've taken away from marriage, it's that you really, really, need to know somebody well before you do something stupid like link your lives together. My blue-green algae pushing ex did some horrifically stupid things while we were married. Had I been paying the proper attention to the warning signs, I wouldn't have had to deal with the flotsam of his disasters. Imagine what could happen when you have children with an idiot who believes:

Seatbelts cause more harm in an accident than not using them.
Using sunscreen is a hoax and unprotected skin is much healthier.
Bathing in acetone won't hurt you.
Cancer doctors spend their time trying to hide any successful research, because they make so much money from treating it.
Dipping a dog in a barrel full of commercial pesticide (now banned) is a good de-flea/de-tick method.

Oh, how I wish I were kidding. But, no. And none of this was evident until after we were married and had a child. So, to prevent your own disaster, ask lots and lots of what you think are ridiculous questions. If any of the answers seem a tad off, it's probable you've just nicked the tip of the iceberg and he or she is still on their best behavior to hook you – before letting you see the *real* them.

My ex espoused so many bizarre things, it makes me wonder how much of it had to do with the blue-green algae he so fervently believed in.

THANKS A LOT, JOHN GRISHAM

Please forgive me, for I have skimmed. I normally read every word of any book I start. A few exceptions happened—say, three in the last ten years. But lately? Oh, man.

I'm a writer. With friends who are writers. Some of them are really, really good. There are others who are not. Recent changes in the publishing world have shifted everything, causing some seriously awkward moments and creating a mine field of potential fights among friends.

It used to be only people who weren't good enough writers yet (I am adding the *yet* to protect myself from the ones who don't realize they'll never be Hemingway)—who were turned down multiple times by agents and editors—resorted to doing it themselves. The poor things paid megabucks to have their books printed by a small press, then sold them from the trunks of their cars. That caused all kinds of uncomfortable eggshell sidestepping maneuvers on the part of their families, friends, co-workers, waitresses, hardware store clerks, proctologists, the perennial beehive-blue-haired lady with the pointy black glasses at the library, and even their insurance salesmen—who, let's face it, kind of deserved the tit-for-tat.

A notable exception was John Grisham, who,

unfortunately for the rest of us subjected to the do-it-yourselfer, was (and is) actually a terrific writer. I say unfortunately because he fueled a million fires of hope in others. And that shouldn't be a bad thing. Inspiring hope in others is noble—if it concerns beating cancer, helping the addicted, housing the homeless, or balancing the federal budget (we can dream, can't we?). But inspiring horrible writers to self-publish is a special kind of torture for those who know them.

Then eBooks happened. And Amazon made self-publishing not only easy, but essentially free. Now everyone—yes everyone—who's fantasized about having the world laud them for their gripping and touching memoir has a book available. Or a gripping and touching rite-of-passage-teenage-angst novel. Or a gripping and touching plot-to-end-the-world novel. Now, before I go on more about the gripping and touching, I must include an important fact for full disclosure. I, too, am a self-published author on Amazon. *What?!*, you are no doubt exclaiming to yourself right now. In fairness to me, I've been part of a ruthless gang of local authors for the last thirteen years— my critique group. They've mercilessly sliced and diced my writing, and, in the process, turned me into a polished author and a good editor to boot. (And yet, I know I am not Hemingway, either.)

Now I must direct your attention to Aunt Petunia (not her real name and likely not even related to me). Aunt Petunia was convinced her story was so unique and compelling that she had to (had to!) write it down and share it with the world. And Lord help me, she was also convinced that I was the one who was going to help her.

The *why* of that is a whole 'nother story for a different day.

Aunt Petunia's book—that she said was completed and ready to go—consisted of a poorly typed, single-spaced Word document with wildly varying margins, indents, point sizes, two different fonts, and weird returns. It was only twenty-thousand words. Unreadable words. Words that jumbled together, expressing in one of its (very long) paragraphs a conversation between three people, back story on a fourth person who wasn't part of or mentioned in the conversation, a description of her honeymoon in the 1970s, and how her mother taught her to make a bed. No, I am not kidding. Someone coined the phrase *word salad* in 2008 when describing Sarah Palin's particular speech pattern, and it applies here. Plus, Aunt Petunia used plenty of exclamation points and lots of 'ly' adverbs—he said softly, he replied gingerly, she asked tenderly, she exclaimed bitterly!, etc.

When I broached the subject that perhaps, *just perhaps*, her 'book' might not be ready for publication and she might consider taking a writing class or a couple of workshops, Aunt Petunia smacked me down with a powerful verbal wallop. In her ensuing tirade, she informed me that her sister thought it was amazing! Her daughter said it made her laugh and cry! Her best friend assured her it was destined to be a bestseller! (And maybe even an Oprah Book Club selection!)

Since then my policy is to bow out of helping, so sorry. When someone I know gives me their book to read, I do try. I'm obligated to try. For the first time in my life, though, I skim. I've never been a skimmer before. It feels like cheating, but it's the only way to muddle through.

Aunt Petunia's parting words were, "John Grisham had to do his first book all alone. So will I."

Yeah. Thanks a lot, John Grisham.

ROAD TRIP

I dated a very wealthy man for a while. Well, dated a few of them, really. But I never married one, which was stupid, because I *was* asked. Anyway, this particular man had a collection of cars. I never knew if he'd show up in the Mercedes or the Ferrari or the Lamborghini. For a lower middle-class kid who grew up in a family of eight with one car—a battered fake-wood paneled station wagon—the idea of having a wardrobe of them was incredible.

The man may well have been crazy. He insisted I take the Mercedes one weekend to drive some visiting friends of mine around the island. This was on Oahu. Lots of hills to chug up and down when you're touristing. Lots of wild and goofy drivers from all over the world.

Silly me, I thought everything would be just fine. What could go wrong? I'd taken trips around the island many times in my old klunker, a beige Dodge Aspen with bald tires. One of the ugliest cars to ever roll off the assembly line. Nothing happened to it on those trips. Not a ding, not a scrape.

Since I lived in Honolulu, near Ala Moana Beach Park, we started our tour by heading down Kalanianaole Highway, toward Haunama Bay and the blow-hole. From there, we'd progress to the Windward side, snake around to the North Shore, and come back through

Wahiawa, the center of the island, to Pearl Harbor. I took along an empty cooler. We stopped at the grocery store in the Aina Haina shopping center on the way. It was summer and hot, so I thoughtfully looked for and found a parking spot in the shade. My reasoning was it would take less air conditioning, and I'd save a little on gas. The Mercedes was heavy, solidly built. In comparison to my Aspen—which was no more than an overgrown soda can, really—it felt like driving an armored tank.

As we exited the store with our bag of ice and cold drinks, a sudden strong gust of wind hit. I watched in horror as one of the tall palm trees shading my boyfriend's shiny black, perfect vehicle let loose a cluster of cannonball-like coconuts with a loud crack onto the roof of the car. Bam, bam, bam. The hard green shells hammered down, then rolled off and hit the asphalt.

I cringed, afraid to see the damage. My friend, Wendy, stood motionless beside me, her mouth gaping. "We could have been hit on the head," she said. "Aren't they supposed to keep those things trimmed?"

Yes, they were. And they did. But the maintenance company must have missed this tree. I scanned the other palms in the parking lot and found none with coconuts still attached. I'd managed to park under the only dangerous tree. The dents in the hood and the roof weren't deep, but there nonetheless. It occurred to me that perhaps we should turn back, return the car, beg for mercy from my boyfriend, and continue our trip in the Aspen. The eternal optimist in me pooh-poohed that idea. The worst was over, nothing else would happen.

We piled back in and drove away.

We stopped to watch the body-surfing at Sandy's, a beach spot known for the treacherous formation of its shore break. Many adventurists had been injured at Sandy's, some had snapped their necks. My friends declined the opportunity to swim there. We did try bodysurfing at Makapuu, though. We built up huge appetites and went for lunch near the gorgeous Lanikai beach on the Windward side. The restaurant had a rain-forest/tropical theme and a netted, contained outdoor area where parrots and other exotic birds flew around cawing to the delight of the tourists. Outside, peacocks strolled the grounds, shrieking and chasing anyone they didn't like the look of.

Seems peacocks like expensive cars, too. When we returned after lunch, a large male peacock sat atop the car roof, hissing at us, daring us to come closer. It looked like he and his friends had quite a party while we ate. Thick white goopy bird poo was splattered all over the windshield and the roof. The stubborn bird would not budge from his spot, until the restaurant manager came out and did a female peacock bird call. It must have been authentic, because that male bird couldn't get over there fast enough. The manager laughed and handed us some wet paper towels. "It's not the birds' fault," he said. "It's the tourists. We have signs all over asking to please not feed them. I caught a guy yesterday giving them pieces of his cheeseburger. Can you imagine what that does to their digestive tracts?"

We nodded, the understanding becoming ever clearer as we tried to wipe the chunky, sticky stuff from the windshield. After cleaning enough area so I could see to drive, we gave it up and hit the road. I planned to visit a carwash before I returned.

Not thirty minutes later, we were on the sleepy two-lane road up the coast enjoying the magnificent, primal-feeling views into the mountains when it felt like the front wheel of the car fell into a deep pothole. I hadn't seen one coming up. I pressed on the gas. The car wouldn't move, so I threw it into Park and went outside to check. The wheel, the whole wheel—tire and all, had come off the axle. I screamed my disbelief. My friends jumped out the other side.

We called a tow truck and while waiting, directed traffic around the Mercedes. At one point, there was a long line of traffic coming from the opposite direction, and the drivers stuck behind our vehicle were getting impatient. People shouted and cursed us in multiple languages. Horns honked. A pick-up truck driver decided to not wait a moment longer. He plowed ahead onto the dirt shoulder, moved past all those in front of him, and though we shouted to wait for a moment, he bashed into our car's open passenger door—mistakenly left open, bending it back against the body with an awful metallic screech as he passed, yelling obscenities.

My boyfriend didn't break up with me. He wasn't even mad. Looking back now, I should have married him. But heaven only knows what I would have done to his fancy house and the rest of his cars.

VICTORIA LANDIS

354

ABOUT THE AUTHOR

Victoria Landis is an author and artist living in South Florida with a tree in the front yard that seems intent on swallowing her neighborhood.

She is the author of two novels, *Blinke It Away*, a suspense novel set on Oahu, and *Alias: Mitzi & Mack*, a humorous crime novel set in South Florida. She has written a monthly humor column since 2008.

A member of Mystery Writers of America since 2003, she served as the Raffle Chairman for the SleuthFest Writers' Conference for nine years, and as Co-Chairman of SleuthFest itself for four years.

As an artist, she does graphics (book covers, ads, logos), oils on canvas, murals, and specialty faux finishes.

Email:
victoria@landisdesignresource.com

Facebook:
www.facebook.com/Victoria-Landis-356968881052071/

Made in the USA
Columbia, SC
13 February 2018